Ogata-mura

Asian Anthropologies
General Editors:
J.S. Eades, Emeritus Professor, Ritsumeikan Asia Pacific University;
Professorial Research Associate, School of Oriental and African Studies; Senior
Research Associate, University of Kent
Shinji Yamashita, Professor of Asia Pacific Studies, The University of Tokyo

OGATA-MURA

Sowing Dissent and Reclaiming Identity in a Japanese Farming Village

❧

Donald C. Wood

Berghahn Books
New York • Oxford

Published in 2012 by
Berghahn Books
www.berghahnbooks.com

© 2012 Donald C. Wood

Library of Congress Cataloging-in-Publication Data

A C.I.P. cataloging record is available from the Library of Congress

British Library Cataloguing in Publication Data
A catalogue record for this book is available from the British Library

Printed in the United States on acid-free paper

ISBN 978-0-85745-524-6 (hardback)
ISBN 978-0-85745-526-0 (ebook)

Contents

List of Figures and Tables

❧

Figures

Tables

PREFACE

❧

My relationship with Ogata-mura began in the summer of 1995 with my placement there at an Assistant Language Teacher (ALT) in the Japan Exchange Teaching (JET) Program (see McConnell 1996, 2000). What I knew about Japanese villages at the time came mainly from studying the canonical works in the English-language anthropological study of them: Embree's *Suye-mura* (1939) and Smith and Wiswell's *Women of Suye-mura* (1982), Beardsley, Hall, and Ward's *Village Japan* (1959), Dore's *Shinohata* (1978), R. Smith's *Kurusu* (1978), and Norbeck's *Country to City* (1978), as well as more recent monographs like those by Bailey (1991) and Moon (1989), and also works by Kelly (1986) and Knight (1994a,b). I had also benefited much from reading Jussaume's (1991) and Hayami's (1988) analyses of Japanese agriculture. However, I was quite unprepared for what I found in Ogata-mura. The place almost seemed to be suffering from multiple personality disorder; its calm atmosphere was frequently interrupted by major events—the local government appeared to be more concerned with pumping up the village's image than anything else—and there was some kind of tension that I could not quite put my finger on. During my first year in Ogata-mura, there were car races, and boat, bicycle, and foot races as well. In addition, a hotel opened and an international solar energy conference was held there—all in a village small enough to completely circle by foot in about thirty minutes. I soon realized that there were things that certain people could not talk about in front of certain other people. I became intrigued by the place, and began snooping about and asking questions almost immediately, prompting many residents to wonder why their ALT was so interested in their community, of which most seemed to think very little. And fortunately, I have managed to continue my relationship with the village far beyond my two-year term as an English teacher.

The book, therefore, builds on a succession of research projects carried out in Ogata-mura from 1995 to the present. My first fieldwork period stretched from 1995 to 1997, during my employment there. Data I collected then enabled me to write my M.A. thesis at the Department of Anthropology, Texas A&M University (Wood 1999a). At the time, I was primarily interested in the process of adjusting to Ogata-mura on the part of the settlers, the problems of inheritance and succession, and the social effects of the big projects that the village had been undertaking for a few years prior to my initial arrival. My second fieldwork period, from September of 2001 to around the middle of 2002, allowed me to write my Ph.D. dissertation in the Department of Cultural Anthropology of the University of Tokyo (Wood 2004). This time, I was mainly interested in the general problem of social solidarity and also the related question of the role of conflict in this. I concentrated on exploring the original social structure of the village that was established during the settlement period, stretching from 1967 to 1974. Just one year before this fieldwork period began a new mayor had been elected, and the community was still reeling from that. It provided a good opportunity to investigate the development of social solidarity and politico-economic associations in the village over time. I was also able to take a much closer look at institutional arrangements in the community than I had before. The third and final fieldwork period upon which this book is based began in October of 2006 and stretched—punctuated by various interruptions—into the early months of 2010. When I started, the election of 2004 had churned up a number of interesting issues, and new events were unfolding before my eyes, so this last period was mainly spent updating my existing data and digging deeper into issues that I had not been able to fully explore before, including the complexities of national government involvement in agriculture, clashing ideologies about agrarian life, and farming trends.

My research methods and activities in the village have been various. In the beginning, I started by asking residents who came to my English lessons at the community center as many questions about the village and about their lives as I could. They were always eager to answer, and just beginning with some questions would usually spark very interesting discussions. At times I visited them privately at their homes in order to speak more comfortably about rice marketing or household matters. Much time was spent simply walking the streets of the village and chatting with whoever happened to be outside. This often took place in the context of conducting neighborhood surveys. As an employee of the village from 1995 to 1997, I had good access to other village employees, and spent a lot of time talking with division heads or their subordinates in the main office. Much personal information I collected in the earliest stages is based on tape-recorded interviews held with various people, generally at their homes, in 1996 and 1997. The recordings were made with their consent, and were fully transcribed by me, with considerable assistance from my wife. Together we translated all of the interviews, a job that required many hours of work. Due to the amount of time needed for transcribing and translating, though, I gradually stopped recording interviews. Most of the interviews and other conversations conducted after 2002, in fact, were not recorded. Instead, I usually took notes and expanded on them immediately after the discussion. Spoken words from these encounters or written text originally in Japanese used in this book were translated by me. I also used questionnaires on a number of occasions—in 1997 and in 2001 for students in the junior high school (approximately 100 students each time), in 1997 and 2001 for members of the Young Wives' Association (*wakazumakai*—127 and 101 responses, respectively), in 2002 for the parents in the elementary school PTA (111 responses), and also in 2002 for the twenty-nine members of a particular rice marketing organization. Beyond these methods, a variety of conversations were held at parties and other occasions, or over lunch, etcetera—encounters too numerous to recall.

Finally, a few technical notes: in this book Japanese names are written with the given name first and the family name second. In addition, I have used pseudonyms for people about whom any personal information is revealed—information involving family affairs or information given in a private setting or situation. Several exceptions aside, public figures and officials, and other well known people, are represented by their true names. Private information on these individuals is not revealed here, and attempting to disguise their identities would have been pointless. In addition, generally following the Modified Hepburn style of romanization, I have used diacritics where needed on vowels in most Japanese words in this book in an attempt to convey the correct pronunciations. This includes all personal names and also lesser known place names such as Tōhoku, but I have not used them in words that are now very common in the English language, such as judo or sumo, or in extremely well known place names like Tokyo, Honshu, Kyushu, or Hokkaido. In addition, although the *o* in Ogata is actually long, I have omitted the superscript line on this vowel because using it would have been cumbersome and because this proper noun appears with such great frequency here. I have also omitted diacritics on all cases of capital *o*, as in some names. Also, Japanese-language words are generally set in italic type, with the exception of proper nouns. Last, all photographs appearing in this book were taken by me, unless otherwise noted.

Acknowledgments

A number of people deserve credit for making it possible for me to complete this project. First, I would like to thank Takeo Funabiki, who retired from the University of Tokyo in March of 2012, for encouraging me to arrange my Ogata-mura material in book form in the first place, and Jerry Eades for getting the ball rolling by taking time to review the dissertation and advising me on preparing a suitable manuscript, and for keeping that ball rolling along the way. I am also very grateful to three anonymous readers who commented on previous versions of this book—experienced authors who helped me in various ways to see the forest when my view was blocked by trees. I profited more than they know from their encouragement and criticism. My gratitude also goes out to Marion Berghahn, Ann Przyzycki DeVita, Mark Stanton, and everyone else at Berghahn Books for their generous support, and also to the copyeditor who helped me improve this manuscript at the final stage.

I am heavily indebted to Abito Itō, formerly of the Department of Cultural Anthropology at the University of Tokyo, for granting me a place among the many excellent graduate students there so that I could benefit not only from his instruction and support but also from that of his colleagues. If he had not trusted and encouraged me in the first place, I would never have been able to finish my degree at the department, or this book. I am also grateful to all other members of the department, but especially to Shinji Yamashita, Masato Fukushima, and Teruo Sekimoto, for their feedback on my dissertation and for putting up with me in their classes over the four years I spent at the university. I learned much from them. In my original fieldwork period in Ogata-mura and in designing and composing the M.A. thesis—my first serious attempt at writing about the village—I received much guidance from Norbert Dannhaeuser, chair of my committee at the Department of Anthropology, Texas A&M University. My own research has been influenced by his instruction, research, general mentorship, and friendship, in no small way. Dr. Dannhaeuser also helped me later by reading and commenting on early drafts of two chapters of my dissertation. Other people formerly at Texas A&M University—namely James Copp, Lee Cronk, Jeff Cohen, and Sylvia Grider—also deserve my gratitude for their instruction and guidance. In addition, I thank Richard Moore of The Ohio State University for sharing thoughts on the village with me and for reading and commenting on some of my writings that formed part of this monograph.

The residents of Ogata-mura who hosted me as a teacher in their village and tolerated my intrusions in their lives over the years also deserve considerable credit for the completion of this book. I cannot list everyone here, but they include Suzuko Nitahara, the Kimura family (and especially Masumi Kimura), Yōko Toyoda, the Satō family (and especially Hiroshi Satō), Keiko Kōchi, the Murasaki family, Shōko Kaneko and her family, the Noro family, Fumiko Tanno, Shigeki Konno, Tokuko Asanuma, the Haga family, Hiroki Sugawara, the Takahashi family (and especially Hiroto and Mina Takahashi), Isao Kobayashi, Nobuo Tsushima, Seiki Miyata, Tsutomu Tani, Tōru Wakui, Sadayoshi Miyazaki, Tadashi and Kita Kurose, and Shinichirō Sakamoto. I am particularly grateful to Toshiko Mimura for her time, effort, and enthusiasm.

Above all, I owe the greatest debt to my wife, Akiko Takahashi, my daughters, Seiko and Motoko, and my parents-in-law, all of whom helped make it possible for me to study at the graduate level, and who endured the effects for far too long. Without my wife's support and understanding (and behind-the-scenes assistance) I would not have been able to complete this project. Finally, I would like to express my gratitude to the Japanese Education Ministry (MEXT) for granting me a three-year scholarship to attend the University of Tokyo, and to Akita University for its support of my research. Needless to say, culpability for any shortcomings or errors in this book rests entirely with me.

Introduction

THE VILLAGE AND THE ISSUES

This isn't really Japan—it's Ogata-mura!
                                              – a remark sometimes heard in the village

At the close of the Second World War the occupation government of Japan was heavily concerned with feeding the population. Unable to foresee demographic and cultural changes in store for the country over the remainder of the century, political leaders placed the issue of securing a stable domestic supply of rice high on their list of priorities. However, the repatriation of thousands of citizens who had been living in the imperial state of Manchuria and other colonized areas and the return of soldiers placed an extra strain on already scarce land resources (see Nishida and Kase 2000: 311–314). One way to increase self-sufficiency in food production, and also to deal with the sudden influx of people, was to make new land—something that had already been done many times in many locations. The shallow lagoon of Hachirōgata, just north of the capital city of Akita Prefecture on the Sea of Japan coast, was an ideal candidate for extensive land reclamation. With the help of Dutch engineers, the government created over seventeen thousand hectares of new farmland inside the lagoon by an empolderment method over a twenty-year period beginning in the mid-1950s. In 1964 the village of Ogata-mura was officially founded on the virgin territory as a model for efficient and highly mechanized agriculture, and between 1967 and 1974 about 580 settlers took up residence in the village—bringing their families (if any) with them.[1]

This book explores the process of Ogata-mura's development from the planning stage to the present. It addresses the dominant problem of how a centrally planned, tightly regulated. "synthetic" farming community might grow and evolve within a leading capitalist democracy undergoing rapid social and

Endnotes for this chapter begin on page 24.

economic change, and that has also been selectively opening itself up to foreign trade. Specifically, the book attempts to answer three questions: (1) How have the ways in which the village was planned and settled affected its social and economic development? (2) What results have the central government's agricultural and regional policies had on the community? (3) Can Ogata-mura serve as a model for the future of Japan's agriculture as originally intended, and if so, in what ways? The village is especially interesting with regard to this final question. Since its creation, it has been deeply intertwined with government agricultural policy— both as an agent of change and as an indicator of policy effects. Even in early 2010 the village made headlines because it was at the center of a political fencing match between the head of the Ministry of Agriculture, Forestry and Fisheries (MAFF) and the prefectural government over penalties that were being placed on Ogata-mura farmers.

This book seeks to present as clear a picture of Ogata-mura as can be presented here, while addressing the three questions above—not only as an academic study but also as a story about the creation of a community and its development over five decades. This introduction lays out the approach of the book by introducing Ogata-mura and the primary theoretical issues which shape my analysis. Chapter 1 reviews agricultural policy and regional politics in Japan—necessary for understanding Ogata-mura's place in its larger social, political, and economic environment. Chapter 2 explains the creation of the village and the establishment of the original social structure of the community, showcasing the settlement process and its inherent problems, and examining why the initial project could not be called a success in all respects. Chapter 3 explores the collapse of village unity over government agricultural (rice) policy that began in the 1970s and resulted in significant fragmentation of the society, and how this was worsened by fervent image-(re)building efforts in the 1980s and 1990s on the part of the village government, under the direction of a powerful mayor who was backed by a rubber-stamp village council (assembly). Chapter 4 concentrates on the role of rice in Ogata-mura, and specifically on the business and politics of its production and marketing, both across the entire village and in one particular neighborhood. It highlights the social divisions within the community of settlers and explains their reconfiguration into new networks and institutions. Chapter 5 builds on the discussions in preceding chapters in investigating Ogata-mura's general political situation, mainly by tracing the mayoral elections and related developments since 1992, when the first signs of real change began to appear. The chapter completes the goal of the previous chapter in demonstrating how the settlers and their heirs became rearranged in a new way—"the new social order"—reflected in the ways in which they market their rice and cast their votes. Finally, chapter 6 provides a wrap-up to the book and offers answers to the three central questions that guide it. The stories of several entrepreneurial settlers and their families are woven through the chapters so that we may be able to better grasp the experience of settling and farming in the village, and to more fully understand why some settlers decided to move to Ogata-mura in the first place and later to risk all they had gained and defy the national and local governments.

Putting Ogata-mura under the Lens

Akita Prefecture is one of six political units that comprise the Tōhoku region of northeast Japan, an area that has been the subject of much anthropological attention (Bailey 1991, Guo et al. 2005, Kelly 1986, Matanle et al. 2011, Moore 1990, Rausch 2001, Shimpo 1976, Thompson 2003, Thompson and Traphagan 2006, Torsello 2002, Wood 2009). Tōhoku is rich in natural resources and offers a refreshing alternative to the more crowded areas of the country. On the other hand, Tōhoku suffers more than many other parts of Japan from the "graying" phenomenon resulting from the current low birthrate. Population loss is a serious issue, not only because it increases feelings of loneliness and unease but also because it disrupts services as well at the flow of money from Tokyo to the regions. In addition, the "brain drain" also hits the area hard. Able hands and nimble minds tend to migrate toward the leading cities. Although the so-called "u-turn" effect has helped bring some young people back to regional places from the major population centers in recent years, farmers and people in all kinds of self-employed professions have to worry about whether they will be able to count on a son or daughter staying around to take over their work. Even in the capital city of Akita favored restaurants are constantly closing down because so many proprietors have no heirs to pass them down to. Similarly, many young women complain about not being able to find a suitable mate (females outnumber males by about sixty thousand). Akita, which possesses about 11.5 million kilometers for its one million residents (compared to Tokyo's 2 million kilometers for thirteen million residents), is known for having plenty of space, cold and snowy winters, delicious rice and sake, and the most beautiful women in the country—so-called "beauties of Akita"—who are said to have especially fair skin. These beauties and their male counterparts are divided into twenty-five different municipalities today— thirteen cities (*shi*), nine towns (*machi*), and three villages (*mura*)—although there were many more in the past. The capital city, home to about one-third of the prefecture's residents, is located on the Sea of Japan coast, roughly midway along the prefecture's coastline.

About one hour's drive north of the capital city of Akita lies Ogata-mura, just to the east of the Oga Peninsula (Figure I.1). Ogata-mura is different from any other community in Akita, or in the country, for that matter. First, there is its history. As mentioned above, the land it occupies was created by filling in a natural lagoon—by far the largest reclamation project ever undertaken in Japan.

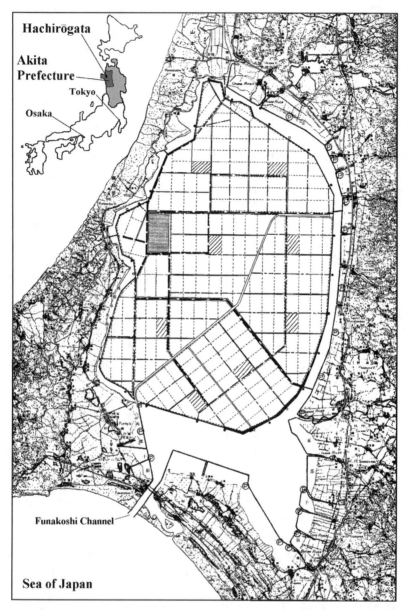

Figure I.1: The Hachirōgata region today. The inner reclaimed area is the administrative territory of Ogata-mura. Outer reclaimed areas are discernible by their geometric straightness. The shaded rectangle on the left side of the inner reclaimed land is the settlement of Ogata-mura itself. Shaded rectangles spread throughout the inner reclaimed territory are spots where separate hamlets would have been built according to an early land-use plan. Inset: Japan (minus Okinawa and the Kuril Islands claimed by Japan) with the Tōhoku region in gray and Akita Prefecture in darker gray.

Source: Hachirōgata map adapted from original provided by Ogata-mura; inset map adapted from WorldAtlas.Com.

The residents were chosen through a national, competitive selection process and they settled in the new village over a relatively short time span, from 1967 to 1974. While there have been other settlement communities founded in the country, none of them compare with Ogata-mura. For one thing, the rice farming system was of an especially vast scale from the start. Individual holdings measured ten hectares—roughly ten times the national average—but this was later increased to fifteen. The system was also supposed to be a model for modern agriculture—rational and efficient farm management and a high degree of mechanization. Furthermore, in contrast to the typical Japanese postwar agrarian situation of small, privately owned farms dependent on household-based labor, in Ogata-mura the settlers originally worked their large, privately owned farms collectively—in work groups of five to ten men. Major equipment was owned by the group, and the earliest settlers even lived in group clusters within the neighborhoods. Rice was also sold to the local, government-backed grain elevator corporation and marketed *en masse*.

With property being in private hands from the start, the village only experienced a very mild decollectivization as the cooperative work groups were disbanded in the early years of the village's history—a process that probably helped maintain smooth social relations between the neighbors more than anything else. Moreover, the national government did not oppose the settlers' desires to work independently. However, Tokyo became incensed when about one-half of the settlers refused to initiate cutbacks in rice production beginning in the mid-1970s, and started marketing their grains through nongovernment (black market) channels as well. They even sold rice directly to consumers, an unprecedented development in Japan's long agricultural history. The mandatory rice quotas were not limited to Ogata-mura—it was a nationwide affair—but being the model farming village that it was, Ogata-mura received much scorn from administrative officials. Yet, a significant proportion of the village's settlers disagreed with their law-breaking neighbors, and deep divisions appeared within the fledgling community. Finally, in 1995 it became legal for farmers to produce as much rice as they wanted, and also later to market it as they pleased, although penalties for overproduction continued to be placed on them by the prefectural administration. In sum, the smooth shift away from collective farming that occurred in Ogata-mura was followed by a difficult and painful transition from public to private marketing methods and a more varied economic base, which resulted in considerable fragmentation of the village society (see also Cancian 1992).

Second, there is the village's demographic situation. One of only three remaining villages in Akita Prefecture, each with populations of about three thousand, Ogata-mura is among the smallest municipalities in terms of people—but the village has not suffered much from outmigration. Its population peaked in the 1980s when the middle school's walls bulged with approximately three hundred students, but has since leveled off and today remains fairly steady. Loss of people has not been a great source of worry. In addition, although finding brides for young farmers tends to be a problem in most Japanese villages, this has not worried residents of Ogata-mura so very much, either. Many sons (and grandsons) have gone away to school in Tokyo or some other place and found a wife there before returning. In other cases young men have been introduced to partners from the surrounding area by their friends. There are, after all, quite a number of small towns ringing the reclaimed land of Hachirōgata. I know of no Filipina brides in Ogata-mura (there are many in Japan's less populated regions today). One woman from Kanagawa, near Tokyo, said that she had been attracted to the village partly because of the chance to ski nearby: "My husband said that if I married him and came to the village, we could ski all the time." But this did not quite pan out. "We never ski anymore," she complained years later.

Partly related to the national population drop, a major problem facing farming families in Japan today is the issue of securing an heir, or the "successor problem" (*atotsugi mondai*). Anthropological and sociological studies of Japanese agrarian communities are largely concerned with this matter, and upon the completion of his fieldwork in Miyagi Prefecture, Moore (1990) concluded that it was the single greatest problem facing Japanese farmers. In Ogata-mura, individual farming families may have fretted at times about securing an heir, but in contrast to small-scale farmers in imperiled towns and villages they have not had to worry after securing one—an industrious successor can at least make a decent living with a farm of fifteen hectares or more, and can do even better by buying additional land. In addition, since they all bought their farms and do not have the pressure of tending to ancestrally inherited property, they can always back out in the end and part with their fields—they have plenty of business-oriented neighbors who would be happy to purchase a plot or two.

There is also the physical layout and general appearance of the village. It is flat, the roads are straight, and the farmers' homes are arranged in neat rows (Figure I.2). The settlement can be conveniently divided into east and west halves, defined by two long streets running north to south, parallel to one another, between which are located most of the public facilities and institutions, including the local branch of Akita Bank, the police department, the village government office building (Figure I.3), the agricultural cooperative (Ogata JA) and the grocery store it runs (Agri-Plaza Ogata, Figure I.4), the community center (Figure I.5), the clinics and the schools, and also the shopping strip, which includes the post office. Settler houses on the east side are basically divided into two large sections, and beyond this into a number of smaller blocks, and then into streets. This is the same for the west side, but there are three large sections rather than two.

Finally, Ogata-mura is extremely clean. Although there are some abandoned houses, these cannot be seen from the main roads but must rather be sought out.

Figure I.2: The layout of Ogata-mura. *Source:* Adapted from original map provided by Ogata-mura.

Hotel

Assisted living facility

Schools

Clinics

Prefectural housing

Bunkajin
neighborhood

Houses for village employees

Shops

Ogata JA

Community
center

Bank

Police

Gov't office

Village-owned
rental properties

Training
Center

0   300 m

Figure I.3: The village government office buildings, September 2008. The wing on the right is the original section. The large wing on the left, partially obscured by trees, is newer, and houses the mayor's office and most administrative divisions.

Figure I.4: Utility trucks lined up outside Agri-Plaza Ogata.

Figure I.5: The community center (*kōminkan*) in early 2008 after a much needed paint job.

This can also be said of piles of refuse, which are exceedingly rare. The village looks not unlike photos of the reclaimed areas of the Netherlands, but the part of Japan that it most resembles is probably Hokkaido, which was settled mostly after the dawn of the Meiji era in 1868 (see Mock 1999 and Takata 2000, 2001). Traphagan and Thompson (2006: 6) write of cultural differences in Japan— "cultures" over "culture"—and in a way Ogata-mura can be said to have its own culture; I have heard the words quoted at the beginning of this chapter spoken by more than one villager.

Throughout the first few decades of the postwar era, U.S.-dominated, foreign anthropological research on regional ("rural") Japan focused on farming villages and the subsequent changes they underwent, within a general modernization and development framework (see Traphagan and Thompson 2006). This was under- standable, since so many people in Japan still lived in villages at the time, since there were so many villages, and since change was occurring at such a rapid pace. But of course there was another reason—intense interest in the effects of the postwar occupation government's land reforms and in the modernization of agri- culture (Ryang 2004: ch. 3). This tradition gave way in the 1980s to a slightly dif- ferent approach—still focusing on change, modernization, and development, but less concerned with agriculture as the base of community and more with politics and local tensions, and also more nuanced. Dore's *Shinohata* (1978) and Smith's

Kurusu (1978) hinted at the start of this movement, which (arguably) came to its fruition around the start of the Heisei era with the appearance of (now well known) books by Moon (1989) and Bailey (1991).

Following this, the anthropological study of regional Japan exploded in many different directions—too numerous and too complex to adequately summarize here. Researchers have written much on the important topics of development, farming, aging, politics, population loss (and demographic change), tourism, and more, and Tōhoku has featured prominently in this work (see chapters in Guo et al. 2005, Thompson and Traphagan 2006, and Traphagan and Knight 2003, for example). In addition, a strong concern with nostalgia, amidst modernity, and its various conundrums—a highly symbolic approach (see esp. Ivy 1995)—is interwoven through much of this body of research. One can say that these trends inform one another. Schnell's fine 1999 study of a public festival in a Gifu Prefecture town makes good use of the symbolic approach but in a very concrete way.

My analysis of Ogata-mura shares this anthropological concern with modernity, for it was created as a modern version of something generally seen as not modern by definition—the Japanese farming village. The national government upheld Ogata-mura as a model for the nation's agriculture, rationalized from the beginning in terms of both irrigation and land, and also highly mechanized; as Kelly (2006) recently demonstrated, this is a modernization process that most rice-producing parts of Japan had to struggle with over many decades. Latour (1993) proposes that to be "modern" is to maintain a (false) mental separation of culture (the human realm) from nature (the world of nonhumans) while also recognizing the messy entanglements of these ("hybrid networks"), yet at the same time ignoring the fact that this rigid dichotomy is itself a product of the proliferation of hybrid networks (making "the modern" a fallacy). This scenario seems to dovetail with Ogata-mura—a gigantic cultural project that was, quite violently, impressed upon the landscape. The enterprise has always been infused with rhetoric of the domination of human ingenuity over nature—the transformation, even, of a "worthless" swamp into a valuable national resource—the creation of a "productive" expanse of land where only "nonproductive" water stood before. Yet, it is generally acknowledged within the village that the cultural and the natural are deeply interconnected.

Scott (1998: 4–6, passim) writes of "high modernism"—"muscle-bound," turbo-charged, scientific positivism that originated in the West and spread across the world, leading to the enactment of grand plans entailing massive expenditures of money, reconfigurations of the landscape, and relocations of people that usually ended in failure (see also Kuwayama 2004: 13).[2] This also relates to what was done at Hachirōgata. However, Ogata-mura does not exactly fit into Scott's category of great failures. Therefore, in the present study, "modern" is considered to involve: (1) a degree of anxiety over an unresolved dichotomy between "culture" and "nature" amidst rapid change; and (2) updated, "improved" versions of things, conditions, or ideas (that can only exist in juxtaposition with the earlier versions). The real problem lies in the reconciliation of these two (related) meanings. As a modern place, Ogata-mura has come to mean different things for different residents—those who long for something more "pure" and "natural" are less pleased, while others are happy with the modernist *inaka* (a rural, down-home kind of place) that it is. Individual reconciliation with Ogata-mura as a modern place—even a substitute for something more natural—has therefore been a major factor in community formation and farming success there. It has also been a central problem in the political struggles over the identity and history of the village.

What counters (and eases the anxiety of) "the modern" is the nostalgic symbolism and intentional packaging of *inaka* Japan as a place to visit, and perhaps as a place to live, and of course as a place where food is produced. Probably the most nostalgic spot in Japan is the kind of place that can be called a *furusato*—a place strongly associated with *mukashi*—an ambiguous and amorphous past that can only exist in opposition to *ima* (the present) (Itō 2007: 94–95). *Furusato* has a number of meanings. According to the Kōjien dictionary/encyclopedia, it can mean "a place of ancient events" or "an ancient capital." In this sense, a *furusato* might be a general homeland or a place to which a number of people are connected historically or ancestrally. Indeed, Tamanoi explains that *furusato* can refer to "a collectivity of Japanese" (1998: 195). Travel agents and local governments often use images and rhetoric that evoke a sense of nostalgia when advertising the Tōhoku region, presenting the entire area as a spiritual and cultural *furusato* for the nation (Schnell 2005: 213–214, see also Graburn 1995). Contemporary *enka* ballads, overflowing with longings for past times and sentiment for a rural homeland, conjure up images of an imagined, but usually unreachable, *furusato* (Occhi 2006, Yano 2002). *Furusato* can also be a concept that a person has internalized within himself or herself—a feeling of nostalgia and comfort, usually based on memories of a hometown.

Most commonly, and in its most practical sense, *furusato* refers to an individual's or a family's hometown or area, usually stretching back at least a generation or two (see Kirby 2011: 76–77 and Robertson 1991: 14–17). Ideally, the graves of a person's ancestors are located in his or her *furusato*. Every year in mid-August millions of Japanese people leave the big cities and head for their *furusatos* to pay respects to their ancestors and reaffirm ties with family members and other relatives who remain behind (Media Productions Group 1991). Ogata-mura began as nobody's *furusato*, but today, whether an Ogata-mura settler (or a settler's children or grandchildren) can call the village a *furusato*, and if so how long this takes, is a strong indicator of adjustment and community formation. On the other hand, the nostalgic aspect of *furusato* that normally accompanies the invocation of the concept—either by individual actors, by the media, by travel and tourism industries, by a government body, or by scholars—is notably absent in the village because of its origins. Rather, it is Ogata-mura as a modern place that receives attention. In fact, academic studies can be divided according to how they treat the village as a modern farming model.

In 1965 Douglas Gordon submitted an M.A. thesis to the Department of Geography of the University of Hawaii on the reclamation of Hachirōgata. Although the official founding of the village occurred during his 1964–1965 fieldwork period, the land-building was far from complete and settler selection procedures had yet to begin. However, Gordon was able to at least evaluate the reclamation process and the initial proposals for human settlement on the new territory. He was unable, though, to view the great experiment with complete optimism—being especially concerned about the early settlement plans calling for the founding of numerous hamlets in the new territory, and the transferability of the modern model to the rest of the country, even if successful at Hachirōgata. In other words, the massive, prepackaged rationalization being created before Gordon's eyes failed to move him.

It is important to remember, however, that Ogata-mura was from the start the ultimate in rationalized rice agriculture in Japan, and this was not lost on the various government offices and agencies that assembled books on the project in its wake. In 1969 a large volume covering the reclamation and the history of one of the offices that oversaw it (the Hachirōgata Kantaku Jimusho) appeared. It was edited by that office and published by the Japanese Society of Irrigation, Drainage, and Reclamation Engineering (Nihon Doboku Gakkai—JSIDRE). This dense monograph covers the history of the reclamation from the planning stages to the actual building of the settlement itself in painstaking detail, including the design of the houses and other structures. In 1970 a much slimmer and highly technical survey of the history and geology of the reclamation was published by the Agricultural Experiment Station (Akita-ken Nōgyō Shikenjō) of Akita Prefecture. Neither of these went out of their way to lavish praise upon the project, but they helped support Hachirōgata as a new agrarian model, and this trend continued throughout the 1970s: the official history of the reclamation and the founding of the village from the point of view of the temporary government office (Hachirōgata Shinnōson Kensetsu Jigyōdan) responsible for the project appeared in 1976, and the following year saw the release of an updated version of the 1969 volume mentioned above (MAFF 1977). While these volumes (Hachirōgata Kantaku Jimusho 1969, Akita-ken Nōgyō Shikenjō 1970, Hachirōgata Shinnōson Kensetsu Jigyōdan 1976, MAFF 1977) are loaded with interesting technical information on the reclamation process and the planning of the farmland and the village, they do not take critical positions (as would be expected), and there is considerable overlap between them. By the time the last volume was published, the settlers of Ogata-mura were starting to become divided over the issue of rice production, with some secretly defying the government's orders to destroy a certain amount of rice plants in their fields, and some doing so openly. Yet this threat to the government's utopian aspirations for the project was not mentioned—the modern model remained insulated from reality.

As of 2003 Ogata-mura could hardly have been held up as a successful pattern for a new Japanese agriculture without some justification, considering the struggles over land, production, and personal rights that had taken place there by that time (two settlers had even lost their fields to the government after lengthy legal battles), but that year the Hachirōgata project—not to mention the very problematic one at Isahaya Bay in Nagasaki Prefecture—was lauded by the managing director of the Land Improvement Construction Association of Japan (LICA) in a paper extolling the many virtues of such massive reclamation initiatives (Ueda 2003). While some obvious local troubles are acknowledged, such projects are heralded by the Director as "the creation of national asset in Japan" (*sic*) (ibid.: 284). The emphasis here on the benefits of large-scale land reclamation for the state is unmistakable.

The triumph of the modern model—or at least one of its results—is also elaborated on by Mizuki (2002: 144–150) in an optimistic book on national development across Japan—not only the regions. Formerly with the *Nihon Keizai Shimbun*, and a prolific writer and essayist, Mizuki's consideration of the village is highly positive, and he focuses on the contrast between a large, relatively new rice-marketing firm in the village (the Akita Komachi Seisansha Kyōkai, founded by settler Tōru Wakui—see later chapters) and the older Country Elevator Corporation that originally purchased rice from all settlers until many of them defied the government and broke the law, leaving the reader to imagine the village as an agent of change for the nation's agriculture as a whole—change for the better within the current environment. Hiroshi Nara, a long-term resident of Akita and formerly with the leading local newspaper, *Akita Sakigake Shimbun*, also echoes this trend in his discussion of Ogata-mura in a book on recent development in Akita (Nara 2006: 214–222). Although his coverage of the village is brief, he does not focus only on agriculture but also examines the general development trajectory the village has followed since the early 1990s, paying much attention to large-scale projects initiated by the powerful former mayor, who left office in 2000. Nara points out that the village has spent a great amount of money on such projects, but avoids taking a critical stance, emphasizing rather the village's position as the municipality with the highest annual per capita income (3,739,000 yen in 2002), the highest birthrate (10.4 births in 2003), and the youngest population (39.7 years in 2003) in Akita Prefecture (ibid.: 217). The author avoids sticky political issues and glosses over recent internal problems.

While positive treatment of Ogata-mura as a model for Japanese agriculture abounds, with modernity or modernization theory underlying many arguments, nostalgia and a yearning for something that might have been lost does guide some early studies of the reclamation project and its effects. In the mid-1960s an Akita University professor and his colleagues spent much time researching the communities in the surrounding area as the reclamation was progressing, reporting on social problems and change in the wake of the colossal project (Handa 1968). They focused on the worries and objections of the fishermen and the ways in which the government appeased them with cash remuneration, promises of land within the reclaimed territory, and explanations of regional economic benefits, and they also considered other issues relating to the ongoing development of the area. Their stance on the government's handling of the social problems caused by the reclamation was mildly critical, going somewhat beyond Gordon's pessimism in its detail. In addition, although they were not critical of the reclamation, government researchers with the Resource Preservation Division in the Agency for Cultural Affairs (Bunkachō Bunkazai Hogobu) visited the area over the course of the reclamation process and carefully investigated the culture and lives of the residents for whom the lagoon's existence had been so important. Unlike Handa's mission, their project was primarily a salvage operation—to document the local culture before too much of it was lost. They looked into the lifeways of the region, studied fishing methods and beliefs, and mapped the geographic patterns of the fish trade, compiling in the end a rather interesting ethnological volume (Bunkachō Bunkazai Hogobu 1971).

Akita native Jihei Chiba did not focus on nostalgia, but he took the theme of loss to the next level when he penned a general-interest book (1972) at the request of a publisher on the reclamation, the settlement, and various problems related to both of these. The monograph was written at a very chaotic time for Japanese agriculture and the new village; the government was hurriedly rethinking its policies to cope with a sudden and unexpected surplus of rice and demanding that growers dramatically reduce output by letting fields lie fallow, and it had also temporarily halted the Ogata-mura settlement program. Furthermore, Tokyo was just starting to question the philosophy behind large-scale land alteration projects, and local residents' opposition to these (especially dams) was mounting. Overall, although hopeful, Chiba assumed a fairly critical stance in his analysis of the entire project, ending with a warning against going too far with schemes to alter the nation's natural lakes, bays, and inlets. Criticism of the project continued with geographer John Rutherford, who suggested in the 1980s that Hachirōgata had been set up more for efficiency of construction and management than for the emotional satisfaction of settlers. He pointed out that the "suburban approach" to designing and building planned farms is considered to prevent residents from engaging in small-scale intensive gardening and animal husbandry in the immediate vicinity of their homes—something usually seen as a basic part of farm life (Rutherford 1984: 94).

This has in fact been one complaint of Ogata-mura settlers. Rutherford concludes, "It seems that planners involved in the creation of the Hachirōgata project have not considered cultural problems as much as they might have" (ibid.: 95).

Finally, two related popular books on Ogata-mura also looked at the village from critical perspectives, not in reference to its design but rather to the role of the state in its development. The first (Shimizu 1978) was penned by an Asahi Shimbun journalist who visited the village numerous times while posted in Akita. The author focused largely on institutional arrangements and reclamation issues, and also investigated the appearance of political strife in the new community. To its credit, the book casts light on the struggles of individual settlers as they pioneered a new kind of agriculture and built a new community for themselves, and it draws attention to the central role of the state in the creation and early management of the village, witnessed partly in the installation of a prefectural bureaucrat as the village's first mayor (who was also elected to serve a two-year term in the first mayoral poll in 1976). Thirteen years later, the publisher of the previous book produced his own story of Ogata-mura (Anbai 1991), based on his personal experience of growing up in Akita and viewing the village from the outside, and on many later experiences in Ogata-mura itself. By the time this monograph appeared, the village's political problems had become quite serious, and internal resistance to the state and to the village administration had become very visible. An interesting read, the book is quite fair in its humanistic portrayal of Ogata-mura as a living community, and of its leading residents, despite the fact that the author was personally opposed to the lifting of the state rice production and marketing controls.

The present study draws on this entire body of work in its consideration of how Ogata-mura was created, how it developed, and how it might serve as a modern model for Japanese agriculture and rural life. I do view the village and the project that gave birth to it critically, but I do not see it as a complete failure. Modernity balances with loss and nostalgia to a degree because some settlers still long for something that was never achieved with the village, but where Ogata-mura is concerned the modern outweighs nostalgia in all respects. Moreover, I am concerned with community formation and economic action in relation to the geographical setting and government agricultural policy. This has also been the interest of some Japanese geographers. Kudō (1969) investigated the village when the settlement process was still underway, and looked into the early formation of the community—focusing especially on the settlers of the first wave. He found that about 90 percent of the settlers had been farmers before immigrating, but that there were great differences in family composition and in the amount of capital each household was able to bring to the village to get itself through the first couple of years. Around the same time, Hōjō (1969) researched land use and output in the new village, finding that the original direct-sowing method espoused by the national government produced very low yields compared to the age-old, trusted, but laborious method of transplanting seedlings by hand—a stab at the modern village model. At the time this made many settlers very anxious about the future of their adopted home and it was an important part of the early development of the village's agriculture. Furthermore, it may have helped to sow seeds of distrust in the government's ability to manage the village and its production system in the minds of many settlers.

Shirai (1976) later investigated Ogata-mura as an example of large-scale planning gone wrong, concluding that future planners should pay more attention to natural village arrangements, traditional farming lifestyles, and the individual satisfaction of settlers rather than to what appears nice, neat, and efficient on paper—foretelling the comments of Rutherford cited above and also those of Scott (1998) many years later. In 1976 the JSIDRE published a special edition devoted entirely to studies of the Hachirōgata area, the land reclamation project, and Ogata-mura. Topics covered included reclamation technology, advances in farming methods, the planning of the settlement and the farmhouses, and terrestrial and aquatic animal life. Most notably, Hōjō (1976) contributed a paper on the social organization of the settlers. This was based partly on the central points of his 1969 paper, but it covered changes in the village's agricultural and economic situation, and also considered the lake's remaining fishing industry. Regarding change in the village, it was already clear by that time that the quality of life of the settlers had improved dramatically, with a more solid infrastructure than most farming villages, 2.5 cars per household, and (reportedly) more drivers' licenses in the hands of women than in any other municipality in the country (Hōjō 1976: 41). The edition is also notable for its inclusion of articles written by nonacademics, such as village employees, and an edition published earlier in the year (in the same annual volume) stands out for its inclusion of short essays and commentary by settlers themselves. About ten years later, Yamashita (1987) looked into land-use patterns and changes in dry-field farming, noting an increase in pumpkin and soybean production. More recently, Dennō (1999) has also investigated trends in land use in Ogata-mura. Finally, Yamano (2003) researched the settlers' decisions to obey or disobey the national government regarding rice production and marketing.

Relating somewhat to the body of literature generated by these Japanese geographers, Richard Moore made passing references to Ogata-mura (although not by name) several times in his book on Japanese agriculture (Moore 1990: 119, 230, 274), but dealt with it more thoroughly in a 1991 report comparing settlers' resistance strategies to those of farmers in two other communities, and then even more intensively in a 1993 piece, which I discuss more below and rely on throughout this book. In addition, I have compared some of the village's image-building and development projects to those of a neighboring town (Wood 1999b), discussed the effects of the shifts in rice marketing on the village society (Wood 2003) and examined the village's land reclamation museum as a regional tourism venture (Wood 2005).

A number of settlers of Ogata-mura have expressed their own struggles with the village as a modern version of a traditional place in writing. By far Ogata-mura's most prolific resident writer is Shinichirō Sakamoto, a settler of the fourth wave who hails from Sendai, who graduated from the Department of Economics at Tōhoku University, and who spent part of his childhood in occupied China. A polarizing figure in the village, Sakamoto has a strongly socialist orientation and he represents the political Left; a number of like-minded settlers have rallied around him since the village's society first became divided over government agricultural policy. In his many books—decidedly one-sided and flavored with poetic passages, literary expressions, and lengthy musings—he has consistently argued against the lifting of the government's protectionist rice policies, the industrialization and commercialization of Japanese agriculture, and increased international trade in agricultural products. A common theme in his writings is derision for Japan's mass media, which he blames for ganging up on the country's farmers when issues revolving around the protection of agriculture as a lifestyle versus industrialization and international trade come into the spotlight. Sakamoto has faithfully maintained a position from the beginning that farming is a lifestyle and not a business and that these cannot coexist peacefully, and that resistance to the state in Ogata-mura was mainly driven by selfish egoism. He identifies himself as a peasant (*hyakushō*) and stresses that he is not a profit-oriented farmer (*nōmin*). His personal calling card bears the title of *hyakushō*, and when I remarked in 1997 that he had yet to replace his original village house with something larger, he said, "No, not me—I'm just a poor peasant." In the words of Moore—who knows him personally—Sakamoto "favors a link between the farmers and the laborers," "theorizes that farmers have a close relationship with nature[,] and advocates self-sufficiency in rice for Japan from the standpoint of ecological and cultural values" (1993: 291).

On the opposite end of the ideological spectrum is Tōru Wakui, also a fourth-wave settler (but from Niigata), a two-time candidate for mayor, and a leading businessman among the disobedient faction. In his 2007 book, he argues strongly that rice farming can in fact be a good business, and that the farming life does not necessarily have to suffer for that to be so. Wakui and Sakamoto are often contrasted with one another. Each symbolizes the hopes and dreams of different settlers. Other less political residents have also published books on the village. For example, taking a mildly critical stance on the government's handling of the rice production issue and the local media's coverage of the village's social divisions, one fifth-wave settler wrote a book (Tozawa 1993) telling his version of the village's history. His humanistic vision for the future of Ogata-mura depended on the actions of the villagers themselves, and emphasizing that it was up to them to make Ogata-mura a better place, he concluded that there was plenty of hope. Finally, another settler (T. Saitō 2001) published in book form a collection of messages he included in shipments of rice he sent directly to his customers over a ten-year period from 1990 to 2000, the book being a chronicle of the village, his own farm, and his personal observations and reflections on the general region. The monograph steers clear of politics, but it does come across as a celebration of a new kind of agriculture that can be household-based, reliable, and consumer-friendly, and yet profit-oriented (and capitalistic) at the same time. This is only a small example, but there are as many opinions of what Ogata-mura should be, and what agriculture is, in the village as there are villagers.[3]

Problems—Community Planning, Transition Economy, and Conflict

One of the main concerns of this study is the role that Ogata-mura's origins and settlement have had in its development. It is very unusual in that it was planned from the start and did not grow out of any pre-existing village, in that it was basically a single experiment and not one of an array or cluster of such communities made for political ends (such as a kibbutz), and in that it still stands alone today—it has neither dissipated as have so many newer Japanese villages nor been swallowed up by growing metroplexes as have most other new settlements in the country (see Nishida and Kase 2000). In fact, compared to most planned farming communities around the world, it has been quite successful. Ogata-mura's planning and settlement conditions have strongly affected its development, and the results are tightly intertwined with social and economic relations amidst change, and with conflicts that have arisen.

When drawing up blueprints for a new, small community—even within a capitalist, democratic state—it is not uncommon for planners to strive for heterogeneity in the population and in the economic base of each household. This was attempted in the U.S.A. during the 1930s under the New Deal Administration. Destitute miners and other workers were resettled in planned communities by the government with the hope that transforming them into self-sufficient farmers and tying them down with mortgages would prevent socialist ideologies from taking root among them (Ghirardo 1989: 127). In Norvelt and Penn-Craft, Pennsylvania, settlers lived in individual houses and held small farms with which they were supposed to support themselves. However, although these communities did not end in failure, conflicts arose in some cases between settlers and managers over the communal nature of the farming plans, with rather serious consequences (Hoagland and Mulrooney 1991). Unlike these examples, in building *kolkhoz* farms the Soviet Union under Stalin forced a complex, pre-existing social system to fit an idealistic model for communal agriculture, which was met by much resistance and which did end in failure (Fitzpatrick 1994, Scott 1998: 193–222). Another tragic case—a massive villagization program in Tanzania that affected over five million people during the 1970s—was supposed to create heterogeneous, large-scale, heavily mechanized farming communities. Not surprisingly, this failed miserably due to ignorance of geographic, economic, and cultural factors (Scott 1998: 223–261). Many of the villages bore a striking resemblance to Ogata-mura (see especially p. 250).

Stanbury (1987) provides valuable details on a settlement project in north-western India. Caste was important in social relations and economic success in the case described by her, but kinship and village of origin appeared as major factors in relocation and in social organization. In fact, spontaneous settlement by people who simply moved in, outside of the government settlement scheme, turned out be a powerful force in the development of the local agricultural system and these settlers also appear to have achieved greater overall success. Due to these processes, Stanbury reports, settlement planning in the end "had only a minimal effect on the social and economic composition of the village" due to the formation of kinship and other social networks that greatly altered the original plan (Stanbury 1987: 290). This makes Ogata-mura an even more special case because of the very high degree of government control over the settlement of all farming households in the village. But, as in Stanbury's study village, Ogata-mura's social organization was largely determined by place of origin and kinlike cooperative group ties at the beginning. And, in Ogata-mura, these ties have continued to influence the social structure and economic success over time, despite the revolutionary changes that have occurred in the local economy. In addition, as with Israeli kibbutz communities (Gavron 2000, Near 2008, Talmon 1972), individual settlers who were supposed to be roughly equal to one another from the beginning began to grow apart both socially and economically as each found his own footing amidst the village's shift from a controlled to a more liberal economy—as, that is, the forces of capitalism grew in strength. Considering these and other examples (Pryor 1992, Sachs 1994), it should be no surprise that the initial heterogeneity of Ogata-mura society has largely disappeared—a phenomenon related to economic transition.

When an economy goes through changes involving a loosening of central control and an increase in the power of market forces, and when state-owned entities start to give way to private enterprises, the economy is commonly said to be in transition, or to be a "transition economy." Prime examples are the former Soviet territories of Eastern Europe and Central Asia, and of course China and Vietnam (see Dana 2002, Pomfret 1996). The term *transition economy* has come to mean a variety of things, and does not necessarily indicate that all such economies are moving in the same direction or at the same pace. Pomfret (2002: 1) explains:

The key elements of transition are the replacement of physical allocation of a nation's resources by allocation in response to price signals, which requires both price liberalization and enterprise reform. These are complementary, because without enterprise reform there is unlikely to be the desired response to relative price changes and with artificial prices reformed enterprises' decisions will not be socially optimal.

Here, Pomfret is referring mainly to entire states as transition economies—the most easily found examples and those usually studied by economists. However, due to the high degree of central planning and control and the collective nature of the original farming operation, and also the shifts that have occurred, Ogata-mura can be said to constitute a small, localized transition economy. The relationship over time between planning, policy, social organization, and conflict, are all most clearly seen in the context of Ogata-mura as such an economy; and viewing it as such economy helps us to understand better why things happened in the village the way they did. We do not have to be particularly surprised by the overall course of development seen in the village. Even as a capitalist democracy, Japan relied heavily on central control and planning, including market protection and state support of institutions, to achieve the spectacular economic growth it experienced following its recovery from defeat in 1945, and the stagnation that deepened in the 1990s helped expose the pitfalls of the system, and brought about calls for deregulation and greater freedom for market forces (Vogel 2005). Deregulation and privatization—sometimes known collectively as "neoliberalism"—were major goals of Prime Minister Jun'ichirō Koizumi during his tenure (2001–2006), and he pursued these even at the cost of splitting his own party, the then-dominant Liberal Democratic Party (Jimintō, or LDP). Ogata-mura started out with a high degree of central planning and control, and was situated squarely in the middle of Japan's protectionist agricultural policies that have attracted so much attention from economists and political scientists.

Ogata-mura can also be viewed as a transition economy in that it became a hotbed of political subversion and illicit marketing activities. As Dana (2005: 2) puts it, "Transitional economies provide a particularly fascinating backdrop for the development of entrepreneurship." In such environments, economic initiatives often occur within an area of hazy legal status, or are rather completely out of accordance with the law. Indeed, studies of emerging entrepreneurialism in economies in transition (Dana 2002, 2005, Pomfret 1996, Pryor 1992) have shown that it is extremely difficult—if not impossible—for a state or other administration to prevent people from engaging in illicit market activities. In fact, a clandestine parallel economy often appears in transition economies that are lacking in developed market frameworks (Dana 2005, Feige and Ott 1999), participation in which allows individuals to circumvent regulations and avoid taxation.

Dissenting Ogata-mura settlers were not interested in tax evasion, but most were so convinced that the state was wrong that they were willing to risk persecution—and prosecution—in order to farm and sell rice as they liked. Likewise, it has been noted that in many transition economies entrepreneurialism and efficiency have come to be popularly equated with escaping regulation and skirting the law (Dana 2005: 8–9), and in Ogata-mura the word *entrepreneur* still has a very negative meaning for many. Furthermore, the village began with a collective farming system that underwent a decollectivization process—albeit a very quick and painless one—that bore many similarities to those common to centrally planned agrarian systems (Pryor 1992: 265–295).

However, although Ogata-mura fits into the typical transition economy model in a number of ways, at least one way in which it does not fit the model makes it an even more interesting case study. In many instances of high central control, illicit entrepreneurial activity has had the unintended effect of helping the system work more smoothly—allowing formal, inefficient systems to survive longer than they otherwise might have by boosting their distributive potential (Grossman 1977). In Ogata-mura, granted, the issue was not the overall economy but only the rice marketing system, but it is notable that the illegal marketing and production activities of the defiant farmers of the village did not help maintain or prolong a rigid, centrally controlled system but rather, if anything, helped to break it down in the long run. In the short run, these illegal activities fractured the community itself. For most of the country, the state has led the way in agrarian reform—dragging farmers this way and that—but in Ogata-mura entrepreneurial settlers have led the way. Even though the defiant farmers were but a tiny minority in the grand scheme of things, they managed to take a large chip out of the foundation of a system that still held the trust of millions. Most avoided legal responsibility for their actions and, moreover, they were all but vindicated when the head of the MAFF chastised the Akita Prefecture government for imposing penalties on the overproducing farmers of Ogata-mura in late 2009, which again thrust the village into the local spotlight—a place where it appears to be comfortable.

In a controlled economy undergoing rapid liberalization, there is the question of exactly who will engage in entrepreneurial or clandestine activities, and who will be most successful in the long run. After studying entrepreneurialism in transition in many locations for a number of years, Dana (2005) concludes that it will always occur unevenly, even in a single locality such as Ogata-mura. Yamano (2003) has shown that settler wave number and place of origin appear to have been factors in the economic choices and successes of the immigrants there. This book elaborates on these findings. Close, kinlike ties between settlers were established due to the way in which the village was planned and to the settlement and initial work conditions. These ties guided the early development of the village. Place of origin directly affected social relations and economic choices—and also relative success—over time. Finally, conflict arose, based at least in part on these divisions, and caused greater divisions that in some cases transcend the earlier arrangements.

On conflict as a social phenomenon, works of the "classic" body of anthropological literature on rural Japan—beginning with Embree (1939) and stretching through the 1980s—tended to concentrate on social cohesion, emphasizing harmony and cooperation over strife and division (see Ryang 2004). This is not to say that these studies were without merit; quite the contrary, together they painted a vivid, detailed picture of Japanese village society, and they traced postwar change carefully, paving the way for later work. Historians, on the other hand, have been quite eager to focus on social conflict in Japanese villages. Hane (1982: 7) mentions more than 2,800 peasant "disturbances" between the years 1590 and 1867, and T. Smith (1959: 183–187) details numerous petitions and protests occurring throughout the same period. Partner (2009) also reminds readers that the Meiji and Taishō eras were tough times for most producers, who occasionally became violent towards landlords, and Dore (1959: 72) counts more than seventy-two thousand land disputes between the years 1917 and 1941.

Anthropologists have recently begun to focus more on conflict as an agent of change in small Japanese communities, a trend that can be detected in Smith's (1978) study of a Kagawa Prefecture village and that became more noticeable with the appearance of books by Moon (1989), Robertson (1991), Bailey (1991), and Schnell (1999)—the third of which particularly relates to Ogata-mura in that social conflict was a product of national government policy in the village in question, and also in the irresolvable nature of that conflict. Theoretically, internal conflict has been seen as deleterious to a community's social fabric (Dahrendorf 1959). But it has also been pointed out that conflict increases solidarity within groups, binding like-minded people together, even if at the expense of a community's overall cohesion (Coser 1956). The conflicts in Ogata-mura have done both, and in addition they conform well to the cultural framework proposed by Ishida (1984), which dictates that conflict among members of a single group must be hidden from the outside (because it should not exist), but a solid in-group must not make concessions in the formal arena when clashing with outsiders, though concessions can be made in the backstage area, as long as neither party is seen as losing too much face. Dore's comment on this, written over fifty years ago, runs parallel to Ishida's argument: "Competition within a group which is in theory harmoniously united tends to become fiercer and more emotionally involved than in one where competition is accepted as normal. As such it leaves scars after the event in the resentful humiliation of the defeated" (1959: 343, quoted in Smith 1978: 237).

Yamano (2003) has analyzed the nature and role of the rice-related quarrels in Ogata-mura and concluded that settler wave number and place of origin were significant factors in the divisions that emerged between households there. He also found that settlers born in the 1930s showed a higher tendency to defy government orders than others, and that free-market-oriented (noncompliant) settlers were more likely than compliant settlers to have increased their land holdings by 1999 (2006: 49–80). The strength of his research lies in his methodological attempt at finding explanations for individual action—especially decisions to defy the government or to comply with its orders. However, while Yamano's findings are useful in understanding the village's development, he has not investigated the village's society in great detail, and factors such as those he has identified need to be understood as parts of a greater whole. Furthermore, Yamano's analysis lacks a strong political economy perspective and overlooks the cultural significance of rice as well as the symbolic significance of the "ideal farming life" and community and personal identity as they relate to business-oriented production.

Richard Moore (1991, 1993) has recognized the importance of conflict, as it related to resistance to government policy, in the course of Ogata-mura's brief history, and he has investigated its role. In Moore's analysis, grounded heavily in Scott's discussions of everyday peasant resistance (1985, 1989, 1990), cultural resistance to hegemony centering around class relations takes central stage, and this is shown to have been a powerful force in the development of the village's society. He details the ways in which the settlers became polarized, the two camps completely unable to agree with one another over the issue of free rice production and marketing, and places Ogata-mura well in its larger political context, paying especially close attention to the effects of government policy—one of his strongest contributions to the anthropological study of Japanese agriculture. Moore shows how some among the faction of Ogata-mura settlers who obeyed the national government, led by Shinichirō Sakamoto, engaged in a subtle form of resistance by overcomplying with policies and emphasizing their "peasantness" and relative paucity of income—partly by holding off on making improvements to their houses—in relation to their overproducing and free-market-oriented neighbors. Also, he explains how the disobedient faction first engaged in organized resistance by surreptitiously overproducing and illegally marketing their rice before switching to more overt tactics.[4] In many ways, this book builds and expands on the foundation laid by Moore (1991, 1993).

In sum, Ogata-mura is a very special community with its own qualities. It stands out because it was carved into the geography, because it was centrally planned, and because it was "modern" from the start. Moreover, it was meant to be as egalitarian and homogeneous as possible. Due to its particular origins and the events that have taken place there, Ogata-mura has been the subject of much consideration on the part of a variety of chroniclers—government researchers, university professors, graduate students, popular writers, reporters, and villagers themselves. In fact, there might not be another community of such small size in the entire country that has been scrutinized to the degree that Ogata-mura has. This makes it easier to carefully study the village's development over time. But despite the volume of information available, there has yet to emerge a comprehensive, objective, "thick" study of the village as it stands today. I hope this book will serve that purpose.

Notes

1. Although 589 men were accepted for the national settlement program, several dropped out early on.
2. "Modernism" here is closely tied to mid twentieth-century "modernization" as discussed by Gudeman: "economic reorganization after the pattern of the 'advanced' industrial economies, such as the United States" (2008: 148). Importantly, Gudeman proposes that "modernity" has come to mean an increase of individual agency and reason—basically, freedom to think and behave as one pleases in an open economy. This meaning of modernity also underlies the development of Ogata-mura, and the reorganization alluded to above is a source of anxiety over rapid change in the village.
3. It is possible that those who applied to the settlement program were already somewhat "different" from other farmers from the beginning. Also, a side effect of the selection process may have been the creation of a village with a large number of outspoken and active people. In addition, the fact that the settlers had free time during the winters from the beginning to engage in hobbies may be a factor.
4. In addition, Moore points to the possibility of a religious factor in the motivations of this faction—the influence of the Sōka Gakkai, to which a number of them are known to belong. I have not been able to verify this as a powerful ideological factor, but it may have helped some secure rice marketing channels.

1

AGRICULTURAL POLICY AND REGIONAL POLITICS IN JAPAN

Saying "don't grow rice" to a farmer who depends solely on rice production
is basically taking away his livelihood. . . . It's equal to a death sentence.
                                                            –Tōru Wakui[1]

For centuries Japan's food producers, and the regions in which they live, have had
relations with a central government (Tokugawa, Meiji, Taishō, etc.) marked by
high degrees of control and regulation. Policies formulated at the center have been
at times designed to boost outputs and at times designed to do the opposite. In the
years immediately following the Second World War, building and maintaining
an egalitarian farm base took precedence over all else. Soon, though, it became
more important for the ruling Liberal Democratic Party (LDP) to keep farmers
happy and to ensure that their incomes would not merely remain stable but in fact
grow slowly over time, in order to secure the rural votes needed to keep itself in
power; after all, the party's decades-long domination of Japan's government was
based on promises of stability and security (Gill 2001: 196). However, keeping
farmers happy grew more and more difficult as their average age rose (it is now
over sixty-five), as village population dropped, and—especially—as pressure to
accept foreign rice imports increased, just as a surplus of domestic rice began to
appear. By the close of the twentieth century it had become quite unclear to most
Japanese farmers exactly what their leaders wanted them to do, and—even more
critical—how they could protect their lifestyles. In many cases it came down to
saving their very communities, as more and more of their neighbors either gave
up and moved away, or died without any successor to take over their farms—for
the days when having multiple sons was enough to ensure that at least one would
stay on the farm were largely over even by the 1980s. Ogata-mura cannot serve
as a case study of these exact processes, for it is not a "normal" village, but as a

---

Endnotes for this chapter begin on page 41.

planned farming project it reflects the hopes of the central government and serves as a flash point where these hopes collide with reality. It is something of a laboratory test case, a case which has generated some very special and unique results. But these results are not unrelated to the effects of policy in other farming areas of Japan, and the village does not exist in a political, economic, social, or historical vacuum, either, so here I briefly consider Japan's major agricultural and regional policies, starting with the end of its feudal days but focusing especially on the postwar period.[2]

Agricultural and Regional Policy

At the dawn of the Meiji era, which lasted from 1868 to 1912, the fiefdoms (or *han*) of the feudal Edo period were abolished and the population of Japan found itself organized into a vast number of new administrative bodies scattered across the land. As of 1883 there were 16 cities (*shi*), 12,194 towns (*machi*), and 59,284 villages (*mura*) (Shichōson Jiji Kenkyūkai 2002: 1). Towns and villages were further divided into numerous hamlets. Keeping track of the population and building a new nation required continuous reorganization—by the turn of the century there were 48 cities, 1,173 towns, and 13,068 villages. Males over the age of twenty-five who had at least two years' residence in one place and who paid at least two *sen* in taxes were considered to be citizens in the full sense of the term (*kōmin*).[3] Constituting a mere 10 percent of the population as of the early 1890s, they were the only voters in the nation (Fukutake 1980: 147).[4] The Meiji government placed high priority on boosting rice outputs. As part of the solution, it initiated a four-year land-tax revision program in 1873. Mechanization was encouraged, and it progressed rapidly, but reliance on draft animals remained constant.[5] Rice yield per unit of land grew slowly: a 1,000 square meter tract (ten ares, or one-tenth of a hectare) yielded an average of 247 kilograms in the period from 1900 to 1909 and 287 kilograms in the period from 1920 to 1929 (Asahi Shimbun-sha 2001: 66).

However, the farm life was not an easy one. Although credit associations for small producers were established in 1900, farmers experienced many bad years after artificially adjusted prices of farm products began falling in 1919. To make matters worse, serious crop failures and famines plagued farmers of the northern territories, forcing them to eat whatever they could find and to sell their daughters as well (Hane 1982: 120). In order to cope with these kinds of problems, the government took measures to increase its control over the marketing of agricultural products. With the passage of the 1921 Rice Law (Beikoku Hō), Tokyo gained the power to regulate rice prices across the board; to buy, store, and sell rice as necessary; and to regulate imports (Moore 1990: 286). This trend culminated in the more comprehensive Food Control Act (Shokuryō Kanri Hō) in 1942, which granted the government even greater managerial powers over rice marketing (ibid.: 288, Solt 2010: 188–189).

Indeed, during the 1930s, as the government strove to perfect Japan as a militarist state, control over production and distribution grew tighter—perhaps as tight as it had been under the Tokugawa regime in its heyday. Moreover, the pressure of having to make mandatory rice "donations" for war efforts (not to mention the loss of their sons) placed an especially heavy burden on farmers. The war years were lean, and even the very concept of the kind of agricultural system that exists in Ogata-mura today would have seemed like a far-off dream, or a joke, to most people. At the close of the war in 1945, the Japanese population was divided into 205 cities, 1,797 towns, and 8,518 villages (Shichōson Jichi Kenkyūkai 2002: 1). Increased efforts on the part of the central government at amalgamating smaller communities, combined with general population movements away from these, resulted in a nearly equal number of cities and villages by the start of this century; as of April 2002 there were 562 of the former and 575 of the latter, with the number of towns remaining fairly steady at 1,981. But as of February 2010 there were only 189 villages, compared to 787 towns and 784 cities, for a total of 1,760 municipalities (Government of Japan 2010).[6] There are today many towns and villages comprised of numerous scattered hamlets which have changed little in their composition since the early Meiji years, but even so these are hardly the isolated, self-governing bodies that they once were, and although names of hamlets are still often used, they no longer carry the legal meanings they once held. On the other hand, a large number of such communities have completely vanished. One Ogata-mura farmer has written books documenting the recent disappearance of 125 hamlets (K. Satō 1997), seventy-five post-Edo era pioneer settlements (K. Satō 2005), and many dozens of small elementary school branches (K. Satō 2001), all in Akita Prefecture.

The greatest immediate postwar change for most agriculturalists was their transformation from tenants to small-scale owner-farmers. As is widely known, the occupation government initiated a series of sweeping land-reform measures during the first few years after the end of the war, which has been well covered by Dore (1959). One of the main goals was to free the country's producers from the shackles of tenancy and to break up the rigid class divisions between tenants and landlords, thus creating a more egalitarian society of relatively small-scale, enthusiastic owner-farmers upon which a stable democracy and a strong national (capitalist) economy could be built. Initially landlords were limited to renting out only five hectares, but this figure was lowered to one, and eventually the total amount of land in tenancy came to be set by county (about three in most of the country and about twelve in Hokkaido), while the problem of absentee landlords was all but eliminated (Moore 1990: 288). Land was redistributed through a complex system that went through a number of adjustments, and did achieve most of its

Table 1.1: National average rice yield by decade, 1940–1999

Years	1940–1949	1950–1959	1960–1969	1970–1979	1980–1989	1990–1999
Yield (kg per 1,000 sqm)	310	345	410	460	478	494

Source: Asahi Shimbun-sha (2001: 66).

goals. However, it failed in many cases to protect former tenants, and excessively harmed many landowners as well, prompting numerous complaints and legal actions. In Dore's view, that the land reform was imposed by an alien entity—the occupation government—was a major reason for its successes; former tenants were able to take land without feeling responsible for doing so (1959: 172).

At the time of the first land-reform measure in 1945, nearly 30 percent of Japanese farmers worked land owned by another person, but this had dwindled to a mere 1 percent by 1975 (Fukutake 1980: 8). Although tenancy was nearly erased by the postwar reforms, the amount of land farmed by each household remained nearly the same: in 1946, 39.2 percent of the farmers worked fields measuring only 0.5 hectares, compared to 40.5 percent in 1975. On the other end of the scale, nine-tenths of 1 percent of Japanese farming households held fields amounting to at least five hectares in 1946, compared to 1.4 percent in 1975 (ibid.: 10). In 1960 the average farm size was nine-tenths of a hectare, and this had increased to only 1.2 hectares by 2000 (Yamashita 2004). The yield per area, however, increased more dramatically throughout the twentieth century (Table 1.1).

But just as yields have increased, so has the minimum field area needed to maintain a viable farm. In 1960 this figure was about 2.4 hectares. It rose to about 3.5 hectares in 1970, 5.5 hectares in 1980, and 5.6 hectares in 1985 (Hayami 1988: 80).[7] Since purchasing new farmland has been nearly impossible for most farmers—both because of availability and price—these conditions have helped encourage farmers to seek regular full-time employment and thus become part-time producers. In 1990 the government began counting farmers in a new way. Now, those who have at least 0.3 hectares (three thousand square meters) of land or earn at least five hundred thousand yen annually from farming are considered to be "sales-oriented farmers" (*hanbai nōka*) and those who fall below this threshold are "self-sufficiency farmers" (*jikyū nōka*). These comprised 75 percent and 25 percent of the farming population in the year 2000, respectively (Asahi Shimbun-sha 2001: 63).[8]

National figures show almost no change in the total number of farms in Japan over the tumultuous thirty-five year period from 1938 to 1973 (5,336,000 in 1938 compared with 5.1 million in 1973—Tsuchiya 1976: 34). This reflects the determination of Japanese farmers to maintain ownership over their fields and the general postwar shift to part-time production as a strategy to achieve this. But data from the northern frontier island of Hokkaido—where serious settlement began only towards the end of the nineteenth century—is indicative of a different pattern. There, influenced at least in part by a lack of adequate wage-labor jobs that would have otherwise helped some farmers avoid quitting and selling their fields, the total number of farm households decreased by nearly half (from 233,634 to 119,644) between the years 1960 and 1980 (Yamamoto et al. 1987: 54). It also seems clear that a lack of long-standing social relationships and deep ancestral ties to farmland in Hokkaido made it easier for settlers there to quit and part with their land—a situation which well relates to the case of Ogata-mura. However, recent information shows that, largely due to government encouragement, farms in parts of Hokkaido have increased dramatically in scale—the average size for dairy farms in the Tokachi region now being over thirty-five hectares (Takenaka 2004).

In 1949 the government enacted the Land Improvement Law (Tochi Kairyō Hō), which established regional offices for overseeing land consolidation and improvements in soil quality and irrigation. The following year saw the appearance of the 1950 Act to Promote Agricultural Mechanization (Nōgyō Kikaika Sokushin Hō), which sought to increase the number of machines in the fields for better efficiency and productivity (Moore 1990: 289). A major mechanical component of Japanese rice farming since this time has been the power tiller. Its increased adoption following the 1950 law (3,150 hp in 1953 compared to 8,109 hp in 1965) has been related to a dramatic drop in the overall amount of human labor (from about 16 million hp down to about 10 million hp) for the same period, while draft animal power actually shows fairly little change (Tsuchiya 1976: 170–172). On average, the total number of mechanical tillers in use per one hundred farming households increased from 8.6 in 1960 to 56.0 in 1967, but there was significant variation in their adoption—due to public inputs—between high rice-yield areas and lower yield areas across the country (ibid.: 174). Japanese farming today is fully mechanized, although the small size of the landholdings has led to a large number of small machines rather than larger ones—most farmers own their equipment, but even in Ogata-mura there are no machines quite as massive as some of those used in the American Midwest.

In 1947 the occupation government passed the Agricultural Cooperatives Act (Nōgyō Kyōdō Kumiai Hō), which reorganized the old credit associations that had been established at the turn of the century and allowed for the creation of new local organizations. Today these agricultural cooperatives, which are tied together through a national association—Nōkyō, or "JA" for "Japan Agriculture"—play an important role. They sell seeds, fertilizers, and chemicals, offer repair services for equipment (including automobiles and bicycles), organize social associations, and provide banking services for farmers. Local agricultural cooperatives operate on a membership basis, and most producers belong to their local cooperative.

Members hold shares, but these are not tradable stocks. The cooperatives own and maintain storage elevators and other processing facilities for grains and legumes, which the members use. Until the passage of a new law in 1995, local cooperatives purchased rice from farmers in their area at prices set by the government. Today, prices on domestic rice are decided by market forces and not by the government, although the amount buyers will pay is often influenced by their knowledge of subsidies available to farmers.

During Japan's economic boom years, the national JA association ballooned into a massive corporation. It opened up a chain of supermarkets across the country and started printing and shipping operations, competing on some levels with private companies. Individual JA entities expanded tremendously. However, after the bursting of the bubble economy and the changes in rice marketing (plus the drop in rice demand and prices) in the mid-1990s, the JAs across the country began to suffer. Therefore, at the beginning of the current century the government started encouraging them to merge with one another, as municipalities were being pressured to do. It used to be that each city, town, or village had at least one JA, but as of April 2012 there were fifteen JAs in Akita Prefecture for its twenty-five separate municipalities.[9] Only several, including Ogata-mura's, had yet to merge with any other. A local JA can serve as a focal point for the political power of the voting population of a town or village, so they have often been singled out as causes of stagnation in agricultural reform.

The year 1961 saw the ratification of the Agricultural Basic Law, which was primarily designed to prevent the nation's farmers from dropping behind people in other professions in terms of income. It protected the agricultural sector and offered the farmers security in the form of automatic price supports, which was a good thing for the dominant LDP because it wanted to be able to count on the farm vote to maintain power and settle the turbulent political situation caused by the renewal of the Japan–U.S. Security Treaty the year before (Mishima 2004: 260). Moore (1990: 291) explains the main points of the law as follows: "Agricultural productivity should increase in such a way as to reduce the disparity in productivity between agriculture and other industries. Persons engaged in agriculture should earn higher incomes enabling them to make a living comparable to those engaged in other industries." The basic law empowered the government to restrict imports and adjust tariff rates: imports of rice and wheat were heavily restricted. Under the law, farmland was rezoned and redistributed to form more efficient, contiguous parcels, on a scale never before imagined (see Moore 1990: 63–105). Dairy farming and horticulture were especially targeted for expansion, and both increased exponentially, but production of feed for cattle dropped dramatically and the country became more dependent on related imports. In fact, the nation's overall self-sufficiency in foodstuffs declined from 79 percent in 1960 to a mere 40 percent in 2002 (Yamashita 2004).

Following on the heels of prewar attempts at lifestyle improvement in rural areas, the government began a new program, known as *Seikatsu Kaizen Fukkyū Jigyō*, focused on bringing rural conditions up to par with the standards of living in urban areas. Infrastructural and economic problems were central, and production and marketing received the most attention. Often called *mura-zukuri*, the program was usually planned at the national or prefectural level. Generally, *mura-zukuri* projects focused on bringing better agricultural machines to towns and villages, building and repairing roads, preparing facilities such as meeting halls and playgrounds, and other infrastructural improvements. Social projects included outdoor markets where locals could sell their farm products and the establishment of production-oriented fairs and festivals, but they were few until the 1980s. Household improvements were also considered by the government to be very important.[10]

One major aspect of postwar rural life in Japan on which *mura-zukuri* was supposed to have an effect was the *dekasegi* phenomenon. *Dekasegi*—working away from home on a seasonal or otherwise temporary basis—has been a typical income supplement for many Japanese farmers due to a lack of local jobs for decades, but it was especially prevalent from the 1950s through the 1980s (Bailey 1991: 146, Dore 1978: 106, Gordon 1965: 26, Nozoe 1994, 2006a, H. Satō 1966). This is why *dekasegi* is generally seen as a postwar phenomenon. It is also strongly associated with the general Tōhoku farming lifestyle. Part-time farmers have been encouraged to engage in *dekasegi* work for a variety of reasons, with poverty always at the core, but an increase of seasonal off-time brought about by mechanization and greater reliance on chemical fertilizers and pesticides, and the diminished need for extra help in the fields due to the same developments, have also contributed. Also, the implementation of rice crop reduction (*gentan*) policies in 1970 compelled farmers to allow fields to lie fallow, thus resulting in less on-farm work. Furthermore, extra activities such as raising silkworms and making charcoal that farmers have traditionally done to supplement their incomes gradually became less and less profitable as the national economy expanded from about 1960 onward. Although *dekasegi* has diminished in terms of occurrence and importance, it is still practiced to a degree today—nearly thirteen thousand people left Akita for such work in 1955, a figure that had expanded to seventy-three thousand per year by the early 1970s, and then dropped to under three thousand by 2005 (Nozoe 2006b: 251).

The most notable agricultural acts passed in the wake of the 1961 Basic Law were a string of laws designed either to take farmland entirely out of commission or to shift it away from rice production, promulgated in response to an unforeseen surplus of rice. These laws were marked by the appearance in 1971 of the Rice Production Control and Diversion Program, which offered cash incentives of up to about four hundred thousand yen per hectare to divert to perennial crops, but less to simply allow land to lie fallow (Moore 1990: 298). This law established the government's *gentan* policy—inspired partly by foreign pressure to import rice—which had an enormous impact on the development of Ogata-mura. In 1978 the *gentan* policy was effectively repealed by a new law that set forth the government's plan to encourage producers to grow crops other than rice (to do *tensaku*) at levels adjusted for each prefecture, or region. For example, while an average of 24 percent of the entire nation's rice paddy land was to be diverted, specific figures ranged from 16 percent for Miyagi Prefecture to 48 percent for Hokkaido, with Akita falling exactly at the national average. Like the previous *gentan* policy, farmers were offered subsidies for complying (Moore 1990: 299–301). However, Ogata-mura farmers who defied the government throughout this period were never offered such incentives. At any rate, most Japanese farmers did not care about the difference between *gentan* and *tensaku* but simply cared whether they could continue to make a good living by farming. As explained above, though, by the time these policies were enacted the overwhelming majority were producing on a part-time basis and not depending wholly on farm income.

The law that made it legal for producers to sell their rice directly to consumers was the so-called "New Food Control Act" (Shin Shokuryō Kanri Hō), thus nicknamed because it reversed the terms of the 1942 Food Control Act to such a great degree. The official name of the law, which went into effect on November 1, 1995, is the "Law Regarding the Stability of Supply, Demand, and Price of Principal Foodstuffs" (Shuyō Shokuryō no Jukyū Oyobi Kakaku no Antei ni Kansuru Hōritsu). Both external and internal pressures were responsible for the ratification of the law in late 1994. First, foreign governments—especially that of the United States—had been pressuring Japan to open its rice markets under the General Agreement on Tariffs and Trade (GATT) for years (Horiguchi 1990). Second, many farmers wanted the freedom of a more open market, and a number of researchers and lawmakers felt that allowing overseas growers to compete with domestic producers would not necessarily harm Japan's internal situation.[11] Shinichirō Sakamoto, the socialist settler-writer of Ogata-mura, has likened this law to a poison, gently administered to the farming populace with sweet words like "freedom to grow" and "freedom to sell"—a deceptive concoction that will eventually kill Japanese farming and farming communities as they have been known up to now (1998: 68).

In addition to the passing of the monumental 1995 law, in 1999 the government repealed the 1961 Basic Law, officially relinquishing its right to control the prices of agricultural products—most notably, rice. It did this by promulgating the New Basic Law, which declared that prices would henceforth be set by the market and not the government, but still promised to help protect farmers by offering an income insurance scheme and programs for direct income compensation (Mishima 2004: 267). Rice price support policies were considerably relaxed due to the passing of this law, the promulgation of which was partly inspired by the establishment of the WTO in 1995. Because of the rice price support structure (and tariffs), Japan's agricultural markets have always been rather well insulated from the rest of the world, and this was important in its rise to the ranks of other economically powerful nations, but it led to imbalances that caught the attention of its trading partners; although Japan had become a major importer by the mid-1970s, it is reported to have had the largest number of restricted-import goods in the world at that time (Tsuchiya 1976: 228). There were also arguments that one result of the government's long-term, artificial rice-price inflation was that Japan's rice farmers had become unable to compete with imports. The release of rice prices from government control had been foreseen by many prior to 1999. Nearly a decade earlier, Ogata-mura settler Shinichirō Sakamoto had argued vehemently against it in a book whose title can be translated as "I Cannot Tolerate the Liberation of the Rice Market" (*Kome Jiyūka Yurusazu*, 1991). In it, he vilified GATT and harshly criticized the national media based in Tokyo for its support of compliance with outside powers and the forces of globalization.

Carrots from Heaven

The central government has long controlled Japan's agriculture and regions by mere command. But simply giving orders and expecting them to be followed does not always work, as a close look at Ogata-mura shows. In recent years, Tokyo and the MAFF have demonstrated an ability to impose some change in Japan's regions by employing different combinations of carrot-and-stick policy formulas—combinations that rely less on the latter than the former.

One of the most critical implications of the New Food Control Act of 1995 was that the national government had finally given up on forcing the nation's farmers to comply with *tensaku* policies—to divert agricultural land to nonrice crops. Actually, the policies ceased to be such and became mere guidelines. Dropping the stick and waving the carrot higher, the MAFF began to offer farmers the chance to become "accredited agricultural producers" (*nintei nōgyōsha*). If a farmer becomes a *nintei nōgyōsha* (or if an agricultural corporation acquires the accreditation and becomes a *nintei nōgyōhōjin*) then access to a variety of assistance from the government, including long-term, low-interest loans, can be obtained. For example, "Super S" loans are limited to five million yen (twenty million for corporations with the necessary accreditation—*nintei nōgyōhōjin*), and must be returned after one year. Borrowed money can be used for purchasing agricultural machines and various farming supplies, and also for training or other, production-related, educational costs. "Super L" loans, on the other hand, have a cap of 150 million yen for individuals and 500 million yen for corporations, and must be paid off within twenty-five years. Money can be used for a variety of purposes, including the purchase of farmland, the construction of agricultural facilities, the repair of machines, the processing of agricultural products, and even patent applications. Money loaned under these schemes originally flowed from the Agriculture, Forestry, and Fisheries Finance Corporation (AFC), a public institution established in 1953 under the Agriculture, Forestry, and Fisheries Finance Corporation Law. In 2008 the AFC became the Agriculture, Forestry, Fisheries and Food Business Unit of the Japan Finance Corporation (JFC)—a government enterprise—so today loan applications must be submitted to the JFC, and it is the JFC that makes the payments. Therefore, municipalities are not directly involved in the flow of public monies into or out of the accounts of *nintei nōgyōsha* (or corporations) under the agricultural support system—they only decide who has the accreditation.

In order to become accredited, a farmer must fill out the appropriate forms and file them with his or her local municipal administration, where the application will be considered. In Ogata-mura, this is done by the nine-member Production Management Recommendation Committee (*keiei seisan taisaku suishin kaigi*). Six members are directly involved in village politics and agriculture (including the mayor, an assembly member, and the head of the village agricultural cooperative association) and three are employees of the prefecture government. In deciding who can receive the accreditation, the primary factor (not surprisingly) is whether the applicant is complying with the MAFF's *tensaku* guidelines. Even the smallest-scale farmers are expected to do so. However, proving that he or she (or it) is complying with *tensaku* policies is not enough for a person or a corporation to receive the accreditation. An application must also show that the applicant has concrete plans for improving their production in terms of efficiency and competitiveness, especially with respect to imported food products. Plans must he explained in detail, and anticipated increases in production must be clearly stated. All accredited individuals or corporations must have their status reviewed every five years, but in Ogata-mura accredited farmers have generally maintained their status for some time, and this is probably the case for most municipalities as well.

The number of sales-oriented farming entities (individuals and corporations) in the country with the accreditation has been growing; there were 191,633 in March of 2005 and 246,026 at the same time in 2009 (MAFF 2005, 2010). This change is even more notable when we consider that the total number of such entities dropped from 1,736,000 in 2005 to 1,555,000 in 2009 (Government of Japan (Sōmu-shō) 2011). Yet, as these numbers show, the proportion of accredited entities to non-accredited entities remains fairly low. In other words, many sales-oriented farmers have chosen not to apply for accreditation, for one reason or another. This is something that Tokyo has wanted to rectify. Perhaps some individuals who have gained the status have done so with their children in mind—it is rumored that should the son or daughter of a farmer try to obtain a government position, they will have a better chance if their farming parent is a *nintei nōgyōsha*.

Another way in which the government has attempted to reduce the amount of high-quality rice for the table produced in the country has been to encourage farmers to grow rice to be used for making other kinds of food products, such as *sake*, *miso*, and even bread. This rice is known as *kakōyōmai*, or simply *kakōmai*, and allowances for it fluctuate from year to year. Generally, though, farmers with *nintei nōgyōsha* status have been allowed to grow a certain amount of rice that they officially declare to be *kakōmai*. Many Ogata-mura farmers have responded to the MAFF's encouragement by increasing their production of *kakōmai*, although the overall amount has remained low. Of the nearly eight thousand hectares of land being used for rice cultivation in the village in 2003, a mere 108 were dedicated to *kakōmai* that year—a number which had grown to only about four times that amount in 2006 (Akita Sakigake Shinpō 2006). However, in 2010 the number of hectares used for *kakōmai* in Ogata-mura shot up to a point above two-thousand due to the sudden participation of many village farmers in a new support program initiated by the Democratic Party of Japan (DPJ), which had assumed power the previous summer (Nagahama 2011: 122). Nevertheless, an ongoing problem with *kakōmai* which many Ogata-mura farmers acknowledge is that the government is unable to make certain that all rice a farmer declares to be of that category is actually sold as such. There are allegations of *kakōmai* being sold as regular, table-grade rice, as there is no real difference between the two.

One more recent program intended to increase efficiency encourages small-scale producers to band together, consolidate their fields, and share equipment and labor in an arrangement called "hamlet-level farm management" (*shūraku einō*). It is interesting to note that what this program strives to create is very similar to the joint farming groups into which the first settlers of Ogata-mura were originally arranged, and which they chose to disband as early as possible (see chapter 2 in this volume). In *shūraku einō*, interested farmers are supposed to form a core group (ideally containing at least one farmer with *nintei nōgyōsha* status), recruit others in order to build as large a farm area as possible, and then seek incorporation under one of several programs offered by the government. Once established, such a "hamlet-level," incorporated farm can receive low-interest loans for land and equipment improvements and machine purchases, and also special guarantees for subsidies should it fail to generate a profit.

The MAFF has been touting these arrangements as ways to streamline farming in general, to counteract the effects of depopulation and aging by spreading labor over a greater area, and even to strengthen the local sense of community in farming areas. The government makes available a variety of publications on *shūraku einō*, including some designed to help interested producers spread the word among their neighbors and build new, incorporated, joint farms.[12] The *shūraku einō* movement caught on earliest in the Hokuriku and Chūgoku regions, where production efficiency was especially low even in the 1960s. Kusumoto (2007: 20–22) shows that in Toyama Prefecture there were already forty-four such incorporated farms by 1971 (and 589 by 1998) and that overall efficiency was higher for such farms than the prefectural average. In Akita the establishment of community-centered incorporated farms under the program has not progressed much compared to places like Toyama and the Chūgoku region that lies further to the west—probably due in no small part to the greater overall yield per area—but there have been some attempts. For example, in the Rokugō area of Misato Town, two different incorporated farms were formed in 2007. In one case, thirty households banded together to form a sixty-nine hectare farm, and in another three hamlets (twenty-four households) formed a thirty-five hectare farm—involving about 77 percent of the total land area of the three hamlets—with two members of the latter having *nintei nōgyōsha* accreditation (MAFF 2007). Ventures such as these have received some coverage in the local media, but problems tend to be stressed over positive points. For example, full-time farmers have found it hard to work well with part-time farmers who have regular jobs—sharing labor evenly has proven difficult due to their different schedules and lifestyles.

Notably, differences in work ethic and background have been widely cited by Ogata-mura farmers as reasons for their decisions to disband their cooperative farming groups in the early years of the village's history. In addition to the *shūraku einō* program, the government also encourages farming entities (individual people or incorporated farms) to take leading roles in regional agricultural development by becoming designated producers (*ninaite*). To become such a producer, a person must possess at least four hectares of farmland (ten if he or she lives in Hokkaido) and an incorporated group farm must have at least twenty hectares. The entity must also have *nintei* accreditation. A *ninaite* entity can have access to a range of special perks, including short-term loans requiring no collateral or guarantor, interest-free loans, and discounts on costs associated with land improvement.

Recent municipal amalgamation (*gappei*) programs have carried with them various monetary rewards, without which they would be largely unable to attract the attention of most small communities—even those facing heavy population loss. When a municipality's population falls below a certain level, it gradually becomes less and less able to support itself by its own tax revenues. It is then forced into the situation of playing "population politics" (Thompson 2003), as it attempts to keep residents from leaving, tries to lure new and returning settlers, and strives to demonstrate progressive leadership and sound management, through the construction of facilities or the hosting of events, or by merging with another municipality, for example. There are many reasons why a given municipality might consider merging with another. For instance, several isolated mountain villages might be better off existing under the same name and sharing the same services. If one village has had success in developing local tourism, the others may benefit by joining with it. The local tax base may also be strengthened through merging. In addition, by merging a municipality can cut its number of public employees, thereby trimming the payroll. Considering these points, it is easy to see why a small village that is losing people might choose to merge with an economically healthier town or city. But even this is not trouble-free—when a small town or village becomes but a peripheral community on the edge of a city it might actually wind up losing more people, and public offices (and representatives) may grow more distant (Rausch 2005). Mergers can also be especially difficult when a number of roughly equal municipalities try to get together (Bailey 1991: 67–68). One of the most enticing reasons, however, for a municipality to seriously consider a merger is the chance to distribute its revenue shortages over a greater population and also to get a shot at receiving larger subsidies from the national government.

Population shifts notwithstanding, virtually all cities, towns and villages in Japan operate in the red because their tax revenues rarely cover all of their regular annual expenses, and because many carry debts stemming from large public-works projects, among the most costly of which are road and port improvements. In fact, if a municipality can cover at least 30 percent of its operational budget from its own tax base, coupled with de facto government subsidies determined by population, it is considered by the central government to be in an "acceptable" financial state (Thompson 2003: 96). Therefore, the national government offers additional monetary help in the form of regional tax grants (*chihō kōfuzei kōfukin*, or simply *kōfuzei* or sometimes *kōfukin*), which are usually allocated for certain purposes and calculated on the basis of factors such as population, geography, and the degree of depopulation, and for which municipalities and prefectures vigorously compete with one another (Onoda 2007, Thompson 2003, Traphagan and Thompson 2006: 12–13).

The general situation with local tax grants reveals a great deal about the financial status of Japan's regional municipalities, and the relationships between the center (Tokyo and the southeastern Pacific coastal belt) and the periphery.[13] For example, areas like Okinawa, parts of Hokkaido, and smaller, isolated islands receive special consideration from the government, which picks up varying proportions of their bills, for they tend to rank highest on the national revenue shortage list. At the top of the list for 2005 was a small, isolated, island village in Kagoshima Prefecture, with a population of about six hundred and a per capita debt of over 11.5 million yen. This might seem like a lot of money, but a full 17 percent of all municipalities in the nation owed over one million yen per resident in 2005. At the bottom of the list was a village in Saga Prefecture which hosts a nuclear power plant, with a population of nearly seven thousand and a per capita revenue shortage of only 22,538 yen. Other small municipalities occupying low positions on the list are home to large corporations or hydroelectric dams. As for Akita, national figures for 2005 show that the three municipalities in the prefecture with the greatest per capita revenue shortages were all villages. Coming in at number three, Ogata-mura registered a per capita debt of 1,004,000 yen, making it number 317 out of nearly two thousand municipalities in the country—just barely falling into the 17 percent of (or 320) municipalities owing more than one million yen per resident. A look at Ogata-mura's budget illustrates the situation. The village's total budget for the year 2005 was 2.65 billion yen, 72 percent of which was covered by tax revenues, with 940 million yen flowing in as regional tax grants (*chihō kōfuzei*) and 715 million yen coming from its own tax base. In addition, the village paid 578 million yen to the government as loan repayments and as interest. Without the regional tax grants, even Ogata-mura would be hard-pressed to make ends meet.[14]

Several small municipalities that have successfully merged with one another to form a new, more efficient, and regionally competitive community—especially one having a population of at least one million—have done quite a lot to prove to the central government that the entire new municipality is progressive and soundly managed. Making such efforts at the local level to shore up the local tax base impresses policy-makers in Tokyo, and helps ensure the receipt of larger tax grants (see Mock 2006: 40–42). A town that gave up its identity as a separate municipality to become part of Akita City in January of 2005 was carrying a debt of 6.2 billion yen at the time of the merger but had seen its tax grants coming from Tokyo fall year by year, from a peak of two billion yen in 2000 to 1.6 billion yen in 2004 (Nara 2006: 139). It may have lost its identity, but this town also lost its debts and gained much in return for its action, for by increasing its size Akita City was set to receive more from Tokyo that could be distributed across its area. Furthermore, new municipalities formed through a merger, or pre-existing towns and cities that grow in size, can receive significant aid packages (*gappei tokurei-sai*) from the national government to cover up to about 95 percent of the costs associated with merging, including construction work, communications arrangements, and other infrastructural matters. For example, Akita City incurred 2.8 billion yen in construction-related costs from taking in two towns in January of 2005, and received 2.6 billion yen to cover this (ibid.: 120). However, the catch is that the extra financial assistance must be used within ten years of the merger—something that sometimes proves difficult for newly formed municipalities (Akita Sakigake Shinpō 2008a). Failing to successfully negotiate a merger may imperil a town or a village in a situation like that faced by the aforementioned town, for this is not a progressive or efficient action in the eyes of the national government. Indeed, the merger question can be seen as a litmus test of the ability of regional politicians and municipalities to adapt to the ever changing environment.

Delicious carrots will also flow forth from Tokyo if municipalities agree to do other things besides merge with their neighbors. For example, allowing the construction of a nuclear power plant or related facility is a sure-fire—but risky, as many people learned on March 11, 2011—way to shore up the economy of a small community, evidenced by the example of the Saga Prefecture village mentioned above. Even just the promise of such a reward has been enough to make local politicians salivate. A recent case from Akita illustrates this. The mayor of Kamikoani-mura—one of only three villages left in Akita, with heavy revenue shortages and the highest percentage of elderly residents in the prefecture (43.1 percent)—publicly announced in July of 2007 that the village was going to consider allowing the construction of a high-level radioactive waste disposal facility inside the village, arguing that it would benefit the community financially while avoiding the more serious risks associated with the building of a nuclear power plant. Indeed, the village stood to receive about six billion yen in subsidies over the same number of years simply for becoming an official candidate, and its immediate neighbors would have received several billion yen between them (Yomiuri Shimbun 2007a). However, public opposition was strong, with even the governor of Akita coming out against the prospect (the prefecture has no nuclear facilities). The local media watched the situation carefully, covering it well in the papers and on the evening news programs. By the end of the month, the mayor had announced that the village would not seek candidacy after all, and apologized for the trouble his initial announcement had caused –which brought relief not only to residents of that village but also to those of the entire prefecture.[15]

On the other hand, regional governing bodies do not always have to jump through hoops or perform other tricks to obtain financial support from Tokyo. As its power waned in the latter half of the first decade of this century, the LDP began to show more signs of concern for their welfare, especially after its surprising defeat at the hands of the DPJ and other smaller parties in the Upper House election of July 29, 2007—due in part to the neoliberal policies of Prime Minister Koizumi and a string of gaffs committed by numerous ministers, and the sudden resignation of Prime Minister Abe following that rout. In the autumn of 2007 the government announced that it would redistribute about five hundred billion yen in tax revenues collected in major cities, many of which enjoy a surplus, to the regions (Akita Sakigake Shinpō 2007b; Yomiuri Shimbun 2007b). This plan even met with the approval of Shintarō Ishihara, the powerful and controversial governor of Tokyo since 1999 (Yomiuri Shimbun 2007c). However, the gesture did not help the LDP avoid losing the majority of house seats—and the prime minister's office—in the August 2009 general election.

Agricultural Policy and Regional Politics—Reflections

Japan's agricultural sector has to a great degree been coddled by its government, which is not a unique, or even unusual, phenomenon on the world stage—it is actually quite common in cases where a country's agrarian sector is inefficient and lags noticeably behind the industrial sector (Mulgan 2000: 2–3). In the case of Japan, this gap is very pronounced. The Japanese government first set about modernizing its agriculture, and this progressed slowly until the economy kicked in following the reconstruction. But land reorganization and increased mechanization combined with rising yields and highly protectionist policies designed partly to preserve the farm vote as the base of LDP power resulted in farming shifting to a largely part-time endeavor—an enterprise that is now facing a number of problems, inheritance being one of the greatest. Mulgan (2005a) argues that although the national government under the leadership of Prime Minister Koizumi appeared ready to make significant changes to the agricultural sector—primarily in the form of injecting it with large amounts of economic liberalism—"traditional," business-as-usual political practices have stymied change. It is true that the national government has backed off quite a bit in recent years from directly controlling what—and how much—is grown in the fields and paddies of the country. It has also relinquished much of its control over prices. In July of 2011 Tokyo even granted two commodity exchanges permission to begin listing rice futures (exchange-traded contracts) for the first time since 1939 (Kyodo News 2011a).[16]

This trend of relinquishing control over the rice market and making it more transparent is closely related to foreign pressure—as a former member of GATT and as a founding member of the WTO Japan is obliged to do these things. But, simply speaking, going too far imperils the farm vote. As a matter of fact, many farmers across the country are sympathetic to the views of Ogata-mura settler Shinichirō Sakamoto on the WTO. In 2006 he strongly argued against it in an essay in the *Akita Sakigake* newspaper. According to Sakamoto, in the decade since its founding, the WTO and its "forced trade" practices (in his words) had resulted only in lower rice prices and a greater area of unplanted paddies (under Tokyo's *gentan* policy) (Sakamoto 2006).[17] Mulgan shows that Tokyo has tried hard to appease both the producers and the consumers with a rhetoric centering on increased self-sufficiency, while pushing the former to become more efficient and encouraging the latter to consider the regional areas as sources of reliable and healthy products. Yet the farm vote and the political power of JA (Nōkyō) have weakened considerably in recent years, and farmers have been turning away from the LDP—some of the reasons for the party's heavy loss to its opponents in the July 2007 general election (and its heavier loss two years later). Mulgan (2005b) also argues that much of what the MAFF does politically is designed for self-protection—to ensure its own survival.

Whatever the MAFF's motivations, on a basic level it is as heavily involved today in the national agriculture as it ever has been. It no longer tries to force farmers to reduce their rice production, but it puts pressure on regions and communities to do this, and thereby still pits neighboring farmers against one another. And, although it does not force the issue, much farmland does remain unused today, and this is mainly rice paddy land. In Akita, considering such land owned by sales-oriented farmers, 2,564 hectares went unused in 1995, and this number had risen to 13,008 hectares by 2000 (Akita Keizaihōkadaigaku Keizaigakubu Keizaikenkyūjo 2002: 112). Eight years later, in 2008, the amount of unused rice paddy land in Akita hovered at just above 15,000 hectares (Akita-ken Kōsaku Hōkichi Taisaku Kyōgikai 2009). Moreover, even though the MAFF no longer decides rice prices on its own and has given producers a considerable amount of legal freedom compared to the pre-1995 situation, it still controls the markets for wheat and many other foodstuffs (under the provisions of the same 1995 law that nearly reversed its position on rice).

Overall postwar regional and agricultural policy in Japan can be characterized as a movement towards amalgamation and consolidation; a quest for rationalization and increased efficiency. Wherever and whenever possible, rice paddies have been sorted and re-sorted into more easily managed units (Brown 2006: 202, Kelly 2006). Much progress toward the rationalization of the nation's agriculture has been made, but as a sector of the economy agriculture is dragging. Tokyo's treatment of the regions and the agrarian sector appears to be best characterized as a mixture of coddling on the one hand and "tough love" on the other. It is deeply involved and concerned, but vacillates between doling out financial support (especially when it is available) and withholding it (especially when times are tight). The national government also rewards municipalities for doing what it wants them to do (merging with neighbors, for example) with money, and punishes those that collapse (like the city of Yūbari in Hokkaido) with a painful debt payoff scheme. Those occupying the middle ground (or that cause trouble) may get nasty looks or visits from officials. But in a free market economy, individuals who move quickly and take advantage of a situation may find great success, and likewise in a capitalist democracy, regional public bodies that play the game well can also benefit. The key is managing to unite residents on an issue and gain their support—for a merger, or for forming *shūraku einō* associations, for example. As will be seen in the remainder of this book, uniting all Ogata-mura settler households on anything relating to agricultural policy and rice marketing has proven to be nearly impossible, although in the middle of 2010 the village was able to boast that nearly 85 percent of its rice farmers were participating in a new agricultural program (see chapter 6). Beyond this, though, there seems to be only one agricultural issue on which all can certainly agree—rice prices are too low.

Notes

1. Wakui 2007: 10.
2. For more on the early postwar situation and its precedents, see T. Smith (1959), Dore (1959), and Fukutake (1967, 1980). Also see Samuels (1983) on regional policy, Thompson (2003) and Knight (2003) on local population shifts and responses, and

Traphagan and Thompson (2006) on the general situation in Tōhoku. For greater detail on agricultural policy up to 1990 see Moore (1990) and on the details of GATT (the General Agreement on Tariffs and Trade) see Moore (1993). For detailed analyses of current agricultural policy from a political science perspective, see Mulgan (2000, 2005a, 2005b). Also see P. Smith (1997) for a revisionist viewpoint on modern Japan in general.

3. One *sen* is equal to one one-hundredth of one yen.

4. Therefore, local governments were basically under the control of the landowning class.

5. Indeed, while the period from 1907 to 1920 saw an increase in total farm-machine horsepower for the entire nation of one thousand to thirty-seven thousand, the number of cattle and horses actually grew from 2,163,000 to 2,266,000 (Tsuchiya 1976: 171).

6. These categories can be deceptive, however, for the overall population of villages may range from fifty thousand to about two hundred, thereby overlapping greatly with the category of "town" (*machi*). Even many smaller cities have fewer than fifty thousand residents (Shichōson Jichi Kenkyūkai 2002: 6–27).

7. An elderly couple I encountered on the outskirts of Ogata-mura in late 2001 as they harvested their rice estimated that a minimum of about seven hectares were necessary for independent, full-time farming.

8. Jussaume (1991) has argued that shifting to part-time production has been an important, rational adaptation to uncertain situations for Japanese farmers—allowing them to keep their fields while stabilizing their household economies.

9. Two JAs in the city of Yokote announced a plan to merge in June of 2011, and finalized the union on April 2, 2012. Also in June of 2011 the prefecture declared its intention to reduce the number of individual JAs in Akita to five by the end of the following year (a very ambitious goal unlikely to be met).

10. The installation of gas stoves, for example, along with other kitchen upgrades, was hoped to improve the relationship between mothers-in-law and daughters-in-law (Aoki 1985, see also Kushner 2010: 148–151).

11. This was based partly on faith in Japanese consumers to continue purchasing high-quality rice at high prices (Kome Mondai Kenkyūkai 1990: 160–169, Ohnuki-Tierney 1993: 26).

12. See the MAFF's website at http://www.maff.go.jp/ninaite/.

13. Unless otherwise noted, information on regional debts and tax grants here comes from Akita Sakigake Shinpō (2007a).

14. This general situation, and these figures, have changed little since 2005.

15. Following the nuclear disaster in Fukushima in the wake of the March 11, 2011 Great East Japan Earthquake, even people who had been politically opposed to the prefecture's governor at the time were glad that he had come out strongly against the idea of allowing a nuclear facility of any sort to be built in Akita.

16. See McMillan (2002: 23–24) for a historical example.

17. See Gudeman (2008: 156–158) on the WTO and GATT, and see McMillan (2002: 211–212) on the WTO.

2

RECLAMATION AND THE OLD SOCIAL ORDER

"The origin of Ogata-mura-utopia lies in the agricultural policies that created it. The feelings of brightness and unbounded possibility that pervaded the village at the beginning: these are exactly what were needed in the agropolitical utopia. This utopia was created through promises of a lifestyle equal to that of cities in the new model farming village—a village sporting industrial agriculture of such a scale that dekasegi would not even be part of the picture."

–Shinichirō Sakamoto[1]

The reclamation project that transformed Hachirōgata into Ogata-mura is particularly notable not only for its creation of a new and rather unique village but also for its vast scale. But it does not stand alone in its greater regional and historical environment—it was actually part of a large postwar movement that began with a focus on rejuvenating Tokyo and the heavily populated Pacific belt and then spread toward the outlying areas, resulting in a flurry of regional development projects, of which dam building and land reclamation have probably been the most noticeable and politically charged. This was made possible by the passage in 1950 of the National Land Development Act (Samuels 1983: 125), which resulted in a series of five National Comprehensive Development Plans (Zenkoku Sōgō Kaihatsu Keikaku), running from 1962 to the present (Government of Japan 2003).

However, Hachirōgata was actually born of a different directive—the emergency resolution (Kinkyū Kantaku Jigyō Jisshi Yōryō) passed by the occupation government in November of 1945 which called for the reclamation of seventy-five thousand hectares of inland lakes and lagoons and twenty-five thousand hectares of coastland, and which was intended to affect virtually all areas of the country

---

Endnotes for this chapter begin on page 89.

(K. Saitō 1969: 9, Torsello 2002: 39). This marked the real start of Japan's post-war efforts at expanding its territory through technical means. That even histori-cally important Biwa-ko, Japan's largest lake, was earmarked for reclamation at the beginning illustrates how radical the terms of the resolution were. Fortunately, most of the work called for was never actually carried out; some plans—such as the one to reclaim a large portion of Naka-umi on its Shimane Prefecture side— were discontinued and others were simply canceled outright. Much of it, however, was finished, and by 1986 no fewer than thirty thousand hectares of new land had been created in the country since the end of the war (Yamano 2006: 39). The massive project that brought Ogata-mura into being was also a direct result of the 1945 initiative. It was the largest single land-reclamation work ever undertaken in Japan, and it may well maintain this distinction far into the future.

Hachirōgata before the Reclamation

According to local legend, Hachirōgata was inhabited by a dragon since time immemorial. The serpent, Hachirō Tarō, was said to leave the lake each winter and spend the coldest months of the year in another, much deeper body of water—Lake Tazawa—further inland, in which his mate dwelled. Therefore, Hachirōgata never failed to freeze over in winter, having no dragon to warm the waters, while the surface of Lake Tazawa always remained free of ice.[2] This legend is still cherished in the general region, but Hachirō Tarō has probably found his accommodations rather small since the mid-1960s—if he still lives there at all.

Originally, Hachirōgata was about twelve kilometers wide and roughly twenty kilometers long (from north to south). It was about five meters deep in a small area on the eastern side and four to four-and-a-half meters deep in the center, but in most places the sandy bottom was only one to three meters below the surface. Fresh water reached the lagoon by way of the many rivers running from the moun-tains to the north and east, and some salt water came in from the Sea of Japan through the Funakoshi Channel, roughly circulating in a clockwise direction. The lagoon was an excellent source of fish for centuries. It also nourished a rich local culture of fishing techniques and tales.[3] Nets have long been used to catch fish in Hachirōgata—even from the frozen surface in winter today. When the lagoon was in its natural state, the ice on the surface was thick enough to support rather com-plex practices. In some cases, groups of eight or more men operated a single net together (Takeuchi 1948: 131). Among the communities surrounding the lagoon, approximately thirty-four thousand different nets of at least eight different types were estimated to be in use at the time the reclamation work began (Bunkachō Bunkazai Hogobu 1971: 21). Total membership of the twenty-five fishing coop-eratives surrounding the lagoon in 1949 came to 2,716 (ibid.: 38). Rutherford

(1984: 84) reports that about three thousand fishermen relied on the waters of the lagoon for their livelihoods and that they provided about 13 percent of the national supply of freshwater fish prior to the reclamation. As many as one-half of fishermen fished without boats, but there were about 1,250 vessels registered in fourteen towns and villages along the banks—54 percent without sails and 46 percent having them (Bunkachō 1971: 18). The most famous boats used in the lagoon were the *utase*—wooden, single-sailed boats. Hundreds of these dragged nets across the surface in the past, but only a few remain today for show. Other fishing methods included operating nets while walking in the shallows using stilts. Smelt (*wakasagi*) have been caught by net in warmer months, or by pole and line through holes in the ice, to the present day. Other types of fish caught in the waters of the lagoon have included whitebait (*shirauo*), types of trout and carp, and more recently black bass—a problematic import. There was also a complex fish market supported by the lake prior to its transformation (Bunkachō 1971). The main points of consumption were the cities of Oga, Noshiro, and Akita, but fish were also sent on further from such nodes.

The Reclamation

Reclaiming Hachirōgata had been considered for over a century before it actually occurred.[4] The earliest recorded case was the creation of about thirty hectares of rice fields along the lake's banks in 1826 by a man named Onomatsu Watanabe, a resident of a small village that is now a part of the city of Oga (Ogata-mura 1994). Later, in 1853 and again when a rice shortage hit the country in the 1860s, plans for larger-scale reclamation projects were drawn up but a lack of money foiled them (Gordon 1965). Following the start of the Meiji era in 1868 several plans for complete reclamation appeared, but once again funding was lacking and no actions were taken. A particularly interesting proposal, the Kachi Plan, was unveiled in 1923. It called for a relatively simple, encroachment-type reclamation project, leaving the Funakoshi Channel and the original banks essentially untouched with a drainage canal surrounding the proposed new lands. The plan also left a section of the lake in the center. According to Gordon (1965: 33), another scheme was prepared by the Ministry of Agriculture in 1925. Other unrealized proposals included the Kanamori and Morooka Plans, both drawn up around 1941, which were prompted by concerns about self-sufficiency during the war years. The second of these two called for a complete fill-in, erasing the Funakoshi Channel as well as the original banks of the lagoon and leaving only a system of irrigation canals inside the new land.

When the war ended, the loss of Japan's colonial territories exacerbated the already bleak domestic situation and the desire for increasing the nation's rice-producing land area was strengthened.[5] Finally, in the early 1950s, the Ministry of Agriculture began to seriously consider a major alteration of the lake, and to this end it established the Hachirōgata Reclamation Investigation Office in Akita City in 1952. Dutch engineers, among them a Professor Yansen—highly revered in Ogata-mura and featured in its land reclamation museum—visited the area in 1954. The report submitted by Yansen was favorable. He and the other experts pushed for the construction of a polder dam, following the main reclamation pattern found in the Netherlands, and the final plan they devised turned out to contain elements of both the 1923 Kachi Plan and the 1941 Morooka Plan. Construction was to have begun in 1956, promises of financial support having been secured from the U.S.A. as well as the International Bank for Reconstruction and Development, but domestic worries over funding caused a delay, and construction of the outer polder dam along the banks of the lagoon (resulting in the creation of about 1,500 hectares of new land) and the foundations for the north and south water-control pumps actually started in 1957. Work on the inner dikes began in 1959, just when the nation finally reached near self-sufficiency in rice (Allen 1981: 192).

In order to obtain the materials for building up the land inside the polder dam, a small mountain near the town of Hachirōgata-machi was destroyed by dynamite and machine and the rocks and soil were carried to the lake. Special barges were used to dump everything in the right places under the water. The Funakoshi Channel was rerouted as well. Whereas it used to meander diagonally through the strip of land that partially separated the lagoon from the Sea of Japan on its southwest side, it now cuts straight through, and it has been tamed by a set of gates and pumps that prevent salt water from entering the waters remaining inside the lagoon today. Although the original plan had called for total drainage and drying of the area within the inner polder dam by 1963, the task of pumping water out of the center area only began that year, upon the completion of the dam, the pump houses, and the sluice gates.[6] Draining the water from the impoldered area took two years, and when the last of it was removed in 1965 a total of 15,600 hectares of fresh, soggy land—all below sea level—had been exposed (Figure 2.1).

The problem of how the new lands would be settled, and by whom, had already become a point of contention between Tokyo and Akita by the time Yūjirō Obata became governor of Akita Prefecture in 1955. Still its most famous governor even today, Obata took an active role in the reclamation efforts. He was in a difficult position—caught between the anxiety of the fishermen of the Hachirōgata area and the stern resolve of the Ministries of Agriculture and of Finance, but he secured promises of compensation for local fishermen and permission to fill at least one-half of the settler spots with people from Akita.[7] Regarding the settlement pattern for the new land, the Jigyōdan retained control. An early idea involved building a central town that would contain retail shops, administrative

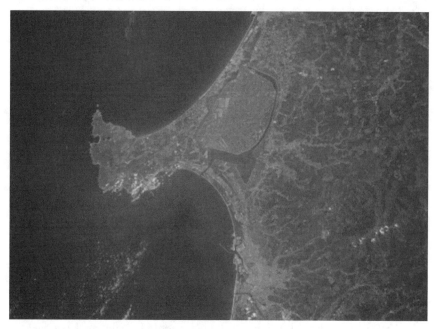

Figure 2.1: The Hachirōgata region photographed from space. The reclaimed land is clearly visible inside the remainder of the lagoon, and the Funakoshi Channel can be seen emptying into the Sea of Japan to the south. The peninsula of Oga juts out westward, and the city of Akita and its port are visible on the shore to the south of Hachirōgata.

Source: Image Science and Analysis Laboratory, NASA-Johnson Space Center. "The Gateway to Astronaut Photography of Earth" <http://earth.jsc.nasa.gov/sseop/efs/photoinfo.pl?PHOTO= STS040-72-54> (03/12/2008 14:55:08).

offices, agricultural support centers and businesses, and anything else that would be needed. Surrounding this town would be eight hamlets, giving the residents living environments that would probably have been more like most "natural" farming villages, as well as the satisfaction of being fairly close to their fields. Sites for the eight hamlets had already been selected and prepared for house construction by dumping sand in order to strengthen them and elevate the spots as of 1965 (Gordon 1965: 59) (see Figure I.1). According to this plan, perhaps as many as nine thousand people could have lived on the new land of Hachirōgata, farming fields of about 2.5 hectares—only slightly larger than the national average. Other proposals involved accepting about five thousand settlers.

In time, the Jigyōdan scrapped the idea of dispersed settlement and reduced the number of settlers it planned to accept, partly because of the prevailing opinion among government planners that Japan's small-scale agriculture was keeping the nation from developing a more efficient system. There was also concern about being able to compete on world markets. Another nail in the coffin for the small-scale farming pattern was the Income Doubling Plan (Gordon 1965: 63) initiated by Prime Minister Ikeda in 1960—designed to stimulate industries and increase investments in heavy equipment over a ten-year period from 1961 to 1971 (Allen 1981: 193). As for the question of what kinds of seeds would be sown on the reclaimed lands, the Jigyōdan concluded that most vegetable crops would not grow as well as rice would on the poorly drained soil, and that grasses necessary to support a livestock industry would take at least ten years to develop. Therefore, despite early signs that rice might not be so badly needed, it was selected as the main crop for Hachirōgata—perhaps an unwise decision, but one that would shape the village's development to no small degree.

Thus, Tokyo became determined to pioneer a large-scale rice farming system on the newly created lands. Influenced in part by the gargantuan agricultural projects that both Soviet and North American planners had dreamed of since the 1930s (Scott 1998: 196), the new system was to be as rational and as heavily industrialized—as modern—as possible. Indeed, this concept better fit into Tokyo's 1960s shift of emphasis from agriculture to industry (Sakamoto 1990: 47). Instead of having thousands of farmers growing rice on small fields in ways not too dissimilar from the ways in which their ancestors had done it, the government decided that settlers would be brought in to grow rice with large machines to make for an efficient production system that could be held up as a model for the future of Japanese agriculture. The planners of the Hachirōgata Jigyōdan, the agency charged with the administration of the project, decided to build only one settlement and have fewer settlers than originally planned. Each household was to receive (purchase) ten hectares of farmland.[8] The Jigyōdan decided to organize the fields of Hachirōgata into great blocks consisting generally of five to eight of the ten-hectare units. Each block would be farmed communally by teams consisting of five to eight members—depending on how many ten-hectare units there were in the block. Each team member would have his own ten-hectare unit, taking out a twenty-five year loan on the farming and residential land, but machines were to be owned and utilized communally. All settlers, the Jigyōdan decided fairly early on, would come alone first and undertake a lengthy training course before being joined by their families.

Finally, a name for the new settlement was needed, so the government solicited ideas from across the nation. Eventually, the name "Ogata-mura" was selected from over sixteen hundred suggestions. The *o* in *Ogata* means "large" or "great," and *kata* means "lagoon." Before the reclamation, the larger, open area of Hachirōgata was known as Ogata, while the smaller section to the southeast was called Kogata, or "lesser lagoon." The name *Ogata* therefore pays tribute to the marine origins of the new land and settlement. The village itself was officially founded on October 1, 1964, scarcely a week before the opening of the Tokyo Olympic Games, with a ceremony held on the current settlement site, complete with sumo tournaments and music, and much fanfare.

Settlement

Tokyo began a national search for settlers almost immediately; advertisements and invitations to apply appeared in newspapers across the country. The village was presented to the public as an ultramodern, model farming project, where brave pioneers would carve out their destinies while working to sculpt a new face for Japanese agriculture. In fact, seeking a full break from typical household-based production, the government declared that women would not have to participate in farm labor in Ogata-mura; the men were to handle everything relating to production, leaving their wives to busy themselves with raising children, taking care of the home, or pursuing hobbies in the new community. Over six hundred people applied to enter the first training program, to begin in November of 1966. The Jigyōdan used both written exams and interviews, conducted at regional centers, to screen the applicants and in the end it accepted fifty-eight (twenty-eight from inside Akita Prefecture and thirty from elsewhere).[9] Two of these men eventually dropped out, so there were actually 56 settlers in the first wave. Although Tokyo had initially said that it wanted only high school graduates, some who had not completed high school were selected. Similarly, even though being married, or at least engaged, was a general prerequisite for consideration, single men were also accepted—especially in the later years of the program. These men generally had to promise to get married as soon as possible, resulting in a "wedding rush"—as residents referred to it—through the first half of the 1970s (Akita Sakigake Shinpō 2007c). The settlers of the first wave, like all others to follow them, were required to relinquish ownership of (or claims to) any farmland before assuming the quarter-century loans on their Ogata-mura property—an important issue because about 90 percent were in fact farmers (Kudō 1969). Most of these left their family fields to a brother or other relative if they were the eldest son of the household.

The men of the first wave started their training period, which lasted for about one year, at the Jigyōdan facility in November of 1966 (Figure 2.2). They lived together in the attached dormitory for its entire duration, their families staying behind until it was complete. At the training center, they learned about the vision that the government had for the new land and the scale of the agriculture that they were to pioneer, heard many lectures and had much hands-on practice with the new, large machines—particularly the harvesters—imported especially for the wide fields of Hachirōgata.[10] Importantly, the Jigyōdan wanted to make sure that they were all thinking along the same lines, and also that they fully understood who was in charge. Many have said that there was a somewhat military-style atmosphere at the training center, with harsh instructors, much order, and rigid rules. Although there was variation among teachers, in general there was a sharp line between them and the settlers. They were the representatives of the state, whose

Figure 2.2: The last remaining section of the original Jigyōdan training center (photographed in the mid-1990s).

control over the project was not to be questioned. This relationship between the government planners and administrators of Ogata-mura and the settlers would continue for years.

The settlers of the first wave finished their training in the autumn of 1967 and immediately took possession of their new houses and land, both residential and agricultural—an event they celebrated with a tractor parade through the streets of the village. Their houses were located on the south side of the central section of its western half (*nishi nichōme*). The settlement of Ogata-mura would progress in this manner, with each group's members' houses being arranged in clusters (Figure 2.3). Most members of the first wave were soon joined by their families after moving into their homes. The following spring, the fifty-six men began to plant their first crops in the muddy fields. A helicopter was used to scatter seeds. This did not work very well, but the government insisted on continuing with it even though the settlers complained about the poor results—the new, highly technical and mechanical (modern) means of planting were not supposed to fail. Nobody in the government wanted to see Ogata-mura take a step back to "traditional" ways of farming.[11] However, results were so poor that even during the first year of planting the Jigyōdan found itself with little choice but to grant the settlers the right to plant some of their fields by hand.

Receiving permission to manually plant some fields made the settlers happy, but it opened the door to a new problem—how to hand plant such a vast area quickly enough. A solution soon appeared; the Jigyōdan arranged to bring hundreds of local women to the village by bus to help plant the settlers' crops. It was

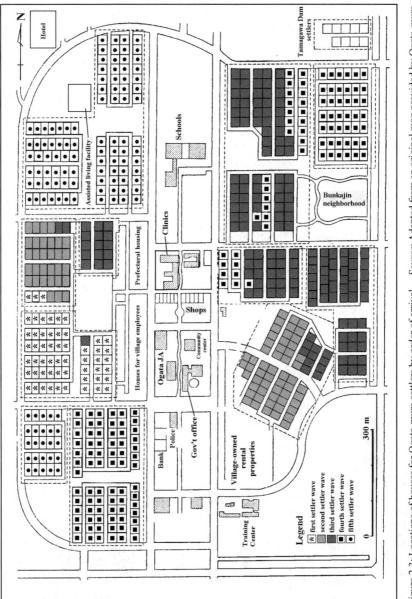

Figure 2.3: Locations of houses for Ogata-mura settlers by order of arrival. *Source*: Adapted from an original map provided by Ogata-mura.

also about this time when the wives and grown-up daughters of the settlers hit the fields in earnest, despite initial government promises of ease and clean hands for them. In those early years, the settlers (the men) would sit on the ground at the end of the day and count out cash to be paid to each worker, setting bills and coins down in little stacks. One settler might have employed as many as fifty women per day for about two weeks. This continued for another six years or so but tapered off as the human planters were gradually replaced by new machines that were able to handle the mud and that were wide enough to plant four to six rows at once. Such machines—the ancestors of those commonly used today by rice farmers with large fields—were partly inspired by the needs of the Ogata-mura farmers. Now, machines can plant ten rows at one time while scattering small amounts of fertilizer as well.

When the time came to harvest their first Ogata-mura rice crop, the fifty-six settlers did so using the large harvesters they had learned how to operate at the training center, and they delivered the grains to the Ogata-mura Country Elevator Corporation, a large silo facility and agricultural institution that had been established just prior to the first harvest. Although it was still rather small at that time, the number of silo clusters in its possession would eventually grow to eight, making it the largest such elevator corporation in the country—at least at one time (Figure 2.4). From the beginning, all commercial rice grown in the village was intended to be sold to the Country Elevator and marketed through government

Figure 2.4: The silos and other facilities of the Ogata-mura Country Elevator Corporation.

channels, with the prices set annually in Tokyo, in line with the general national situation.

While the "first fifty-six" were still struggling with knee-deep mud and constant equipment failures during the earlier half of 1968, the eighty-six members of the second settler wave were doing their time at the training center. That November, after Ogata-mura's first harvest, they moved into their houses. Some were located near the original settlers and the others were on the east side of the village (see Figure 2.3). They also had to endure quite a bit of hardship (mud and machine breakdowns) as they labored to plant their first crops in the spring of 1969, and they joined their predecessors in protesting the helicopter seed-scattering method. By the time the 175 members of the third and largest wave of settlers moved into their square houses in November of that year, however, things had settled down somewhat and the fields had begun to firm up.[12] According to village data, by the middle of the following year 90 percent (2,354 ha) of Ogata-mura paddy land in cultivation had been planted by hand, whereas the ratio of helicopter-planted to hand-planted land had been closer to 1:1 two years earlier.

A few of the third-wave settlers' houses were located on the north side of the central area of the western half of the village (*nishi nichōme*) but the rest were divided among the two major sections (north and south) of the eastern half (see Figure 2.3). Takeru Isono, from Niigata Prefecture, was among this big group of hopeful men (Figure 2.5). Born in 1934, he was the eldest son of his family, and as such carried the responsibilities accompanying the position of heir. His father, a skilled local sumo wrestler, specialized in making charcoal and raised silkworms, but also grew rice. Takeru never attended high school; he began handling the family farming operations at an early age. He also supplemented the family agricultural income by engaging in seasonal *dekasegi* work in winters as soon as he was able. Generally, this took him to Osaka, where he would work as a carpenter for about five months of the year under unsafe conditions. "It was dangerous," he said. "You had a whole lot of guys from here and there, and their backgrounds were really different, so there were lots of fights. There were even murders. I decided to kill rather than be killed, if it ever came down to that, so I carried a long knife!" Fortunately, Takeru never actually had to use it.

The Isono household produced roughly twelve thousand kilograms of rice (worth about eight hundred thousand yen) annually. In addition, Takeru's *dekasegi* work garnered around three hundred thousand yen, while his father earned about the same amount by making charcoal. Therefore, in the mid 1960s the family of seven (Takeru's parents, Takeru and his wife, and their three children) were living on an annual income of about 1.4 million yen, which means that they were faring relatively well overall, considering that in 1967 the average farm household in Japan consisted of five persons and had a total income of only slightly over one million yen per year, with one-half of that being agricultural (Japan Statistical

Figure 2.5: Takeru Isono standing among his fields at planting time in 1997, and posing with his grandson, Kenji.

Association 1988: 548). However, Takeru had neither the time nor the money to take family trips out of the prefecture—a brief excursion with the kids to the capital city of Niigata was the best vacation that he could manage. The Isono house was a large wooden farmhouse, designed with an open area for the ox and horse in the center, the presence of which, according to Takeru, resulted in midnight grunts and other noises, a constant stench, and a plethora of flies.

In 1967 a disaster occurred in Takeru's home area (which eventually turned out to be quite fortuitous for him): heavy rains caused serious flooding in the lowlands, resulting in a number of deaths—eight in his own neighborhood. Takeru's father's rice paddies were submerged by the river when it overran its banks. The region was declared a disaster area and the self-defense forces were called in to help with the relief efforts. Subsequently, the Construction Ministry decided to widen the river and reinforce the levees to prevent future damage, so the government purchased the family's land rights, which left him with almost nothing to inherit. One day, while worrying about what to do, Takeru found information about Rokunosuke Fukui, a local man who had migrated to Ogata-mura as a second-wave settler, in his local newspaper. Takeru became determined to follow in Fukui's footsteps. He applied, and took the written examination along with other hopefuls at the prefecture headquarters.[13] The test was not easy, but Takeru passed and was invited for an interview. This he also passed, thereby earning himself a place in the third wave of settlers, who arrived at the temporary training center in Ogata-mura in late 1968. He spent about one year at the center with the others, learning how to use the large tractors and combines—far greater in size than the mini tillers he had operated before. He had a good time making friends there, but remembers the experience as having been pretty tough, with rather severe instruction—and instructors (as other settlers have also said). After the training period ended, Takeru returned to Niigata and brought his wife and children to Ogata-mura. The new village house was quite a bit smaller than their Niigata house, but all were pleased to find that it featured a flush toilet—an amenity they had never had before. Takeru's parents remained behind for a few years, coming to join the family later.

In November of 1970 the members of the first three waves of settlers were joined by the 143 members of the fourth wave, who had just completed their training.[14] Their homes were divided between the south section of the west half of the village and the north section of the east half, with a small handful in the south section as well (see Figure 2.3). The next, and final, wave of national settlers would not take up residence in the village until four years later. Between the time the fourth and fifth waves entered the village, the agricultural situation stabilized, rice prices rose, and large-scale planting machines were gradually purchased by the individual farmers; in 1974 only 18 percent of the village's paddy land was being planted by hand, with machines covering the rest. Those who had started farming in the village earliest began adding to their houses and building small storage units and garages on their residential property (Figure 2.6). In some cases daughters of

Figure 2.6: Even in October of 1971 many settlers' lots featured extra structures they had added themselves (photograph taken from the tower of the community center by Saburō Yoshida, a farmer originally from Oga).
Source: Courtesy of the Yoshida family.

settlers married other settlers' sons, forming new bonds between village families. This continues today.

The 120 settlers of the fifth wave finished their training period in November of 1974 and they soon joined the members of the four earlier waves in the village's neighborhoods.[15] Ninety-five of their houses filled the north section of the west half of the village and twenty-five more completed the south section of that half (see Figure 2.3). The four-year gap between the arrival of the fourth and fifth waves of settlers was not due to some arbitrary bureaucratic decision or to a lack of funding—it was a sign of things to come. It was becoming clear to both elected and appointed government personnel in Tokyo that previous concerns about rice not being so badly needed had in fact been justified, and ideas about shifting from encouraging its production to discouraging it were starting to take form in Tokyo. Although plans had originally called for the recruitment of at least one more wave of settlers, the Hachirōgata settlement project was cut off after the fifth. In addition, the agricultural land holdings of all settlers were increased by five hectares to a total of fifteen, which helped make use of most of the remaining land within the polder dam. Of course, with the relationship between the representatives of Tokyo and the settlers being what it was, the latter had no choice but to purchase the additional five hectares or quit the village. This development was the first in a series of moves that would eventually impact the community in no small way. Furthermore, it was not the most felicitous consummation of the government's great model-settlement project, which started with a bang and ended with somewhat of a whimper.

Nobuhiro Machida and Isao Satake both migrated to Ogata-mura with the fifth wave of settlers. Nobuhiro was the eldest son of a Toyama Prefecture farming family, but had grown tired of having to hold down a job with his local JA while farming the family's modest 2.1 hectares of rice paddies by the time he ran across information on the Hachirōgata settlement program around 1973. His wife, Takako, was from a nearby farming family, so she was also quite accustomed to hard work, and was not opposed to leaving Toyama and her wage-earning job for a shot at something bigger. Nobuhiro had already heard of Hachirōgata. In fact, he had been there. In 1968, just after the settlers of the first wave moved into their homes but before any crops had been planted, Nobuhiro and a fellow college student traveled by train up the Sea of Japan coast to have a peek at the newly reclaimed land. They were both interested in the possibility of applying for the program, but what they saw made them change their minds. Nobuhiro said:

Back then, there weren't even any pine groves here in Ogata-mura. There literally wasn't anything other than the training center and the first settlers' houses. It was March, our spring vacation, and this place was just a sandstorm—whirlwinds . . . small twisters—just picking up the sand and spinning it around, you know. There was no asphalt. We rode a bus from Akita City to Ogata-mura, and when we reached the village land the road got really rough. It wasn't even gravel—just dirt. When we saw it, we said "this isn't a place to settle and live," and we left!

But by 1973 the original settlers of Ogata-mura had begun to experience some success, and it was clear that the situation was improving. It was also clear that the settlement program would not continue indefinitely. Not wanting to miss his last chance to become a large-scale, full-time farmer, Nobuhiro applied for the program, and proceeded through the selection process. Looking back later, he speculated that the officials who conducted the interviews had been trying to spot idealistic people with strong personalities among the applicants so that they could drop those people from consideration, since signs of trouble had already started to appear in Ogata-mura. Perhaps they failed to spot Nobuhiro's strong will; he passed both the written test and the interview with ease. He went to the village first alone, and then took his wife and young daughter back with him in 1974. As for the family farm in Toyama, he left his younger brother in charge, and he still farms the land today.

Isao Satake also grew up in a farming household, but in northern Akita Prefecture. The fourth born among five sons, there was nothing for him to inherit. Moreover, his father tried to discourage him from following in his footsteps, since the farm life was so tough in the first place. But Isao was not so easily deterred. As soon as he had graduated from a junior college in Akita he set off for the United States, where he participated in a two-year international agricultural exchange program in California and Washington, and where he earned the nickname "Joe." Like Nobuhiro Machida, Isao had no trouble getting accepted for the Hachirōgata settlement project, but he was a member of the unmarried minority (who were strongly encouraged by the Jigyōdan to find a mate as soon as possible). One day, Isao accompanied a friend and fellow fifth-wave settler who had been in the U.S.A. with Isao to Tokyo in order to meet the friend's former supervisor from the States and give him a tour. The friend hailed from the area just to the southwest of Ogata-mura—now part of Oga. His sister, Hiroko, was known to have a fair command of English and was working in Tokyo at the time, so she was asked by her brother to help guide the visiting American. In this way Isao and Hiroko met, and they married about one year later.

Schools and Formal Education

Schools were needed in Ogata-mura from the beginning, as many farmers of the first wave already had children when they entered the settlement program, but since nothing had been prepared by the time they moved into their houses in late 1967 their children had to commute to schools in a nearby town for a short while. Soon, however, lessons came to be held within Ogata-mura's government office building. The kindergarten and elementary school were the first educational institutions of the new village to get their own permanent buildings, in 1969. The junior high school was finished two years later, completing the village's basic education system (Figure 2.7). The kindergarten and the elementary and junior high schools are nearly the same as any other such public institutions in the country, other than the fact that all three are interconnected—an unusual situation. One other odd thing about the junior high school in particular is the ever present environmental and agricultural influence. In their science classes, the students test the water in the Hachirōgata reservoir annually for traces of chemicals and other pollutants and compare the results with those of previous tests. They present their findings to the village government and display them at their annual school festival each autumn as well. This helps to instill in them a strong sensitivity to environmental pollution.

Another aspect of the junior high school that sets it apart from other schools is the one day each year when the students are let off class to help their families plant their crops. Those whose parents do not farm are assigned to help their classmates' families. The teachers have the duty of traveling from field to field for the day, observing the students and cheering them on (Figure 2.8). Most of the students who have no intention of farming in the future dread the day—they would rather spend it at the school (Figure 2.9). Some, however, are happy to have a chance to help their families (Figure 2.10). Like it or not, nearly all of them are the children of farmers—the fields are the muscle tissue of their village and the water is its blood, and they cannot escape this unless they leave for high school and perhaps settle elsewhere.

The Cemetery Park and Buddhist Affairs

As with the schools, the village cemetery (completed in 1973) is somewhat different from that usually found in a small village, where graves tend to be clustered in Buddhist temple grounds.[16] Gravestones vary greatly in age, in size, and in the type of stone. Buddhist temples are also divided into sects (*shūha*). In Ogata-mura, in order to avoid dividing the new settlers, and also out of fairness, the Jigyōdan decided on a simple cemetery park. All gravestones and plots are identical: size, shape, and stone. The park is administered by the village itself, and a rotating committee of residents helps to tend the grounds. Once the park was completed, the village government office began encouraging settlers to purchase plots early, but many resisted for twenty years or more. After all, the settlers grew up elsewhere, and it has taken time for many to feel comfortable enough in the

Figure 2.7: Ogata Junior High School in 2004 (construction of a new building began in 2010).

Figure 2.8: A school teacher enjoys a day out in the fields in spring of 1997, while a student takes a break in the seat of his family's seedling planter. A mat of seedlings, removed from its tray, rests on the rack behind the student. These mats are dropped down onto the tracks behind, which allow them to slide down to the mechanical planting arms.

Figure 2.9: A student unenthusiastically helps her family's planting activities by washing plastic seedling trays in the drainage channel, spring 1997.

Figure 2.10: A student enthusiastically helps his family in the fields. He had already made up his mind to stay in the village and take over the family farm by this time.

new village to think seriously about starting a new family grave on the reclaimed land, for doing so suggests giving up on making their final resting places the same as, or at least close to, those of their ancestors. The fifth-wave settler Isao Satake said: "They bugged me for years, so I finally bought a plot. I don't think I really want to use it, though. This was a lake once, so it has to become a lake again!" On the other hand, third-wave settler Takeru Isono—having lost his ancestral home in Niigata to a natural calamity—did not hesitate to purchase a plot in the village cemetery park and bury both of his parents there.

But the absence of a temple in the village meant that the settlers had to find one by themselves. Although some people do opt for Shintō services, and there is a small number of Christians, the majority of Japanese people choose Buddhist funerals.[17] Yet since Buddhism is divided into sects, the settlers could not simply seek out the nearest temple. What they did, therefore, was to find the nearest temple of the same sect that they had belonged to back home (unless home was very close). To this day, the settler households of Ogata-mura generally call on the temples they selected when they first arrived. In the event of a funeral, they usually use the public facility in the village (the *son-min sentā*), which can be rented at very low cost. A priest will come to officiate from the temple to which the household belongs. *Butsudan* (Buddhist altars) are also found in many Ogata-mura homes—as they would be in almost any farmhouse across the country, and especially if the household head is an eldest son. Again, Ogata-mura residents call on a priest from their temple to come to their home or to go with them to the cemetery park when certain rites need to be performed—interment, forty-nine days after death, one year after death, seven years after, and so on.

Ogata Jinja: The Village Shrine

Not only did Ogata-mura go without a temple from the start, it also got by without a Shintō shrine until one was founded in 1978 (Shimizu 1978: 141). Modeled after the famous shrine at Ise, the small structure stands amidst a grove of pine trees at the far southwest corner of the village (Figure 2.11). A tall gate, or *torii*, marks the entrance to the sacred ground, and running beneath this for about fifty meters or so right up to the front of the building itself is a gravel path. Every year in September, when the preharvest festival is held, small stands selling various kinds of food commonly sold at any public festival, including *yaki-soba* (sautéed noodles), chocolate-covered bananas, and *tako-yaki* (balls made of pancake-like batter cooked with bits of octopus inside), line this path. Young men from the different neighborhoods carry a portable shrine, or *mikoshi*, and children carry a smaller one, around the streets of the village, stopping occasionally to dance along the way, and slowly make their way to the main shrine itself (Figure 2.12). Once they reach their destination, they relax and drink *sake* donated by local

Figure 2.11: The Ogata-mura shrine—Ogata Jinja.

Figure 2.12: Young men of the village (and a foreign guest) carry the *mikoshi* around the village for the annual September festival in 1995.

businesses and enjoy the children's sumo tournament—the necessary dirt ring being located just to the north of the shrine. Behind the shrine is a small reclamation memorial. There is no regular Shintō priest at the shrine. When a need arises—a rare event—one comes from a nearby shrine to officiate. As with the cemetery park, Ogata Jinja is tended and managed by a rotating committee of residents.

Loneliness, Depression, and Tensions

The hardships of dealing with the notoriously thick and deep mud of the virgin fields, very stubborn weeds, the disappointing performance of the seed-scattering helicopters, and chronic equipment failures were not the only sticks in the spokes of Tokyo's shining example of agricultural modernism. For one thing, the houses that had been prepared for the settlers were less than ideal in many respects, even though they sported modern kitchens and flush toilets. They were nearly identical, differing only slightly in size and configuration—relatively small, block-concrete affairs with peaked metal roofs (Figures 2.6 and 2.13).[18] Most families found them to be rather cramped. One problem was that the sharply angled roof design resulted in much wasted space on the second floor—there was only a loft-like area upstairs that could be converted into a room, or perhaps two very small

Figure 2.13: A largely unaltered, triangle-roofed, concrete-block village house stands abandoned in 2006. The front door section in the center and the attached garage to the left were added by the settler after arrival.

rooms, at the owner's expense. "Someone who had never lived in a farmhouse designed those houses," villagers have said, but the design was apparently related to government regulations on the amount of public support available for the building of new settlements—too big or too many rooms, and Tokyo would have been unable to fund their construction.

Downstairs, there were two small rooms that could be used as bedrooms, and one larger area that served as a kitchen/dining room/living room. If a number of settlers decided to have a drinking party there, the entire household must have been kept awake. Another problem with the houses was their concrete-block construction. They sat low to the ground, and were poorly ventilated, so the wood plank floors and straw *tatami* mats that covered them and formed the living surface received too much moisture from below and failed to dry out sufficiently, even though one could detect air flowing up between the *tatami* mats in places. Lack of privacy was another problem. This was caused not only by the layout and construction materials of the houses but also by their proximity to one another and the lack of trees or anything much else between them. One second-generation farmer who came to the village with his parents as a young child remarked, "Back then you could hear everything that was going on in the houses next door and behind—every single fight!"

Most settlers of Ogata-mura with farming backgrounds had lived in much larger houses that offered greater privacy than their Ogata-mura abodes, which made many of them uncomfortable at the beginning. This is why they began enlarging their houses as early as possible, a gradual process that continues to this day. When I first walked the streets of the village in 1995, there were not very many of the old peaked-roof houses remaining, but a surprising number of them were still discernible, embedded within larger structures that had grown outward and upward enough to make the original parts rather hard to spot in many cases. Figure 2.14 compares the situation in 1997 with that in 2002 for the entire village, with the settlers' houses divided into three different types—those with no trace of the original building remaining, those with new sections but also having the old peaked-roof part, and those that had been altered only minimally.

Another early problem was the timing of the end of the training periods and the planned relocation of the settlers' families to the village—always in the late autumn. The school year in Japan runs from April to early March, so children would have had to leave their schools during the academic year to move to Ogata-mura, where no school yet existed (at least at the very beginning). Furthermore, it was not easy to suddenly leave a relatively warm place such as Kyushu to face the icy winter of Hachirōgata. Besides, as explained above, the homes were fairly small and cramped. Of the first wave of settlers, the number of families who actually did move into Ogata-mura right away is unclear, but a February 1968 survey shows that in many cases only the men stayed for the first winter, awaiting the

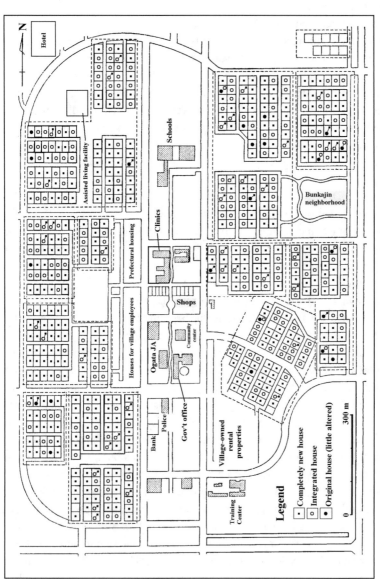

Figure 2.14: Changes in house type, 1997–2002. Only one symbol in a residential lot indicates change from one type to the other—the symbol at the top left representing house type during the earlier period and the symbol at the lower right or lower middle representing house type in the later period.

arrival of their wives and children the following March (Yoshitake and Ura 1976: 245–262). More than this, the survey also showed that at least seventeen houses of the first-wave settlers stood empty for the initial winter, even though the settlers were instructed not to return to their home areas by the Jigyōdan. The settlers who did move to the village right away and who did spend the first winters there had to entertain themselves somehow, for there was no agricultural work that could be done and there were no old friends around—especially for those who had come from far away. Many men got together and drank often at each other's homes or frequented bars in the area—primarily in the town of Hachirōgata; or they would drink at home alone. Either way, most wives were less than pleased with the situation.

Becoming comfortable with one another was also difficult, for both the settlers and their wives, although the former got a head start on this at the training center. One problem was that most people were simply used to following different customs. For example, when the village Women's Association (*fujinkai*) first formed it was hard for the members to decide on basic matters like how much money should be collected from each household for weddings and funerals (Akita Sakigake Shinpō 2007c). In addition to such cultural differences, there were serious misunderstandings among all arrivals due to their different dialects, pronunciations, and expressions, and even their general attitudes, since over one-half came from different places outside of Akita. Some early settlers have said that the fact that most of them used "different words" made it hard to get along with one another at the beginning. Indeed, ways of speaking in some areas of Japan are vastly different from ways of speaking in others, and since the settlers of Hachirōgata were all adults and came mostly from smaller communities it was generally impossible for them to change their ways of speech. In most cases it was simply easier to deal primarily with people from the same home areas. Also, of course, they had an easier time relating to people from similar backgrounds and who were familiar with the same places and foods. Hence, they began to form prefecture-based organizations early on. Although it is technically not a prefecture, the Hokkaido group has been the largest such group besides the Akita group in Ogata-mura. The Niigata group is also fairly big. The communication problems faced by the settlers were mirrored by their children's experiences at the village school later. The son of one settler said: "Those of us from outside Akita had no idea what the teachers were saying when they tried to instruct us in Akita dialect—'What the heck is he talking about?' we'd ask aloud!"

This relates to another social problem that appeared early on in Ogata-mura—the fact that some settlers were able to go back to their old homes in winter, even as a day trip, while many were not. One settler of the first wave said that he and his peers—even if they were from inside Akita Prefecture—had all shared a very strong longing for their homelands (*bokoku no nen*) during their initial years in the village, but that those from nearby were able to deal with this more easily not only because they were better acclimated but also of course because they could simply go back home for a bit to refresh themselves from time to time. He explained that a meeting between the initial settlers and the prefecture governor was held during their first winter. When asked by the governor how things were going, a man from outside Akita complained that those from inside Akita were being mean ("doing *ijime*") to those from farther away because they were going back to their old homes fairly often. But a great many of the settlers had relocated to Akita from very far away, and so the differences between Ogata-mura (and even Akita) and their home areas were as great as, or greater than, the physical distance between them.

Distance from home was indeed a much bigger problem for some settlers than for others, but strong ties to the homelands were maintained for many years by nearly all of them, largely due to the loneliness they felt in the early period of Ogata-mura life. An extreme example: one settler of the first wave left a son behind as the heir to the family land and brought the other son to Ogata-mura, thereby establishing two successors for two different farms. Over the next thirty years he and his wife continually traveled back to Shikoku to spend time with their other family there. With the passing of his wife in the late 1990s the settler decided to reside permanently in Shikoku, traveling to Ogata-mura only for planting or for the harvest, but he eventually stopped visiting Akita altogether. Most others from far away also felt it important to maintain strong ties to their homelands for many years, but even this feeling of need has gradually tapered off. The wife of an early settler who hails from Kyushu said:

> In the old days we used to go back often—nearly always for the New Year holidays and for *o-bon* in August. But eventually we just got tired of making the trip and stopped going. Everyone there has grown up, anyway, and there are fewer people to see. Sometimes they come here, anyway. But the thing is that we come from Kyushu. To get there you have to fly from Akita to Haneda [in Tokyo], change planes, and then fly again. And if I go I have to take gifts with me, too. So when we have time for a trip it's cheaper and easier to just fly to Korea[19] and have fun there instead!

Again, for those from other parts of Tōhoku it is not too difficult or expensive to go back home by car or train. Many still do from time to time, but the original settlers do so less and less today. Some of their heirs, however, may take their own children to visit cousins in the homelands, and younger women who married into the village—especially from large cities—go back when they can.

One of the most serious early social problems in Ogata-mura was the high suicide rate among the settlers. Getting clear information about this is difficult—

people generally do not want to talk about it. Due to distance and other factors, some found it hard to be separated from their families and friends back home, and there were tensions between couples and neighbors that a few people could not deal with. The feeling of *bokoku no nen* made many hearts heavy in the early years. Besides, Hachirōgata winters are long, dark, and cold. The wind tends to blow in from the sea almost horizontally, threatening to shove vehicles off of the icy roads and pelting people with the sleet and snow that it carries. Many of the suicides, however, were related to the political problems that intensified after 1975. The exact number that occurred throughout the first two decades of the village's existence is unclear, but no members of the first settler wave appear to have taken their own lives. A member of the fourth wave estimated that at least six of the men who went through the training period with him committed suicide during the earlier years. Comparing the original list of settlers with residential maps in 1995 revealed that at least two dozen men were no longer present in the village then. Some of them simply gave up and moved away early, but others were among the unhappy few who decided to take more drastic measures to escape Ogata-mura life. There are roughly twenty-five deserted houses or empty plots in the village today, and a handful of other homes that were abandoned but are now being used either as rentals or as the business offices of small rice-marketing corporations that have been formed by settlers or their sons.

Third-wave settler Takeru Isono, despite his excitement over the chance to help pioneer a new kind of large-scale, efficient agriculture, and the fact that Ogata-mura farm work was always easier for him than what he had grown used to in Niigata, had his own difficulties adjusting to the new village. Aside from the coldness and harshness of the winters, the large amount of free time between November and March was especially hard to get used to at first. Since he and the other settlers were not only discouraged from going back home in winter but also forbidden by the government from engaging in *dekasegi* work, he (like many) spent his early winters in the village drinking at local bars, which often led to coming home late and angering his wife. After several years of this pattern, a neighbor who was also from Niigata, Tarō Omori, offered to teach him how to ski. He tried, and was immediately hooked. "If it hadn't been for him," he said many years later, "I would have drunk myself to the grave by now. I'd have at least gone nuts!" Indeed, I initially met Takeru because he was the only person to show up for my first "beginning English" conversation class one September evening in 1995. He explained that he needed to study English in order to travel abroad for skiing, which surprised me. "Why," I asked, "do you need to go overseas to ski when you live in Akita?" Little did I know then of his passion for the sport—a passion which helped him adjust to life in Ogata-mura in no small way.

The Cooperative Farming Groups

Even in 1965 it was clear that the settlers of Hachirōgata would have their own fields but farm them in blocks on a communal basis using shared equipment (Gordon 1965: 66). These cooperative farming groups were critical elements in the formation of the new community, and at least a few of their functions linger today. Since it was known at the beginning of the application process that group-oriented farming was to be the basis of Ogata-mura agriculture, some local governments advised residents who were interested in applying for the program to band together with others in the same community and apply together as a unit in order to increase all of their chances of acceptance; a group of five or six men who hailed from the same town and who were interested in working together had a greater likelihood of being selected.

During the first training period, the settlers who had not already formed groups were instructed by the Jigyōdan to do so. Most who came from places inside Akita made groups with others from the prefecture, but some groups contain only one or two Akita natives. In this system, each settler had his own ten-hectare section of fields—later increased to fifteen—but he and his group were to farm each member's plots as one complete unit, and all equipment was to be owned by the group. Storage facilities for each group were built in an area to the east of the settlement that still serves as a storage area and also is the location of several new marketing associations today. As mentioned earlier, all rice produced for the market was deposited in the Country Elevator silos and the farmers each received the government-set price for their rice. The members of the first two waves of settlers were organized, for the most part, in a different manner from the later arrivals. When the first settlers entered their village houses in November of 1967, they generally had their cooperative group members as their closest neighbors (Figure 2.15). Not only were their fields all in the same spot, but their houses were also clustered together. They could hardly go a day without seeing each other and chatting, or at least greeting each other. When the settlers formed their groups during their training period, they chose names as well. Many of the groups' names either reflect the members' places of origin or indicate their hopes for future success in the new village. Table 2.1 shows the first-wave settler groups, their location on Figure 2.15 ("Code"), their names, the members' places of origin, and the locations of their fields.

The final column in Table 2.1 ("Fields") indicates where the group's rice paddies are located on Figure 2.16. Two of the groups, Tony Farm and Tarō Farm, deserve special mention. They are different from the others in that the members' houses are scattered. The men who formed these two groups requested that the Jigyōdan allow them to have their houses arranged in such a manner so as to not get too tired of each other. After all, they recognized that living so close to one

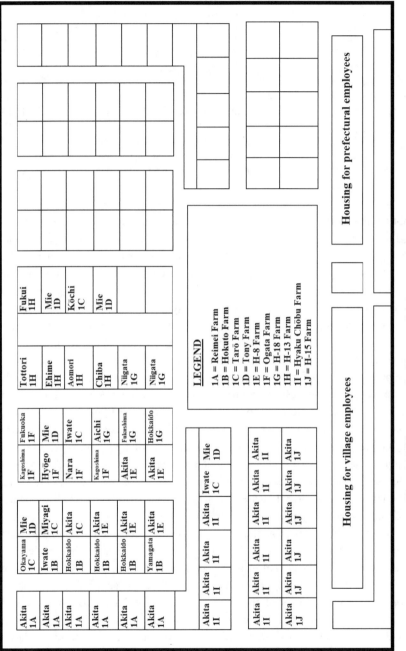

Figure 2.15: First wave settlers' houses and their cooperative group arrangements.

Table 2.1: First-wave settlers' cooperative farming groups.

Code	Group name	Members' prefectures of origin and number of members from each prefecture (if more than one)	Fields
1A	Reimei Farm	Akita (6)	H-16
1B	Hokuto Farm	Hokkaido (3), Iwate, Yamagata	H-11
1C	Tarō Farm	Iwate (2), Akita, Miyagi, Okayama, Kōchi	H-19
1D	Tony Farm	Mie (5)	H-20
1E	H-8 Farm	Akita (5)	H-8
1F	Ogata Farm	Kagoshima (2), Fukuoka, Hyōgo, Nara	H-14
1G	H-18 Farm	Niigata (2), Hokkaido, Fukushima, Aichi	H-18
1H	H-13 Farm	Chiba, Aomori, Ehime, Tottori, Fukui	H-13
1I	Hyaku Chōbu Farm	Akita (Minami Akita County = 5, Yuri County = 5)	H-9
1J	H-15 Farm	Akita (6)	H-15

another and working nearly every day together could become more than a little stifling. Tarō Farm is a group consisting mostly of members who hail from the Tōhoku region (Iwate, Akita, and Miyagi) and two members from much farther away—Okayama and Kōchi. Tony Farm is the village's only all-Mie Prefecture group. The five members shared the experience of studying farming techniques in the United States in the 1960s before applying to the Hachirōgata settlement program. While there, they became interested in the way Americans pronounced the word *twenty*, as in "Oh, you're twenty years old?" To them, this sounded something like *Tony* and they decided to make this the name of their cooperative group. (The other groups of the first wave of settlers, along with all groups in the central section of the western half of the village, are discussed in detail in chapter 4.) These cooperative groups formed the original social framework of the new village society. In many ways, group membership was a substitute for the usual kinds of deeply rooted relations—grounded often in kin ties—found in most small farming villages in Japan. The binding nature of group membership can partly be witnessed in the names that members chose for their groups. For example, the very name of Tony Farm indicates the members' shared experience of living and studying in the United States.

Thirty of the families in the second wave of settlers took houses in *nishi nichōme* along with the first settlers. The other fifty-six families—divided into nine cooperative groups—moved into houses in the east side of the village, fairly close to the training center operated by the Jigyōdan. Table 2.2 lists the cooperative labor groups of the second settler wave. Many of these groups' names reflect the geographical origins of their members. Seishū Farm is composed of three members from Aomori and three from Akita. The *sei* in *Seishū* is another pronunciation for the Chinese character *ao*, as in *Aomori*. The *shū* in *Seishū* is another pronunciation of the character *aki*, as in *Akita*. Therefore,

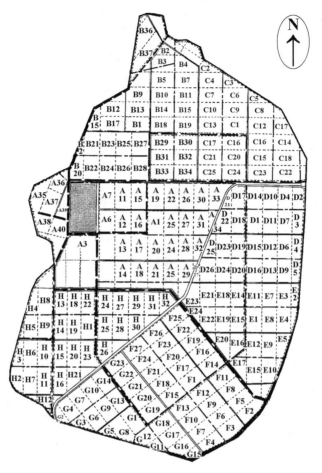

Figure 2.16: The fields of Ogata-mura and original ownership patterns by cooperative group (because the original holdings were increased by five hectares, most settlers actually have fields in at least two different locations).
Source: Adapted from an original map provided by Ogata-mura.

the group's name represents its equal proportions of members from Aomori and Akita. Some members of Chōkai Farm hail from Yuri County, at the foot of Mount Chōkai—the grandest mountain in Akita. Kotohama Farm is named after a settlement to the south and west of Hachirōgata that later became a part of Wakami-machi, which was subsequently swallowed up by the city of Oga and, hence, has disappeared. All six members of the group come from there; they preserved the old name of their community while emphasizing their roots and their unity. Finally, four members of Hokkai Farm hail from Hokkaido.

Table 2.2: Second-wave settlers' cooperative farming groups. "Code" refers to the location of their houses on Figure 4.5. Field locations can be found on Figure 2.16.

Code	Group name	Members' prefectures of origin and number of members from each prefecture (if more than one)	Fields
2A	Taihei Farm	Okayama (2), Akita (2), Ishikawa, Tokushima	C-12
2B	Shinsei Farm	Akita (Iwaki = 4), Niigata (2)	C-8
2C	Kyōwa Farm	Niigata, Saga, Kumamoto, Hyōgo, Akita, Fukushima	C-6
2D	B-14 Farm	Yamagata (3), Miyagi, Mie, Gifu	B-14
2E	Kohoku Farm	Akita (5), Tochigi	C-14
n/a	Hachirō Farm	Hokkaido (6), Akita	C-18
n/a	Seishū Farm	Aomori (3), Akita (3)	C-7
n/a	Mizuho Farm	Tochigi (3), Miyagi, Akita	C-19
n/a	Chōkai Farm	Akita (6) (Yuri County, Moriyoshi)	B-10
n/a	Seiwa Farm	Akita (Minami Akita County = 6)	B-23
n/a	B-7 Farm	Akita (2), Hokkaido, Niigata, Iwate, Miyagi	B-7
n/a	Kotohama Farm	Akita (Wakami = 6)	C-23
n/a	Hokkai Farm	Hokkaido (4), Aichi	C-15
n/a	Kyōshin Farm	Akita (Hachirōgata = 2, Kotooka = 2), Iwate (2)	C-22

By the time the third wave of settlers took up residence in their Ogata-mura houses, the cooperative farming system that the immigrants of the first wave pioneered was already breaking down. One problem was that even though the village was conceived as an egalitarian community of like-minded producers, there were some irresolvable differences between them. For one thing, the first farmers of the new land began to feel a psychological need to work their own fields by themselves early on. There were also practical problems with the cooperative farming system. It was difficult to coordinate the communal labor and machine-use arrangements. Conflicts also arose between the settlers due to differing work ethics. For example, a settler who had a wife, several children, and his own parents in his house would generally tend to feel a greater need to get out early in the morning and take care of the crops but, since all were expected to share equally in the work, he would feel cheated if he were the only one doing so much. If his next-door neighbor and fellow group member arrived in the field at perhaps ten a.m. or so, and he had already been at work weeding for two hours, he would wonder what the point was of trying so hard.

Another problem was the sharing of the storage sheds near the fields. From the beginning, each cooperative group shared a parcel of land near their fields where the storage facilities for their machines, and general workspace, were located. These parcels of land had large concrete tanks installed in them for washing rice husks and small equipment, and perhaps also for soaking seeds. Most settlers found these useless and felt that they took up too much space. In some cases entire groups decided to get rid of them, and simply did so—breaking them up with tractors or digging equipment—but in other cases the concrete tanks became points of contention. One settler reported: "No one used that tank anymore, and it really was in the way, so I decided to get rid of it, but as soon as I said so my neighbor's wife started using that tank again to wash things. I'm sure she did that just to prevent me from getting rid of it!" There clearly were some cases in which arguments erupted over joint use of the land and the facilities. Many groups decided to simply divide up the property and erect their own separate storage units and work spaces rather than to try to continue joint maintenance. Quite a few settlers sold their shares of the common plots to fellow group members and set up their own facilities on a different corner of their own paddy land, away from those of their fellow group members. Thus, when driving though the vast networks of Ogata-mura farmers' rice fields one finds such storehouses and work spaces scattered about, standing independently of one another, although there are no residences among the fields.

In the end, the farmers of the first and second waves helped prevent serious problems from developing between themselves—thereby preserving their cooperative groups in a way—by ceasing to produce their rice jointly and no longer working on each other's fields, after only two or three years of struggling with the system. Even though they went back to typical household-based production, most still lacked the resources needed to purchase machines alone. Therefore, joint ownership was the only production-related aspect of the cooperative groups that continued into the rest of the settlement period. Even today, some rarely used machines and tools are owned collectively, but most settlers already had their own planters by 1975 (415 machines for 460 households).[20] There were many incentives to buy one's own machines as soon as possible. For one thing, if a schedule for using a group-owned harvester had been decided, and then a typhoon began to approach the Tokyo area from the Pacific and was predicted to hit Akita in two days' time, one can imagine the scenario: I am very anxious to harvest my crops as fast as possible before the storm comes and flattens the plants. The problem is that another group member, according to the schedule, has several days to use the harvester first, so I cannot do anything until he finishes. I hope that he will go out in the morning and begin harvesting as soon as the dew on the plants has dried enough, but he does not. Instead, he gets up late and heads out to the fields well after noon and takes his time, quitting early since he knows that there will be one more day of sunshine before the storm hits. This is of course an extreme example, but these kinds of problems with timing and schedules abounded when the neighbors and group members were sharing the most necessary equipment. Once they had bought their own machines—at least the truly critical ones—many found it fairly convenient to continue owning and using a few rarely used or otherwise less crucial pieces of equipment on a communal basis.[21]

The cooperative groups also had social functions that continue to some degree today. When the pioneers entered the village, very few had any blood relatives near them. Even those who came from nearby towns were not able to call upon their family members back home as easily as they were able to call upon the members of their cooperative group. One reason for this was probably the fact that their lifestyles and work schedules had changed dramatically from those of their old neighbors and relatives back home, nearly all of whom either were not farmers or were part-time farmers committed to wage labor. The settlers of Ogata-mura were, from the beginning, very unusual Japanese farmers—free to decide their work schedules and to concern themselves only with agricultural matters since they were not dependent on any other jobs. From the earliest years in the village, the members of one's cooperative group were basically like family. More than once I have heard the expression "closer than distant relatives" or simply "we were like family." If there were a serious problem with one household—the death or other incapacitation of a member whose labor was necessary for planting or the harvest—members of the group would not need to be asked to pitch in and help. Any other serious problems that transcended the private sphere of the household would be handled first by group members.

The groups had no set leaders and no structure of any real sort. They were small enough not to require rotating headships or treasurer positions. The members simply met when needed to decide when and how to fix a damaged machine or to share the cost of repair and, especially in the earlier years, they sometimes took short trips as a group. The traditional *sanaburi*, or postplanting sojourn for relaxation and a little celebration to recover from the crucial and arduous task of getting the crops in the fields, was usually done at the cooperative group level. Often this simply took the form of a day in the sun amidst the newly planted paddies, eating, drinking, joking, and sleeping. In many cases—more so in the earlier years—entire cooperative groups, with families, would travel together. Other times only the wives would plan a trip together and the men would just meet up for drinking and telling tales. These groups no longer travel together as a unit today, but Ogata-mura farming households still rely first of all on their fellow group members when their labor power is suddenly cut short due to death or illness, and funerals at any time of the year call for immediate visits and offers of help from cooperative group members as well as close neighbors.

Due to the problems with the original cooperative groups outlined above, the Hachirōgata Jigyōdan decided to change the labor and living arrangements for the settlers when the 175 members of the third wave took up residence in the village. From that point on, the cooperative groups were only to own equipment on a joint basis. Each farmer was to be responsible only for his own farmland. This seems to have made the third-wave settlers and those who followed them happier, at least where their labor was concerned. In addition to the early shift to hand-planting, the dissolution of the cooperative farming groups also brought the wives and elder daughters of the settlers out into the fields to make their own labor contributions to their households' farms. The settlement situation was also changed for the immigrants of the third, fourth, and fifth waves. Whereas groups with scattered households were the exceptions among the settlers of the first wave, and none at all existed among those of the second, from the time of the third-wave settlers' arrival in 1969 groups with houses clustered together became the unusual ones. Table 2.3 lists the cooperative farming groups of the third wave of settlers.

Table 2.3: Third-wave settlers' cooperative farming groups. Field locations can be found on Figure 2.16. Houses of the members of the first three groups are located in *nishi nichōme* (Figure 4.5).

Group name	Members' prefectures of origin and number of members from each prefecture (if known, and if more than one)	Fields
Essa Farm	Niigata (6)	D-9
Hōei Farm	Hokkaido (4), Aomori, Akita	B-12
Daiichi Farm	Akita (Hachiryū = 5)	B-28
Mutsuwa Farm	Akita (Tennō, Kotooka, Oga)	D-11
Tōhoku Farm	Akita (Wakami, Kotooka)	B-19
Mikuni Kyōei Farm	Saga (3), Toyama, Fukui	D-15
Gokō Farm	Akita, Nagano	B-11
Kōwa Farm	Akita (Wakami = 5)	D-12
B-17G Farm	Tottori (3), Hokkaido, Miyagi	B-17
Shōwa Farm	Akita, Niigata, Shimane, Aomori, Mie, Kumamoto	B-18
Kyōei Farm	Akita (Senboku County—Kyōwa)	D-16
Akita Farm	Akita (Yuri County = 4), Aichi	B-27
Niko-niko Farm	Hokkaido (3), Akita (2)	D-13
Apollo Farm	Akita (5), Shiga	B-32
Shin Nihon Farm	Miyagi (2), Fukushima, Gunma, Yamagata, Akita	C-25
Yamato Farm	Akita (Senboku County = 6)	C-9
Aozora Farm	Akita (Honjō, Kotooka)	B-31
Taisetsu Farm	Hokkaido (5)	C-17
Asunaro Farm	Okayama, Yamagata	B-34
Kita no Hashi Farm	Hokkaido (2), Toyama, Hyōgo, Akita	C-24
Daiei Farm	Akita (Minami Akita County)	B-13
Hokusei Farm	Hokkaido (4)	C-20
Akebono Farm	Akita (4), Hokkaido	B-30
Smile Farm	Tokyo, Nagano, Okayama, Tokushima, Kōchi	C-21
Tsugaru Farm	Aomori (N., W., and S. Tsugaru Counties)	B-15
Hachiei Farm	Akita (Minami Akita County = 5), Miyagi	C-10
D-8 Inter-Farm	Akita (3), Ishikawa	D-8
Shūnan Farm	Akita (Hiraka, Ogachi, Senboku)	B-29
Nichirin Farm	Iwate (4), Hokkaido, Akita (Honjō)	C-13
Iwaki Farm	Akita (Iwaki = 1, Yuri County = 3)	D-7
Takusan Farm	Hokkaido (5), Akita (Tennō)	B-33
C-16G Farm	Hokkaido (4), Akita (Yuri County)	C-16

Many third-wave settlers' group names also reflect place of origin for their members. Tōhoku Farm is a group whose members are all from the Tōhoku region (actually, Akita Prefecture). Likewise, the members of Akita Farm mostly come from Akita. Taisetsu Farm reflects the origins of the members—all five hail from Hokkaido, and at least some from the area around the Taisetsu mountain range—and four members of Hokusei Farm (written "northern star") migrated from Hokkaido. Shūnan Farm, which looks like "Akita south," is composed of members mostly from southern Akita Prefecture, and Iwaki Farm has members from the Iwaki area of Akita. There is also Tsugaru Farm, with members from that region of Aomori Prefecture. One more third-wave group that deserves mention is Essa Farm. The name *Essa* is interesting. It derives from two place names— Echigo, the old name for Niigata, and Sadogashima, the large island in the Sea of Japan off the Niigata coast, which belongs to that prefecture. Putting the first part of the former word with the first part of the latter word forms the compound *Essa*. This, of course, reflects the fact that all of the group's members hail from Niigata Prefecture, with one being from Sadogashima. Takeru Isono is a member of this group. His house is located on the northern edge of the neighborhood— the far right side of Figure 2.15. In addition, Asunaro Farm has a notable name. Asunaro is a type of tree (Japanese arborvitae) that resembles the Japanese cedar (Cryptomeria japonica), a well respected and much revered tree in Japan, but *asunaro* also sounds like "let tomorrow come"—it is a veiled call for a better future that should be possible through hard work and perseverance.

Five cooperative groups of the fourth wave of Ogata-mura settlers show clustering of houses, while the members of the other twenty groups are largely scattered. Fourth-wave settlers' cooperative farming groups are listed in Table 2.4. Some group names of the fourth wave indicate the places from where the members immigrated. The name of Hokuyū Farm, composed entirely of members from Hokkaido, means "northern friends," and the members of Hachiryū Farm all hail, not surprisingly, from the former town of Hachiryū to the north of Ogata-mura. Other fourth-wave cooperative groups with names that are based on the members' places of origin are Wakami Farm (for the former Wakami-machi), Kyushu Farm, Moriyama Farm (named after a mountain in the nearby town of Gojōme-machi), and Yuri Farm (named for Yuri County in Akita Prefecture). Finally, Sakigake Farm means "pioneer farm," Shinome Farm means "dawn" or "first light in the east" (hinting at hope for a new tomorrow), and Utase Farm is named after the most famous type of sailing vessel once used on the waters of Hachirōgata. The name "Laramie Farm," of course, comes from the American West—another frontier land.

Fifth-wave settlers' groups are like those of the fourth in the inventiveness of their names, but different in that none of the twenty-two groups chose to live in group clusters. Fifth-wave settlers dwell only in four neighborhoods on the west

Table 2.4: Fourth-wave settlers' cooperative farming groups. Field locations can be found on Figure 2.16.

Group name	Members' prefectures of origin and number of members from each prefecture (if known, and if more than one)	Fields
Gotoku Farm	Akita (Ogachi County = 4), Miyagi (Sendai)	B-25
Wakami Farm	Akita (Wakami = 5)	A-20
Sakigake Farm	Akita (2), Aomori, Yamagata	A-15
Hokuyū Farm	Hokkaido (7)	A-17
Kyushu Farm	Saga (4), Kumamoto	A-24
Kotō Farm	Akita (Ikawa = 2, Hachirōgata = 4)	A-12
Miyuki Farm	Niigata (4), Akita, Hokkaido, Toyama	A-21
Kamikawa Farm	Hokkaido (6)	D-18
Young Farm	Akita (various counties = 7)	A-14
Laramie Farm	Akita, Nagano, Gunma, Shizuoka	D-19
Fuji Farm	Hokkaido (2), Aomori, Akita (Wakami)	A-23
Himawari Farm	Akita (Yuri County = 2, Kakunodate, Iwaki)	D-6
Takushū Farm	Akita (3), Iwate (2), Hokkaido	D-20
Shinome Farm	Akita (3)	E-11
Hachiryū Farm	Akita (Hachiryū = 5)	E-7
Mikurahana Farm	Akita (Hachiryū =2, Hachirōgata), Yamagata	E-3
Sakura Farm	Akita (3), Miyagi (2), Shiga	A-18
Center Farm	Akita (4), Okayama	A-11
Moriyama Farm	Akita (Gojōme = 4, other = 1)	B-26
Utase Farm	Akita (Hiraka County = 4), Hokkaido (2)	A-13
Yaei Farm	Niigata (4)	D-10
Happy Farm	Aomori (2), Hokkaido, Iwate, Nagano	H-20
Kuroshio Farm	Okayama (2), Gunma, Ehime, Kōchi	E-14
Yuri Farm	Akita (Higashi Yuri = 6)	A-1
Mikago Farm	Hokkaido (4), Kagawa, Kagoshima	A-16

half of the village—one in the southwest corner near the shrine, and the other three in the northwest corner near the hotel. Their cooperative groups are listed in Table 2.5. Group names that reveal the places of origin of the members are fewer than in the previous settler waves, but there are some. Oū Farm takes its name from the Tōhoku region itself, Oū being an old name for the greater part of the region, and also the mountain range running between Akita and Iwate. Members of the group come from these two prefectures. Other group names also reflect geographical locations. Senshū Farm, composed of six members from Akita, is written using the pictograph for *aki* in Akita. "Senshū" means "one thousand autumns." This is also the name of the park and former castle site in Akita City near the train station. Nihonkai Farm means "Sea of Japan Farm," reflecting the fact that its members are all from Akita. In addition, a number of fifth-wave settlers' groups have inspirational names. Takuhō Farm's name is written with the Chinese character referring to land reclamation combined with *hō* or *ōtori*, an imaginary bird from Chinese mythology. Tayō Farm means "Sun Farm" (which sounds a bit like "Sunny Five"), and Yutaka Farm means "Bountiful Farm" or "Plentiful Farm." Phoenix Farm's name speaks of the origins of the land upon which Ogata-mura rests. Finally, Kotobuki Farm's name suggests that good fortune awaits its members, Asahi Farm refers to the morning sun, and Gold Valley Farm sounds very fertile.

Table 2.5: Fifth-wave settlers' cooperative farming groups. Field locations can be found on Figure 2.16.

Group name	Members' prefectures of origin and number of members from each prefecture (if known, and if more than one)	Fields
Takuhō Farm	Akita, Aomori, Iwate, Shizuoka, Okayama, Kōchi	F-22
Godai Farm	Akita (4)	G-19
Taiboku Isseki Dai Farm	Akita (4), Saga	F-17
Shine Farm	Akita (4), Okayama (2), Miyagi	F-14
Green Rowland	Akita, Hokkaido, Gifu, Fukuoka, Nagasaki	F-15
Tayō Farm	Akita (5)	F-25
Oū Farm	Akita (4), Iwate	F-16
Sunny Five	Akita (4), Toyama	F-20
Meisei Farm	Akita (Hachiryū = 6)	F-11
Farm of Japan	Akita (3), Niigata, Ishikawa, Ehime	F-8
Yutaka Farm	Akita (3), Fukui, Toyama, Saga	F-19
Olympia Farm	Akita (2), Iwate (2), Aomori	F-2
Wakasugi Farm	Akita (Kotooka = 5)	F-5
Phoenix Farm	Akita (3), Mie, Okinawa	F-23
Kotobuki Farm	Akita (2), Hokkaido (2), Saga, Tokyo (Meguro)	F-21
Shirakaba Farm	Hokkaido (5)	F-26
Minori Farm	Akita (2), Shiga, Aichi, Hyōgo	F-27
Senshū Farm	Akita (6)	F-24
Kogane Farm	Akita (3), Aomori, Hokkaido	G-21
Asahi Farm	Tochigi (3), Akita, Hokkaido, Niigata	F-12
Nihonkai Farm	Akita (various counties = 5)	G-20
Gold Valley Farm	Akita (Minami Akita County = 4), Miyagi (2)	F-18

In sum, cooperative group membership was an important part of life for settlers in Ogata-mura at the beginning. Along with larger, pan-village organizations based on place of origin, the Niigata Prefecture Club for example, cooperative group membership was the original framework for the small society. Place of origin was also the main factor in the formation of these small, intimate groups, and this can easily be witnessed in the selection of names for them. But relations within these groups were not the only factors in the formation of Ogata-mura.

Social Organization beyond the Group Level

With the arrival of the fifth wave of immigrants, mass settlement of the village was complete and the basic social system was set. Despite the many problems associated with the cooperative arrangements, the farmers knew that they could always count on the other members of their group in times of serious need. This was the case whether the group was clustered or scattered. After all, their fields were in the same place so they saw each other daily, and all of them shared equipment.

Beyond the group level, since all Ogata-mura neighborhoods were set apart from each other and built with straight roads, it is easy to determine street and block sections. Residents of individual streets have no official organizations like the old cooperative groups, but there are cases of street parties (*ocha no kai*) among the wives—now the grandmothers—who live along certain streets. Beyond the street level, there is the neighborhood block, or *jūku* (a block of households usually spanning several streets). At the time the fifth group of settlers took up residence in Ogata-mura there were seventeen of these in the village. Each has an annually rotating headship, a *jūku-chō*, who is in charge of organizing end-of-year (*bōnenkai*) or beginning-of-year (*shinnenkai*) parties, the schedule for communal cleanup work or flower planting, or other matters relating to the entire residential block. In at least one *jūku* of Ogata-mura, the *jūku-chō* is decided each year on the basis of age. When the residents moved into the community, they set up a list of all settlers (household heads) and arranged them by birth date. Even today, each year's *jūku-chō* is determined according to the list, going from eldest to youngest. When a household in which the original settler is no longer living is reached, the surviving wife of the settler may be asked to serve if she is willing, but she is usually skipped and the next settler on the list takes the job for a year. Today, though, the sons of settlers are beginning to take on these responsibilities. There are also cases of simply going from house to house in a set pattern in order to determine the annual *jūku-chō*.

One job that the *jūku-chō* used to have was helping to make wedding plans for block residents. In the earliest years, residents usually held weddings in the villagers' center (*son-min sentā*), where funerals are still regularly held today, and since there was no staff there to manage the affair, it was up to the *jūku* residents or the relatives and friends of the family (or families) concerned to take care of everything. Later, when they could afford it, villagers began holding their weddings in Akita City hotels, where they could let the hotel staff do most of the work and also give relatives from other places comfortable rooms in which to stay. After the village hotel—Sun Rural Ogata—opened in 1996, people began holding weddings there instead. However, the *jūku-chō* has always had to deal with funeral plans, since funerals are not held in hotels and because they usually come up suddenly. Even today, when a household experiences the death of a member, the *jūku-chō* will contact the family as soon as he hears of it, if he has not been contacted by them first, and ask whether they want to have a *jūku-sō*, or *jūku*-style funeral. If they do not opt for this, then they must handle all of the arrangements themselves. If they do choose to do it *jūku*-style, then the *jūku-chō* will notify everyone in the block and begin taking care of necessary matters, such as reserving the villagers' center for the night vigil, or *tsuya*, and making a reservation at a crematorium. He must also prepare the paperwork for the next of kin to sign. Cooperative group members will spring into action first, immediately going to the household that experienced the loss to give comfort and decide how to divide up the important jobs that have to be done.[22] The arrangement works rather well. When residents experience real times of need they can count on the members of their own *jūku* and on those who belong to the same cooperative farming group, even if they live in a different *jūku*. One setter's wife said, "When my father-in-law passed away, my immediate neighbors, people from this *jūku*, and the cooperative farm-ing group members all came to help. My own mother and sister came as well, but there wasn't really anything for them to do—everything had already been seen to. It's a good system." Beyond the level of the *jūku*, some voluntary associations in the village use the larger *jūku* clusters—west section one (*nishi ichōme*), west section two (*nishi nichōme*), and so on—for their administrative organization.

In a typical Ogata-mura farming household, the grandmothers usually help out during the busiest times if they are able, but generally tend more to their small gardens, selling some of their vegetables in the special products center attached to the new museum (see below). Many of the grandmothers socialize often with their neighbors—especially where relations along one street are tight—and participate in village gateball games (see Traphagan 2000: 115–131) or join circles based on particular hobbies. The *Taishō-goto* (a small version of the Japanese harp, or *koto*) group is especially popular among the grandmothers, as are the tea ceremony circles. Settlers (the men) are usually very active in farm labor even into their seventies, but in most cases settlers fortunate enough to have a son taking over their farm tend to back off from the management and marketing aspects once they reach the age of sixty or so. Households belonging to smaller marketing associa-tions are generally represented by the young heir rather than the actual settler who helped build the company in the first place. Older men in the village are gener-ally less organized in groups than the older women, and many spend their free time chatting with their friends and drinking. If they belong to smaller marketing associations, they may associate with other members often. The oldest men and women in the village have the option of joining the Seniors' Club (*rōjin kurabu*), which is composed of many smaller groups. These villagers are generally retired from farming work. Men who are not quite ready to consider themselves retired may join the *kōshinkai*, an association that takes care of trees and other plants on public village land. Other older members of the village participate in sports circles—the ski group is popular—or volunteer to teach crafts to the younger generations.

Young married women (*yome*) of the village are probably the most dynamic and least homogeneous of the villagers, because most of them have married in from outside—from as near as Oga (a five-minute drive) or perhaps as far as the Kansai region, or even farther. While the settlers made most of their adjustments to the new village years ago, the young wives continue to do so today. When they first enter the tiny community, they have to adjust to living in their husbands' homes with their parents-in-law, which often proves to be difficult. Unless they come from a farming background, they may be spared the serious farm work for a while. Most *yome* in Ogata-mura begin helping seriously with the family farms once the smallest child has grown old enough to enter the day care facility (perhaps one or two years) or the kindergarten (at three years).[23] Young wives are very active in social circles, with the sports associations being especially popular among them, and they are probably the most frequent users of the swimming pool during the warmer months when it is open. Young wives sometimes enjoy the English classes at the community center as well. While conflicts between the young wives and their mothers-in-law are inevitable, they are usually able to ask the grandparents to watch the small children when necessary, which is convenient. Even so, many *yome* have complained of not being allowed to move freely—to come and go without offering a good explanation and a good reason. Asking the grandparents to watch the children in order to spend a day shopping in Akita City, in other words, may not be easy for all of them. As their children grow, however, mothers may drive them that far for music, dance, or other lessons. Although it sounds old-fashioned to say so, it is still true in Ogata-mura that once a woman who has married into a farming household produces and raises some children—especially a boy—and also begins helping with the agricultural work in earnest (i.e. making a concrete economic contribution), she can start to assert her independence.

In order to make friends in Ogata-mura, most new brides join the Young Wives' Association (*wakazumakai*). The association has approximately two hundred active members, with a president, a committee of officers, and sections responsible for different activities. The association is divided into *jūku* groups with a leader for each. In the autumn of 2001 I asked the president of the association to help me distribute questionnaires to the members because I wanted some quantifiable data on their demographics and feelings about the village. On my behalf, she sent about 150 forms out to the most active members, and I received 101 completed papers. The average age for *wakazumakai* members was thirty-three, and 87 percent had at least one child. Fifty-two percent hailed from other parts of Akita Prefecture and one-third grew up in Ogata-mura. Fourteen percent were from beyond the prefecture's borders.

When I distributed questionnaires to *wakazumakai* members, I asked those who had married into the village from the outside to indicate on the forms what sort of relationships had helped them adjust to life in Ogata-mura. The responses "people in my *jūku* helped me adjust" and "other members of the *wakazumakai* helped me adjust" each received fifty-two positive responses, while forty-nine of the women answered that people on their street had helped them, and forty-three felt that mothers of children with whom their own children had become friends had been especially important. Only 25 percent answered that members of the same cooperative farming group had helped them, and a small handful reported that they had made friends with their husbands' friends' wives. I asked the members to explain in writing what they liked best about Ogata-mura. Many of them pointed to the clean, natural environment and the open space that the village offers. A number of them indicated that they enjoyed having plenty of free time in the winter, and many others appreciated the fact that the village is a fairly safe place to raise children. As for what they did not like about Ogata-mura, some complained about the lack of privacy and other general problems relating to living with their parents-in-law, such as having to prepare three meals a day throughout most of the year. Quite a few of them expressed much unhappiness over the way that gossip spreads around the village. Some blamed their own mothers-in-law for contributing to the rumor cycles. One wrote of the many "meddlesome old women with nothing better to do than talk about other people," and another penned a lengthy condemnation of villagers who savor gossip and rumors as "delicacies." Five members responded that they wanted to have a heated pool in the village, and a number of others expressed a desire for more facilities that they could use in winter. Finally, I asked the members to explain why they joined the association in the first place. Fifty-seven responded that they had joined in order to make friends, fifteen answered that they had thought it necessary to join, and fourteen responded that they had been invited by other members. Four said that their own mothers-in-law had simply registered them in the association—another complaint.

While many young wives of Ogata-mura do remain at the mercy of their mothers-in-law as they dodge flying rumors, they are actually in better positions than many of their contemporary or historical counterparts. Raising children today is clearly different from the prewar or even the early postwar years, and even from the 1960s or 1970s when most village grandmothers were raising their children. As young mothers of this age, Ogata-mura *yome* have access to a great amount of information that differs too much from that of the past and changes too fast for their husbands' mothers to keep up with. Gone are the days when a new wife would have to put up with all that her mother-in-law said about what to do with her baby. Today, at the very least, she can cite any part of the growing amount of information flowing past her fingertips when faced with a disagreement over childcare. In addition, most young wives of the village have a degree from a university or a junior college, and many of them also have had the experience of working for some years before marrying. There are a number who continue to do so after marrying and even after having a child. Actually, since most Ogata-mura farming households rely entirely on agriculture for their survival, it is helpful if one member works outside the farm for wages to supplement the income a bit. A young wife—or even a young mother—is generally the best candidate for this role because the agricultural labor can be handled well by her husband and his parents, as long as they are able. In such a case, young children may be tended to by the grandmother, or go to the village day-care facility. On the other hand, since the farmers of Ogata-mura are full-time producers, young wives can use the time and space available to grow vegetables for sale and contribute to the household finances, or to their own pocketbooks.

Young men of the village—the sons and grandsons of the settlers—are the most difficult demographic group to pin down. Even in the agricultural down times they are hard to find. As far as group memberships are concerned, many join the village Youth Organization (*seinenkai*). The members are divided into sections that are responsible for organizing different activities. There is a section for arranging fishing events, one for planning group tours, one for disseminating information within and outside of the village, and a special women's section since they are few. Through the *seinenkai*, young villagers may widen their circles of friends and acquaintances. They may even find mates, but most young village couples appear to have either met through arranged meetings (*omiai*), or at college in places like Tokyo, Yokohama, or Sendai. Many sons of settlers who intend to take over their fathers' farms join youth farming associations that are organized at the prefectural level, giving them access to new information and training opportunities. They also may take trips overseas as part of these groups. Village sports clubs—especially ski circles—are especially popular among the sons and grandsons of settlers. Like their female counterparts with regards to raising children, young men of the village are not entirely at the mercy of their fathers or grandfathers when it comes to farming. One interesting aspect of Ogata-mura agriculture is the vast difference between it and that which was practiced by the family's ancestors—or even by the original settlers before they moved to Ogata-mura. The younger generations usually have far more knowledge about matters such as technology and markets than their elders, and it puts the sons who are taking over their fathers' farms in an advantageous position.

The End of the Settlement Phase

Ogata-mura's settlement period came to a close in 1978 with the arrival of nine families who took up residence in a neighborhood in the northeast corner of the village (Figure 2.17). These were the only people from a small hamlet in the mountainous town of Tazawako who decided to accept Akita Prefecture's offer

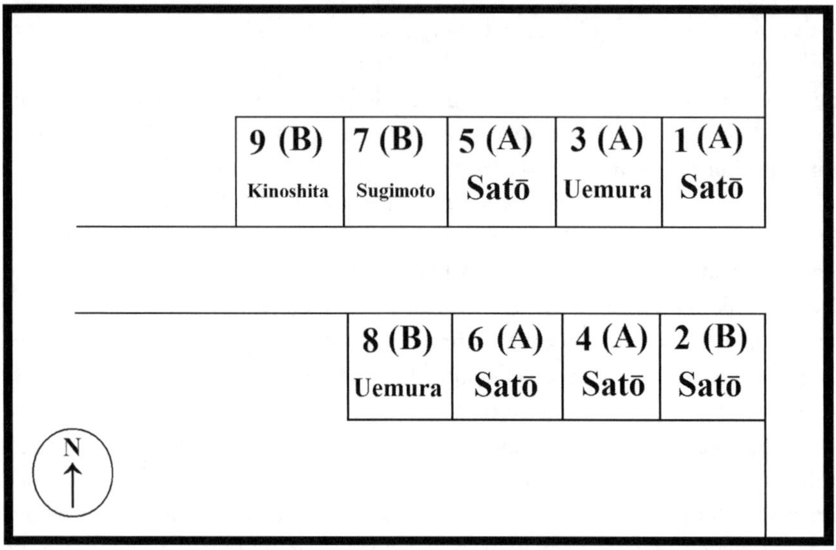

9 (B)	7 (B)	5 (A)	3 (A)	1 (A)
Kinoshita	Sugimoto	Satō	Uemura	Satō

8 (B)	6 (A)	4 (A)	2 (B)
Uemura	Satō	Satō	Satō

N
↑

Figure 2.17: The neighborhood of the Tamagawa Dam settlers.

to become Ogata-mura farmers when they were forced to leave their homes due to the construction of the Tamagawa Dam. Five of the families have the surname Satō, although they do not consider themselves to be blood relatives (a common situation in many small hamlets). These families differ from the other Ogata-mura settlers not only in their late arrival—eleven years after that of the first settlers—but also in that they are prefectural, and not national, settlers. The Akita government prepared houses for the nine families—small but more modern and less uncomfortable than the original peaked-roof houses that the other settlers had purchased—and the nine families took out twenty-five-year loans on their agricultural and residential property just as the other settlers had done before. Unfortunately, however, their story after arriving in Ogata-mura is not entirely one of success and prosperity.

Since land values had risen considerably by the time they settled in the village, they had to pay more for their fifteen-hectare farms than their predecessors had paid. One said the cost had been about 470,000 yen per 10-are plot (one-tenth of a hectare) compared to 300,000 or so for most of the earlier immigrants. Today, only five of the original nine Tamagawa settlers are farming. The nine settlers formed two groups for sharing equipment when they moved into the village— A and B on Figure 2.17. Overall, group B has fared better. All of the members' houses are in good shape, and all of them are still farming—marketing most of their rice, if not all of it, through the Country Elevator.

Only one member of group A, the Satō household numbered five on Figure 2.17, is still farming. Mr. Satō at house number six has sold his fields and is

Reclamation and the Old Social Order | 87

essentially retired—now only helping other farmers during the busy times of the year. When I spoke with him one day, he said that his son was working for wages somewhere in the village, but complained about the low salaries in the area. When I remarked that fifteen hectares of prime farmland must fetch a fair price, he responded with one word: "taxes." He had not been able to build a large nest egg by parting with his fields. The next house to the east, numbered four on Figure 2.17, belonged to another family named Satō, but they sold all of their Ogata-mura property some years ago and went elsewhere. The house is now abandoned and derelict. It is the same story for the house across the street—number three— except that the former owner sold the residence to another Ogata-mura farmer before returning to his home area. The current owner has been renting it out to young women who work at the home for the elderly recently built in the village. The house itself, therefore, is not in terrible shape.

I had the good fortune of finding the wife of house number one on Figure 2.17 in her driveway one afternoon while exploring the area. At first she greeted me with a suspicious frown, but once she found that I was not trying to sell any-thing or proselytize she was quite willing to talk about her family's experiences. Originally her husband had been encouraged to come to Tokyo by a relative after news of the impending dam project broke. He met his wife there, but he was not pleased with the living situation in Tokyo so the two of them returned to his home. "My father was very much against my going to a little farming community in Akita," she said. They lived in the doomed hamlet for four years until the order to leave came. Unfortunately, since they owned little farmland, they did not receive very much cash for their troubles. They did, however, get permission to settle in Ogata-mura. "My father really was against that as well. He didn't think we knew what we were doing—going off to a place like this to be full-time farmers. He knew we didn't have any real experience." Her words were laced with bitterness. Nevertheless, her husband was unwilling to miss the chance to become a "real" farmer. "Anyway," she continued, "men have their dreams."

Life for that Satō family in Ogata-mura has been difficult. They managed to send both of their children to college, but the father hurt his back and became unable to labor in the fields. In the end, they sold them all and gave up on farming. Today the older couple lives in their relatively large house with their son and his wife, who work in Ogata-mura for wages. Mrs. Satō said:

Well, we aren't farmers anymore but at least we can live comfortably here. We couldn't live in such a large house or enjoy having this much space in a place like Tokyo, and I still have a little land for growing vegetables that we can eat at home, so I guess we managed alright. It's not exactly what we had hoped for, but it's okay.

This family's story represents many of the hardships faced by Ogata-mura settlers—health problems, failure at farming and disappointments—and the household has joined the growing ranks of ex-producers in the village. Mrs. Satō's ability to take it all in her stride and appreciate what Ogata-mura has to offer might be a good attitude for many village settlers to cultivate within themselves in the future as the number of farmers decreases while the average farm size rises.

With the close of the building and settlement period in 1978, Ogata-mura already looked much as it does today. Very noticeable facilities had yet to appear, but the neighborhoods and the central section of the community were essentially complete. The original concrete-block houses, with their peaked roofs, were still clearly visible from the tower attached to the community center (*kōminkan*— Figure I.5) at the center of the settlement. Today, tall poplar trees obscure most of the houses on the west side of the village from view, and the height of the new houses also makes it difficult to see very far across much of the east neighborhoods as well. In 1978, however, one was able to gaze out across the entire village from the high lookout, and the roof colors that marked the five different sections of the village—each consisting of three or four separate *jūkus*—must have been quite a sight. On the west side, the two outer sections were marked by blue roofs, and the section in the center (*nishi nichōme*) was all red. On the east side, the northernmost area was red as well, but houses to the south had yellow roofs. Settlers were not forbidden from changing the colors, but the Jigyōdan—and later the village government—strongly discouraged them from doing so. Even today, although the old peaked-roof houses are getting harder to find, the original color of each section is discernible from the air. As of 1980, the village population stood at 3,334—essentially the same as today. Individual households numbered 706, with an average of 4.72 members each. By 1995 the number of households had grown to 762 but the average number of people per household had dropped to 4.35. Of the 762 households in the village in 1995, 560 were listed as farming households, down from 580 fifteen years earlier. This number would drop to about 540 by 2005, and to 523 by 2010.

Utopia Lost?

By the time the settlement of Ogata-mura ended in 1978, although the village itself was esthetically pleasing and a true society was beginning to form, the Hachirōgata project was looking like somewhat of a failure, especially as compared to the initial expectations of the national government and the Jigyōdan that built Ogata-mura and managed it until that year. The original reclamation plans had not been drawn up in haste—they were based on many decades of thought, and also on the expert opinions of experienced Dutch engineers. For better or worse, the land was successfully created without major complications or embarrassment. But a curious social experiment was then imprinted upon the landscape in a somewhat careless manner, with economic concerns taking precedence over social ones (e.g. the choice of clustering all immigrants in a single settlement), based on a desire for homogeneity and egalitarianism. As a result, settlers began to want to live further apart from one another very early on, and inherent differences between them were magnified. Many personal problems detailed above remained secret from the general public, but the suicides among settlers could not be kept under wraps—newspapers across the country ran stories on this.

The government's decision to settle fewer people in Ogata-mura and have larger farms than originally planned, on the other hand, was probably a good one. I have heard more than one settler supportive of Shinichirō Sakamoto—the social-ist writer of the fourth wave—say in hindsight that the village should have been used to settle far more households on smaller farms in order to combat unemploy-ment, but in reality this would only have made the tiniest dent in that problem, and it would also have merely served to create a community of poor farmers with bad prospects for off-farm work. However, many settlers longed for a more "natural" village environment, and at the very least, reconciliation between the modern village and the nostalgic *furusato* came hard for the majority of them. Although community formation was occurring, the utopian model was clearly not working quite as planned. Tokyo's heavy-handed approach, backed by the village government, continued into the following decade, and this had major repercus-sions on the development of Ogata-mura through the rest of the century and into the following one right up to today.

Notes

1. Sakamoto 1990: 32.
2. A scientific explanation for why Lake Tazawa never freezes, despite its high altitude, is based on its depth—at 423 meters it is the deepest lake in the country (see Anbai 1991: 25–28 for more on the legend of Hachirō Tarō).
3. Stories have been recorded from many areas of the lagoon's banks regarding what kind of fish not to feed a young wife, and who should handle nets and how, for example (Mutō 1940).
4. There is evidence of small-scale reclamation along much of the banks of Hachirōgata, similar to the gradual encroachment pattern found in Kojima Bay, Okayama Prefecture (Connors 1963). This may have begun prior to the Edo period.
5. Even so, however, the country's financial situation still prevented any action being taken on a 1948 proposal for reclaiming Hachirōgata, and even at that time fishermen living in the areas along the banks of Hachirōgata were speaking out against the idea (Shioya et al. 2001).
6. Another delay was caused by an earthquake that struck the area on May 7, 1964, caus-ing some damage to the dikes. Vertical slippage of 15 to 20 centimeters was reported (Gordon 1965: 55).
7. Making a transformation to pure farming, it was thought, should not have been too dif-ficult for most of the fishermen, for only 13 percent of the 1,284 households belonging

to local fishing cooperatives were without farmland at the time of the reclamation, and nearly 40 percent possessed at least one hectare (Bunkachō 1971: 22).

8. This was five to ten times greater than the national average but still miniscule in comparison with the 1969 figure of about 158 hectares per farm in the United States (Albrecht and Murdock 1990: 43).

9. According to village data, applicant acceptance rates varied greatly by wave, ranging from a low of 9 percent (wave one) to a high of 57 percent (wave three). The overall rate for the entire national settlement project was about 24 percent.

10. The training course entailed nearly 1,500 hours of instruction.

11. See Scott (1998: 229) on a similar way of thinking regarding the pioneering of large-scale farms in Tanzania.

12. There had originally been 179 men accepted but four quit the program early on.

13. Of his composition for the written test, Takeru said, "Yeah, I gave it my best—the essay. [I wrote,] Just as a peasant, I'll work with all my might. I'll even bury my bones there. . . . With resolve to bury my bones in the land of Hachirōgata, I'll settle there."

14. Three had dropped out early on.

15. There had been 121 but one man dropped out early.

16. Single gravestones or small clusters of them are also often found near rice paddies, but this is not seen in Ogata-mura at all.

17. It should be noted that today an increasing proportion of the Japanese population is choosing quasi-Buddhist or even secular funerals (see Suzuki 2000, Tanaka 2007, and Wood 2007: 6–7).

18. Houses for first- and second-wave settlers measured about 500 square meters, while those for settlers of the third and later waves measured about 700 square meters.

19. There are regular direct flights between Akita and Seoul.

20. The number of tractors in the village jumped from 479 to 1,070, and the number of large combines skyrocketed from a mere 19 to 491, between 1975 and 1980 (Ogata-mura 1994: 8).

21. Even today, dump trucks, water irrigation pumps, and small machines for digging ditches are owned on a group basis in some instances.

22. The involvement of cooperative group members in such matters seems similar to the situation that Miyara (1984) describes for small religious associations (*kō*) based partly on migrants' places of origin in Hokkaido.

23. Their labor is usually not critical on the farm until the older couple have begun to cut down on hard work out of physical necessity.

3

The Storm and the Aftermath

We have two villages really, existing side by side. These days, we don't talk to each other very much.

-Shinichirō Sakamoto[1]

Out of the darkness and into the light—that's the impact that the solar sports have had on the village's image.

-Seiki Miyata

Impediments to Ogata-mura serving as a symbol of all that is good about modernity and as a model for efficient agriculture—an inspiration for farmers across the country—did not end with the kinds of problems outlined in chapter 2. As mentioned earlier, things got worse after the settlers found themselves pitted against one another over rice production and marketing issues. The village became generally known as a focal point for dissent and subversion, and somewhat less as an ideological battleground (Anbai 1991). Moreover, the fighting even spilled over into the district courtrooms in Akita City, and caught the attention of foreign diplomats who used the issue as ammunition in their attacks on Japan's rice protection policies. Consequently, the village's image was badly soiled, Ogata-mura having been harshly criticized in the press and repeatedly chastised by its own elected political representatives.

In order to improve the village's image, the administration of Seiki Miyata—mayor from 1978 to 2000—embarked on a large-scale beautification campaign in the 1980s that intensified in the next decade. The campaign began innocuously enough—as a series of understandable responses to several natural disasters. In July of 1981 heavy rains resulted in significant damage to the (small) wheat crop, and the following month saw the arrival of typhoon number fifteen, which

----

Endnotes for this chapter begin on page 124.

wreaked havoc upon the rice paddies to the tune of about 4.5 billion yen and destroyed over forty-one thousand of the poplar trees lining many of the village's roads, serving as windbreaks. In 1983 a magnitude 7.7 earthquake ravaged the area, badly cracking sections of the polder dam and many of the streets. It would take three years to completely repair the damage. After the quake, some villagers joked that they might have to put lifeboats on their roofs in case another major temblor caused the Hachirōgata reclaimed land area to flood completely, for were the lagoon's water level to be restored to its original state the ground floors of their houses would lie well below it.

In response to these disasters, the village kicked off an intensive four-year tree-planting project in 1984 that eventually resulted in a total of 6,600 cherry (*sakura*), plum (*ume*), and gingko (*ichō*) trees lining various village roads, helping to replace the trees that had been destroyed by typhoon 15 in 1981. Having successfully responded to the natural tragedies, the Miyata administration continued its focus on image-building with the unveiling of the village's symbol—a variation of the phonetic *katakana* letter *o*—and the official song, also in 1984. In addition, that year marked the selection of the red salvia as the village flower, the black pine as the official tree, and the swan as the village bird. Indeed, although the poplars, gingkos, and cherry trees draw more attention from visitors, the ubiquitous black pine groves filling much of the unused space in the residential district of Ogata-mura give the settlement itself a lush, green character. The swan was selected as the official bird because swans have enjoyed the waters of Hachirōgata seasonally since ancient times—a traditional symbol for the new village. From this innocent beginning, the administration's PR campaign grew in strength and intensity—not to mention cost—and in the end it did indeed help to clean up the village's image, but it also served to widen the gap between the mayor's supporters (the obedient faction) and their disobedient neighbors.

Dark Clouds on the Horizon

As explained in chapter 1, the early 1970s marked the beginning of strict government attempts to curtail rice production in Japan. Within this trend, 1975 was an important year in the history of Ogata-mura, for it saw the beginning of a development that would change everything about the village. Since the government had found itself faced with an unprecedented overabundance of rice, amid changing national dietary patterns that included less and less of the grain and a projected population drop as well, Tokyo decided to cut short the Ogata-mura settlement program and cease all recruitment activities. As mentioned in chapter 2, each farmer who had already settled in the village was essentially required to purchase an additional five hectares of prime farmland at the full price for paddy fields—considerably higher than the set price for dry fields (which became a major point of contention). Another serious problem for many was the fact that they were supposed to buy the land with the promise that they would not use it for growing rice.

Next, things got worse. In August each settler who had planted in excess of a previously set limit of about nine hectares was ordered to cut and destroy all rice plants in his fields beyond that amount. Known as the *aogari mondai* ("cutting of green rice problem"), this marked the beginning of a series of political moves by the government that gradually split the fledgling community in half. The *aogari* episode was a part of Tokyo's larger, long-range plan to force farmers to produce less rice through its reduction (*gentan*) program or a crop diversion (*tensaku*) scheme. The former allowed farmers to collect payments simply for letting land lie fallow, while the latter required them to plant certain crops in lieu of rice. However, the government did not offer Ogata-mura farmers monetary incentives to comply with its commands because it felt that the settlers should simply be glad to have been selected for the settlement project and therefore just follow orders. As Moore (1993: 287) explains, these policies "were symbols of injustice to Hachirōgata farmers who sold their family farms as down-payment for their legal contracts with the government to buy land to grow rice on a large scale" (see the epigraph to chapter 1). Many felt that Tokyo had simply tricked them and broken its promises. At this point, divisions between the settlers opened up based on the matter of who complied with the orders to destroy immature rice plants immediately and who did not. Those who refused to follow orders generally waited until their plants were just mature enough to be harvested—albeit early— and then harvested the excess until what remained in the paddies conformed to the set level of rice plants that should be grown. The remainder would stay in the paddies until they had fully ripened. But, even among those who complied with the orders, there were settlers who felt that they had been severely mistreated by the bureaucracy in Tokyo, since they had received no compensation whatsoever for their losses. Takeru Isono was one of the settlers who initially complied with the orders from Tokyo and destroyed about three hectares of perfectly good rice plants, worth about five million yen—something he later described as the hardest thing he had ever done since migrating to Ogata-mura.[2] Something in him seems to have snapped. His trust in the government's agricultural policy began to waver, and this also happened to several other members of his cooperative farming group, so the group began to split apart ideologically. Tarō Omori, who had taught Takeru to ski, remained loyal to the government and to the Country Elevator.

As happened between Takeru Isono and his fellow group members, those who were especially unhappy about the way things were going, whether they had complied with the *aogari* orders or not, started to drift away from their neighbors politically. The village basically became divided down the middle over this issue, and two major factions formed. For convenience, I refer to them throughout this book as the compliant (loyalist) faction or group, and the noncompliant (or sometimes "opposition") faction or group. Associated somewhat with the compliant faction—as noted in the introduction—were certain settlers who were determined to overly comply with the government to force it to notice and protect them. These overcompliant settlers rallied around Shinichirō Sakamoto, and refraining from making noticeable improvements in their homes was part of their strategy.[3] The two main factions quickly developed into political parties of sorts, and they still vie with one another for control of the village.

Despite the *aogari* episode, that autumn Akita Prefecture had a record rice harvest of 717,000 tons and the entire nation produced over thirteen million tons— the largest rice harvest in six years (Government of Japan 2008). Five months after the *aogari* incident, in January of 1976, a new order came out of Tokyo: the farmers of Ogata-mura were to grow only 8.6 hectares of rice on their 15-hectare farms and no more. In response to this, many settlers began planting their rice in "zebra stripe" patterns (*zebura hōshiki*) to make it difficult to gauge the amount that had been planted and also to increase overall crop yields per area (caused by greater air flow between plants, for example) (see Moore 1993: 288). Also, also around this time the disobedient settlers began marketing illegally produced rice through channels that were also technically illegal. Officially known as *jiyūmai*, such rice was also called *yami-gome (yami-mai)*, or "black-market rice."[4] As if intentionally overproducing rice had not been bad enough in the eyes of the government, selling rice freely was a clear violation of the Food Control Act, and Tokyo was not amused. The Country Elevator started refusing to accept rice from overproducing farmers—it would not even purchase the amount of rice that had been legally grown—and the divide between compliant farmers and noncompliant farmers was as if etched in stone. The stage was set for a struggle between these two camps of Ogata-mura settlers that would forever alter the social, political, and economic environment of the village—transforming it from a cooperative community rooted in notions of equality and harmony to one marked by increasingly high degrees of specialization and grounded in differences over rice marketing strategies and political ideologies. The year 1977 began with the arrest of a settler who had been found to be selling rice illegally, which cast a shadow over the official completion of the land reclamation project that summer, and three more suicides occurred in the village during the following winter. In 1978 the settlers who had exceeded the 8.6 hectare planting limit set in 1976 were ordered to cut down and burn their rice plants—the second *aogari* episode. This time, though, most of those who were opposed simply refused to comply, and the egalitarian utopia that the Jigyōdan had sought to create slipped further out of reach.

It was no minor coincidence that Seiki Miyata, a member of the third wave of settlers from the nearby town of Hachiryū, was elected mayor of Ogata-mura in 1978—the year of the second *aogari* episode. Miyata had served on the town council of Hachiryū before becoming a settler in the new village, so he was well-acquainted with municipal politics and understood (and cared about) the feelings that residents of the Hachirōgata region harbored for Ogata-mura (Anbai 1991: 256). He took office on September 5 and would hold it for twenty-two years. Mayor Miyata, an LDP member, sided with the national government and supported its policies from the beginning, as did the village council—controlled entirely by farmers of the compliant faction. Animosity grew among noncompliant farmers, as they were identified by the village government for breaking the law. Government agents visited the village repeatedly to pressure them to comply with production guidelines and marketing laws, and to inspect their fields and vehicles, which of course increased the anger of the disobedient settlers, who accused the bureaucrats of trespassing and other violations. Allegations of government wire-tapping to monitor telephone calls arose, the names of overproducing settlers were announced in regional and national newspapers, and, in a dramatic show of state power, banks in the Hachirōgata area were forced by Tokyo to inform it if any suspiciously large deposits were made to the accounts of blacklisted settlers (Kurose 1988a). Furthermore, since these settlers had become totally unable to use the Country Elevator to market their rice or to use its processing facilities, they had to find other ways to sell their products.

The Deluge

In the early 1980s, Nobuhiro Machida from Toyama (introduced in chapter 2) and a number of like-minded settlers who were selling rice illegally banded together to form a group—the Seiji Keizai Kenkyūkai (Political and Economic Research Association, SKK)—in order to increase their strength. They also joined forces to solve the problem of how to dry, polish, and store their rice following the harvest since the Country Elevator had turned them away after they violated rice reduction policies and marketing laws—equipment had to be purchased, and no single farmer could afford to buy everything by himself. Another problem was that they had found themselves vulnerable to deception by dishonest middlemen—since the entire operation was technically illegal they had no way of defending themselves when payments failed to arrive. There are tales of dubious merchants filling bags with cheap rice and labeling it as Ogata rice for higher profits. Working as a group, they could better protect themselves from such perils.

The administration of Mayor Miyata was also in a difficult position, caught between higher government levels and the defiant farmers, but it remained firmly allied with Tokyo and Akita Prefecture. Illegally grown rice was flowing forth from Ogata-mura under cover of night, hidden in trucks and cars, and everybody knew about it. The main leader of the defiant farmers was Tadashi Kurose, who had moved to Ogata-mura from Shiga Prefecture with the fifth settler group after first spending a short time working for the government of Shiga. The oldest son of a farmer, Kurose entered Ogata-mura with knowledge of both agriculture and bureaucracy, and he was not willing to simply bow down to higher powers. His weapon against the state has always been three-pronged: (1) the government broke its promise first by forcing him and his fellow settlers to reduce their rice production, (2) because of the low elevation and marine origins of Ogata-mura its fields were never well-suited for growing anything but rice, and (3) the Food Control Act was causing low rice prices and stymieing the evolution of Japanese agriculture into something better in the first place (Anbai 1991: 225–232, Kurose 1988a, b). In 1997 he explained his choice to defy the government in the following way:

> You know, you have a bunch of monkeys in a zoo, and they all want to eat. One of them is happy to get whatever the zookeeper gives him. If it's enough, he's all right. Another monkey takes what he can get and complains but doesn't really want to make the effort to try to get more. The third monkey is so unsatisfied that he doesn't even care what he gets from the zookeeper. He'd rather get out of there and take his chances by himself—all for the opportunity to find something better on his own. Win or lose, he has to do it by himself. There just might be something better out there, after all. That's me—I'm the third monkey!

The discovery of *yami-gome* from Ogata-mura in Tomakomai City, Hokkaido, in April of 1985 attracted the attention of the MAFF and other government agents in Tokyo (and exposed a black market route), so in order to stop the illegal flow of rice out of the village Akita Prefecture sent police officers to block the roads connecting Ogata-mura to the outside and inspect cargoes. Known as the *kenmon jiken* (police checkpoint incident) this began on October 7, 1985 and lasted until Christmas Day. Some rice was confiscated, but much was successfully smuggled out. Takeru Isono and Isao Satake—also introduced in chapter 2—were among the latter group. Along with his neighbor Tadashi Kurose, Nobuhiro Machida found himself at the forefront of the legal battles—both men were prosecuted by the government for their deep involvement in organized resistance. An undated article from the *Akita Sakigake* newspaper in a scrapbook in the village middle-school archive room features a photograph of Nobuhiro sitting next to Kurose and another man. Their happy faces contrast sharply with the troubled expressions of the bureaucrats and government lawyers pictured below them. The headline reads: "Big Sensation: No Indictments in Ogata Black Market Rice." A smaller heading reads: "'Our Toils Were Pointless': Obedient Faction Disappointed."[5]

Overall, the *yami-gome* affair strengthened the resolve of many to fight for what they believed in. In retrospect, Isao Satake's wife Hiroko said:

We learned that there were a lot of farmers in Japan who were against the government's *gentan* policies. But, you see, they're small-scale farmers—mostly part-time. There are hardly any full-time farmers in Japan, but here there are many, so we're the ones who could best fight with the government. That's why some of them said, "Keep it up!" They cheered us on.

Figures indicate that 161 households were overproducing and illegally marketing rice in the mid-1980s, while 426 were complying with *tensaku* guidelines and selling all rice through the Country Elevator (Yamano 2003: 124). Other figures show that 309 households were overproducing by 1989, with well over 1,000 hectares of village land illegally planted with rice (Sakamoto 1990: 227). Many, including the members of the SKK, shared a conviction that the government in Tokyo could not be counted on to take care of them, and that they needed to fight for their freedom to control their production and marketing in order to secure their futures as farmers. For them, as for Tōru Wakui of the Akita Komachi Corporation (named after the type of rice most commonly grown in Ogata-mura), farming could be both a lifestyle and a business, and it was better to struggle alone than to comply with government demands.

The bold moves of the recalcitrant Ogata-mura farmers brought a great deal of bad publicity to the young village, and to the surrounding area as well. They also helped push up the prefecture's rice production numbers, which threatened to imperil government subsidies to other producers. This is one reason why the noncompliant farmers were much disliked not only by their compliant neighbors, but also by many farmers in the local area. Some especially angry residents of the Hachirōgata region publicly threatened to destroy the polder dam with explosives and allow the waters of the lagoon to reclaim the surface of the land within its banks. Once again, Ogata-mura farmers joked about having to tie lifeboats to their roofs, as they had after the earthquake struck in 1983.

Inside the village, as evidenced by the comment of Shinichirō Sakamoto quoted at the start of this chapter, residents on different sides of the rice quarrels literally became unable to talk to one another about rice marketing issues—or politics in general in some cases, or anything at all in still other cases. Even in the earliest years of the current century some were bitter about the actions of their neighbors during this chaotic period, freely expressing lingering resentment for people marketing their rice independently: "Oh, yeah. Delivery trucks are always coming and going over there across the street. They have a nice big house, too. Not like us." At the same time, some independent marketeers criticized those who sell their rice in large groups: "I'll tell you, all those people who sell their rice to the Country Elevator or to Wakui's company—they don't even know the taste of their own rice. They can't even be proud of it." Still others defend their actions with condemnation for the government for placing such strict restrictions on them in the past: "Yeah, we sell all our rice by ourselves. You know, as soon as the [national] economic situation starts looking really good, the government always starts bullying [doing *ijime* to] all the farmers. What could we do?" In 1985 Tokyo finally began to relax its policies on rice production, raising the amount of land that the settlers could devote to it from 8.6 hectares to 10 hectares, and this figure was raised again to 12.5 hectares in 1987, but this could not hold back the tide.

Why Did the Clouds Burst?

While it is understandable that Ogata-mura farmers would have been unhappy about the *aogari* episode and other rice reduction policies, it might be difficult to comprehend exactly why things turned out as they did. Initial dissatisfaction can partly be explained by the fact that they were not compensated by the government for letting land lie fallow or diverting fields to other crops (Kurose 1988a, Yamano 2003: 122). Later, though, when monetary incentives were made available, these angry farmers still refused to comply with official policies. It was largely an ideological battle—and disobedient settlers always focus on this when explaining their actions—but monetary incentives cannot be ignored in a consideration of the decisions to obey or to disobey the government. In 1980, a settler who did as he was told by the local office and grew only 8.6 hectares worth of rice, and diverted the rest of his land to dry crops, could earn about twenty million yen for the year, while a neighbor who used all of his fifteen hectares for wet rice farming (far less vulnerable to weather fluctuations) and sold the grains illegally, could expect to bring in closer to thirty million yen (Yamano 2006: 63). Some have said that they were able to earn considerably more than this—even up to fifty million yen. Certain farmers pulled far ahead of their fellow settlers during this time by maximizing production and investing the profits back into their farms: purchasing extra land. This is what Takeru Isono did. So, for many settlers, the end simply justified the means. Yet there was also an ideological barrier to crossing the line. This barrier divides two different sets of philosophies about the role of agriculture in rural life, and about the relationship between farming and business. The fact that rice is a culturally sensitive crop cannot be overlooked, either (Ohnuki-Tierney 1993). It has been very easy for rice farmers to cast themselves as champions of the national character—or for them to be cast that way by others—considering how tightly rice and national identity are intertwined.

Today on television and in the newspapers it is not uncommon to learn of adventurous Japanese farmers who have completely given up on rice and instead thrown themselves into the commercial production of anything from carnations to cabbages, and they are increasingly forming new marketing organizations with neighbors for these alternative products and creating Internet sites in order to sell directly to consumers across the country quickly and cheaply. In certain cases these farmers can receive official kickbacks for not growing rice. And the shift away from rice production seems fairly natural today—a logical response to market realities—but it was quite a shock when the government began initiating its rice reduction policies in the early 1970s, when for so many generations farmers had enjoyed the security of growing the same, reliable crop over and over again. Ogata-mura settlers gave up just about everything they had and knew back home to grow rice on their large fields. They had also taken out twenty-five-year loans on their new properties, and had assumed the responsibility for building garages and extra rooms on their residential land, and even for converting the upper floors of their little houses into living areas. All of this they had done with the understanding that they would at least still be producing the same crop as before—and lots of it. The dependability of rice, they had assumed, would ensure their success and happiness in Ogata-mura. So when they saw signs that this might not pan out, many got angry.

However, there still is the question of why many settlers did not rebel. Yamano (2003) has found that settlers of the fifth wave and those from outside Akita appear to have been less likely to comply with government rice reduction policies than other settlers. The difference according to wave number might be due to the location of the fields and the fact that land values had risen by the time the fifth-wave settlers entered the village. Most of their fields are located farther away from the settlement itself and do not drain quite as well as other parts of the reclaimed area; they are therefore even worse suited to dry-field farming than the fields of other settlers. Also, since land values had gone up, the later settlers had to pay slightly more money to the government for the purchase of their fields. Those from outside Akita may have felt less inhibited about producing, and selling, rice as they saw fit—partly because they had no relatives in the area. Yamano also found that third-wave settlers appear to have been more compliant overall, which is an interesting pattern, but he neglected to note that Mayor Miyata was a member of the third wave. Certainly this must have been a factor in the relatively high rate of compliance among them.

Indeed, the majority of settlers who obeyed the government rallied around the political leadership of Mayor Miyata. They were in control, and they believed they were right. As mentioned above, many settlers also drew inspiration from the socialist views of Shinichirō Sakamoto, even sharing in his lamentations over the disappearance of the egalitarian utopia that he had sought when he quit his government job in 1969 to enter the settlement training program. Like him, they feared further commercialization of farming and the formation of increasingly larger economy-of-scale farms as small producers were bought out by bigger ones. For Sakamoto and others like him, farming is mainly a way of life and it does not mix with business—for that combination in an open market situation, they feel, is too dangerous. That the government made mistakes is not necessarily in question—it never was with Mayor Miyata, either—but the ideological and economic motivations (and perceived selfishness) of the noncompliant farmers were, according to the compliant side, more corrupt than those of the government. So there have essentially been two main trains of thought among those who followed the government's orders all the way: (1) that small farming needs to be protected from the perils of the market, that the government should continue fulfilling that role, and that giving up and going independent—even if the government is not providing that protection anymore—is a poor choice because it will simply help destroy farming as a way of life faster; and (2) that remaining loyal to the government and working within its legal frameworks will be better for all in the long run, provided that others also comply and that all work together with the same understanding.

Basically, therefore, the divide between the farmers of Ogata-mura was about the power of the state, the meaning of farming, the value of the farm life, long-term security, and also short-term profits (at least for some). In 1997, Mayor Miyata admitted to me that, in his view, both the government and the defiant farmers had been in the wrong. Both, he said, had behaved badly, but he fully believed that it was better to find ways to work with the government, or at least within its frameworks, than to fight against it. As explained in chapter 1, post-war agricultural policies in Japan have been rather conservative overall, as has been the general political situation in the country for decades—evidenced by the nearly unbroken control over the Diet and the position of prime minister on the part of the LDP (Jimintō) right up to the summer of 2009. Policies protected rice farmers while keeping their farms small, but they kept the farms from shrinking in size by funneling younger sons and daughters into the workforce rather than encouraging them to take over small sections of the family land. Policies also protected Japanese rice farmers from the effects of open-market capitalism—the government bought essentially all rice produced in the country at set prices each year—so Sakamoto's socialist politics are not as radical as they might be viewed in the United States, for example, but rather are decidedly conservative within the Japanese agricultural environment.[6]

Perhaps, then, we should be surprised that so many Ogata-mura settlers eschewed their conservative backgrounds and struggled for the right to market more or all of their rice freely. It was a very radical move. It may be that a greater proportion of adventurous risk takers than typical, conservative farmers settled in Ogata-mura—that the village has a ratio of conservative to change-seeking/ risk-taking farmers that does not match the national average. After all, over the years it was proven to Japanese farmers that as long as they continued to listen to the government and grow the food that was needed, they would be all right. They would not be rich, but they would be all right. Ogata-mura settlers might have gone on feeling this way even after the government began changing its policies.

But many did not. The timing of the village's creation was probably a big factor in this. Even for risk takers, the risks of relocating to the Hachirōgata reclaimed land were great, and it may be that doing so helped give them more confidence— confidence to do whatever they felt they needed to do in order to ensure their survival and preserve their dignity (for they felt that they had been terribly mistreated). Again, one effect of the relocation experience seems to have been the inculcation of a strong pioneer spirit among most of the settlers.

The Beautification Campaign Accelerates

Continuing its efforts to improve the appeal of Ogata-mura, the Miyata administration reorganized the conspicuously quiet *shōtengai* (shopping strip), positioned between the community center and the schools, in 1988 (see Figure 2.3). Since its creation in 1974 the stores had been arranged in a tight line that bisected the parking lot and ran perpendicular to its current arrangement, so shop owners were generally happy about the rearrangement, for it gave them more space and also made the shopping strip more inviting. After all, many of the business owners had been asked by the village to open stores there in the first place because of a general lack of interest. Business along the *shōtengai* increased in the years following the reorganization, and the new open space (which now faces the community center with its commanding tower) became the staging ground for various events, including the summertime *o-bon* dance, which helped bring more residents and outsiders into the center of the community.

Today the shopping strip is clean and spacious and inviting enough, but it is very quiet (Figure 3.1). One of the busiest shops is the Fujii family's general store, near the eastern end of the strip, and next to this is the relatively popular restaurant, Panda, which has a sushi bar and some karaoke rooms in the back. There is also a small living space above Panda, as with most shops of the *shōtengai*. Both the owner of Panda and the wife of the Fujii store were complaining even in 2002 that business was not as good as it had been in the past. Particularly, according to them, the farmers were not spending as much as they had once spent—especially at the general store—and the young students in the village preferred the atmosphere of the new village grocery or the small shopping mall ("Joyful City") in nearby Funakoshi, about fifteen minutes away by car (this mall, however, closed down in late 2008). On the other side of the Fujii General Store is the barbershop, and next to that is a small clothing store and the chiropractor's clinic. The owner of the clinic, Dr. Satō, is the eldest son of a fourth-wave settler, and he was led into his field through an interest in judo and fitness in junior high school. In fact, the doctor has a judo school behind his clinic, and an instructor comes from elsewhere to teach. The other side of the *shōtengai* houses the post office, a small liquor store, another restaurant—Kinoya—and a beauty parlor. The meat

Figure 3.1: A typical business day at the *shōtengai*. The post office is on the left. Passing under the semi-circular sign decorated with flying swans takes one northward toward the schools. The Fujii store is near the end of the *shōtengai* to the far right, and Panda, the restaurant, is barely visible beyond the store.

and fish markets both went out of business after I left the village in 1997. There was also a bookstore, but it closed at the end of 2006. With this, and also the death of the owner of Panda restaurant in the same year, the *shōtengai* has become slightly quieter, although Panda is still open under the ownership of the original proprietor's widow.

Nevertheless, this and other cosmetic adjustments to the village (including tree and flower planting) had good results on the surface. Ogata-mura came to be known for its spaciousness and general attractiveness. People from across Akita started driving to the village in the springtime to enjoy the flowering trees and the scenery. Many came simply to see the linear arrangement and clean neighborhoods. However, the Miyata administration was not content to stop with the reorganization of the shopping strip. Under Miyata's direction, and with the full support of the council, the office increased its village beautification efforts to a hyperactive level in order to reclaim Ogata-mura's identity as a model farming village and even to rewrite the village's history, leaving the opposition settlers and their families feeling more and more excluded from the political process. They, for their part, struggled for years to reclaim their own identities as settlers with their own histories. Miyata's administration started to turn away from a focus on production and toward the actual products instead, emphasizing their relationship to tourism.

Figure 3.2: A giant pumpkin sits near the front counter of the land reclamation museum in the autumn of 2006.

This new focus on tourism was the start of the "Rurec Plan." It was the mayor's attempt at redefining Ogata-mura as a model village for people to have fun in—to experience recreation in a rural place—and thereby cleaning up its image as well. This might be called the "second reclamation"—a symbolic reclamation of the village's reputation and identity, a very public reconciliation of Ogata-mura's ambiguous position between "nature" on the one side and "culture" on the other (cf. Latour 1993), controlled by Miyata and his cohorts. The establishment of the special products center on the highway outside the settlement in the summer of 1989 is a case in point. In the following years, an annual giant pumpkin festival was begun as well (see Figure 3.2). The nonagricultural events and projects, however, gradually became more visible in the village than the production-oriented ones. Hosting a national high-school sports competition in 1984 was one early example of this. Others include commissioning a popular singer, Kiyohiko Ozaki, to record the Ogata-mura Image Song, hosting a national roller ski competition, establishing a hot spring (*onsen*) facility, attempting to build a golf course (the proposal was defeated by village residents—see Anbai 1991: 60–67), starting the annual solar sports events, and creating a special neighborhood for esteemed specialists, or *bunkajin*. The new projects did even more to clean up Ogata-mura's tarnished "black market rice village" image than had the previous projects. It began to look as if there was nothing that the tiny municipality could not do. But at the same time, the divide between the opposition (noncompliant) settlers and their Miyata-supporting, compliant neighbors only grew.

Big Plans and High Hopes

The Village Hotel: Sun Rural Ogata

April 26, 1996, was a big day for Ogata-mura. It marked the grand opening day of the hotel, Sun Rural Ogata (Figure 3.3). To honor the event, the village hosted a day of music and games both inside the new facility and outside in the "ground golf" area across the street from the building. The hotel has eight floors, the first of which sports a fairly inexpensive and spacious Chinese restaurant, a gift shop, a game room, a lounge, a large hall for wedding receptions, a chapel for ceremonies, a beauty salon, a fitting room for kimono, and a small photo studio. On the second floor are various meeting rooms and a karaoke bar. Guest rooms—both Western- and Japanese-style—fill floors three through seven. On the south side of the eighth floor, commanding an excellent view, is a more expensive restaurant. The food, certainly quite unlike anything that can be found in most small Japanese villages, is rather good. The north side of the top floor is devoted to hot baths—one side for men and one for women. The building was financed jointly by Akita Prefecture and Ogata-mura, the former shouldering two-thirds of the cost and the latter picking up the remainder of the 4.3 billion yen tab. This is why the hotel technically has several names—the main official one being "Akita Prefecture Ogata Sports Overnight Stay Center."

The hotel is managed by a joint-stock corporation, Rural Ogata—founded in February of 1995—which currently claims a capital of 200 million yen. Ogata-mura owns 60 percent of the company's stocks, and the remaining 40 percent are held by various private interests, including Akita Bank. This means that the mayor of the village has long been the president of the company, and therefore the head of the hotel. The actual operation of the facility, however, is overseen by the general manager—an employee of Rural Ogata. Business ventures of this sort are known as "third sector" arrangements—not fully public, and not fully private, but a combination of the two. The formation of such companies was encouraged by Tokyo from the early 1970s in order to stimulate investment in, and development

Figure 3.3: Hotel Sun Rural Ogata shortly after its grand opening.

of, regional areas. Many facilities across the country benefiting rural residents have either been built or managed by third sector companies. However, after the economic bubble burst, and as the population of such areas began to drop, these organizations often found it difficult to function well, and "third sector" eventually came to be synonymous with "running in the red" (Ikuma 2002, Matanle et al. 2011: ch. 9).

The bad reputation of third sector corporations may not have been so much the fault of the organizations themselves, though, as the fault of the relationships between them and local governments. Originally, a municipality would build a facility and then create a third-sector company to operate it. Obviously, in such an arrangement, the managing company would not have to struggle too hard to conserve costs and increase profits as long as the local government was satisfied, or at least willing to bail it out. All of this changed after the national government passed a law in June of 2003 declaring that municipalities must throw open the bidding for the management of public facilities to any entity that wants to tender (Idei 2005). The law established a system known as *shitei kanrisha seido,* or the "designated manager system." According to the law, individuals are not allowed to apply, but nearly any organization can. When Akita Prefecture adopted the system, it decided that the contract period for all such facilities would be five years.

In 2005 Ogata-mura opened the bidding for the management of its hotel, and although one other organization apparently showed interest a five-year contract was awarded to Rural Ogata, which had already managed the facility for nine years. In 2006 the manager said, "When a hotel like this is running in the black, other companies might take interest and, thinking that they can do better, try to take control." Should this happen, though, the name by which the hotel is most commonly known, Sun Rural Ogata, will have to change, for this name itself is the property of Rural Ogata. Therefore, a new management company would mean the loss of this name, new signs for the hotel, and new paint for the hotel's buses, to mention only a few changes. Furthermore, Rural Ogata currently manages no other facilities. The village now has a greater stake in the tiny company than ever before, and it was granted another five-year contract to manage the hotel in 2010.

Fifteen years ago village residents were worried about the new hotel. Opposition farmers (who generally despised Mayor Miyata) saw it as a money pit—a great waste of tax revenues. For more than ten years the hotel and Rural Ogata were able to defy these predictions and hold their own. However, after the hotel celebrated its tenth birthday things began to change. Worsened (but not caused) by the global economic downturn of 2008, the road for both the hotel and its managing company got rocky as that year progressed, and Rural Ogata began to slip—posting a net operating loss of 18 million yen for the annum (Ogata-mura 2010: 17). The village and other investors stepped in and helped out, and the situation was generally understood to be part of a larger problem that would eventually pass—there was no notable public opposition to the hotel itself over this issue. But the fact that the hotel has basically been running in the red since then is generally known, and the disastrous earthquake and tsunami of March 11, 2011 made the road to recovery for the hotel and for Rural Ogata only that much tougher.

Despite these problems, the hotel has proven to be a worthwhile addition to the small community. Many tourists visit it, sometimes staying overnight, and quite a few villagers work there. Furthermore, Ogata-mura farmers now often hold wedding receptions in the hotel instead of in Akita City facilities, which is very convenient, and the gift shop has begun selling more local products, including crafts made by village residents, books authored by Shinichirō Sakamoto, and biodegradable soap produced by a group of village women who originally banded together in 1989 to help defeat Mayor Miyata's golf course plan (also see chapter 5). It only took a very small struggle to bring enough change to the hotel to make it reasonably attractive to the mayor's opponents, and it is now a useful facility. Things have not gone as smoothly, though, for most of the other major projects of the Miyata administration.

The Solar and Electric Vehicle Races

Ogata-mura's involvement in solar race events began with a hair stylist: Hisahiro Yamamoto, an Akita native who owns a posh studio in Akita City and a related enterprise in the Minami Aoyama area of Tokyo as well. Long active in Akita business groups, and maintaining a constant interest in regional development, he had already spoken to Mayor Miyata about the possibility of building a rocket-launching facility on the village lands prior to the solar sports idea.[7] However, Yamamoto changed his mind when he saw a program on television about a grueling solar car race held in Australia every year. He decided that such an event would be good for young people in Akita, and that Ogata-mura would be the perfect place to have it. He took his idea to Mayor Miyata, who liked it, and they formed a committee for raising funds and drumming up interest among local politicians.

Akita Prefecture promised thirty million yen for the event, and Ogata-mura put up another twenty million. PepsiCo, IBM, and the Honda Motor Company were among the major corporate sponsors. After two years of planning and preparations, which included making certain that the rules of the race would be compatible with the rules of other solar races, held in the U.S.A. and in Australia, the first annual event took place in August of 1993 under the name "The World Solar Car Rallye [*sic*] Japan in Ogata" on the public roads of the village. It was deemed an overwhelming success. Mayor Miyata wasted no time in preparing for

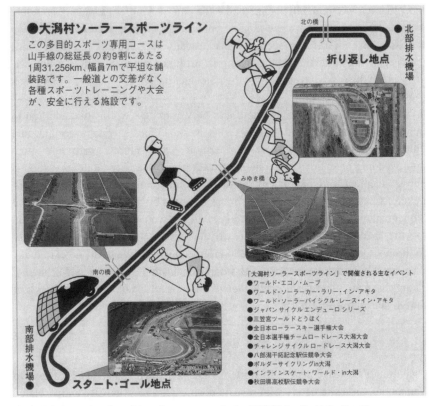

●大潟村ソーラースポーツライン

この多目的スポーツ専用コースは
山手線の総延長の約9割にあたる
1周31.256km、幅員7mで平坦な舗
装路です。一般道との交差がなく
各種スポーツトレーニングや大会
が、安全に行える施設です。

北の橋

折り返し地点

北部排水機場

みゆき橋

南の橋

南部排水機場

スタート・ゴール地点

「大潟村ソーラースポーツライン」で開催される主なイベント
●ワールド・エコノ・ムーブ
●ワールド・ソーラーカー・ラリー・イン・アキタ
●ワールド・ソーラーバイシクル・レース・イン・アキタ
●ジャパンサイクルエンデューロシリーズ
●三笠宮ツールドとうほく
●全日本ローラースキー選手権大会
●全日本選手権チームロードレース大潟大会
●チャレンジサイクルロードレース大潟大会
●八郎潟干拓記念駅伝競争大会
●ボルダーサイクリングin大潟
●インラインスケート・ワールド・in大潟
●秋田県高校駅伝競争大会

Figure 3.4: An explanation of the solar race course in the 1996 "Solar Car Rallye" guide.
Source: Ogata-mura.

the following year's event—he quickly pushed through the village council a plan to build a new, 31-kilometer solar track running from the south pumping station along the primary north–south irrigation canal to a point on the main east–west canal and back (see Figures 3.4 and 3.5).

Such a proposal would certainly not pass today, but at the time the village council was controlled by Miyata's supporters, and the track was ready for use by the time the second event, known as "The World Solar Car Rallye in Akita," was held in July of 1994. From the time of that event a few foreign teams became regular competitors. One from George Washington University, in particular, participated numerous times. The Miyata administration offered special financial assistance to foreign teams in order to bring them to the village, and a team from a more prestigious school or institution could generally receive a larger amount of money. However, changes in the village's political environment in 2000 resulted in the cessation of this generous support. Foreign teams, therefore, are rare today.

Figure 3.5: The starting line area of the track during the 1996 solar car race.

The year 1995 marked yet another change for the solar events: the addition of a bicycle race. The reason for this was so that more competitors—especially those from overseas—could participate. While building a solar car costs anywhere from 500,000 to 3 million yen, a solar bicycle only requires that 70,000 to 100,000 yen worth of equipment be added to a regular bicycle. Furthermore, while the cost of shipping a solar car from another country to Japan runs to about two million yen, a solar bicycle can be taken apart and transported far more cheaply. The 1995 car race attracted eighty teams and the bicycle race ninety-one. The following year saw a slight drop in the number of teams entering the car race but over one-hundred entered the bicycle race (see Figure 3.6).

For the rest of the decade, the number of teams entering the events remained fairly steady at somewhere around eighty for the car race and about 120 for the bicycle event. When the George Washington University team participated in 1996, the members were provided with rooms at the new village hotel, Sun Rural Ogata. This prompted a local journalist to write small piece in the Akita newspaper criticizing the special treatment the Americans received and arguing that removing them from the race-participant community, which generally stays in tents near the track, destroyed opportunities for international interactions (*kokusai kōryū*—important aspects of the big events (Shimomura 1996, see also T.W. Traphagan 2006 on *kokusai kōryū*). Since around this time, foreign team members, when they do come, have stayed in the homes of village residents who volunteer to host them.

Figure 3.6: The cover of the 1996 guide featured an inset showing solar bicycles.
Source: Ogata-mura.

The solar events have been the biggest special events in the village, and they are typical of the kind of planning favored by Mayor Miyata. They did not start at the grassroots level, as do many regional revitalization projects in Japan (Knight 1994a, b), but came from the outside and were mostly externally funded as well. In fact, in this aspect they seem very similar to development initiatives undertaken by the mayor of an Iwate Prefecture town from 1986 to 1997 described by Thompson (2003). Questionnaires I distributed to students of the village junior high school indicate that the events' popularity among young people may have been slipping even during the time of the events' zenith. On my behalf, the principal of the school asked all students in late 2001 to complete questionnaire forms that were essentially identical to forms I passed out to their predecessors nearly five years earlier.[8] A comparison of the results reveals a 10 percent drop in the number of students who stated that they liked the events (see Table 3.1).

Table 3.1: Students' attitudes toward the solar events, 1997 and 2001.

	I like them	I don't like them	I don't know
1997 (N=99)	50%	12%	38%
2001 (N=94)	40%	14%	46%

This change would not be statistically significant, but that it was accompanied by a 2 percent rise in the "I don't like them" category could be a sign; perhaps the wonder of the events was already wearing off somewhat as they became more commonplace for the younger people of the village. Another vehicle race event also exists in Ogata-mura. This is the "World Econo Move," an electric car race held every year in May—to coincide with the Golden Week holidays—since 1995. Vehicles in this race must have electric motors and must be powered by a regulation battery pack, and the event is also held on the special solar course. This event has never been as big as the solar races, but approximately sixty teams have entered every year since it started. Today it is linked with other Econo Move events across the country, so they form a national circuit. Teams travel from place to place to compete against one another on different tracks.

To be sure, on the surface the solar and electric car events—the main events of the Rurec Plan—helped to clean up the village's image. Clean air, clean water, and clean farming—all were interlinked in this package. For the village administration, the solar events were a shining star in the Rurec Plan universe, as Mayor Miyata's comment—spoken in a recorded interview in 1997—attests. But settlers' interest in the events was low from the beginning, and it dwindled over time. A few sons of settlers formed teams and joined in, and younger people of the village enjoyed having something unusual happen. It was also interesting for many villagers to have some foreigners to speak English with. But the events do not last all year, and even though money came from Akita Prefecture and from large corporate sponsors, the village was spending tremendous amounts on the events and on the maintenance of the track. Opposition farmers complained and ran for positions on the village council with anti-solar event platforms, but with little success—the mayor's support base was always too strong. Things only began to really change when Miyata left office and the true scale of the village's investment in the events became fully known. Not surprisingly, the solar and electric vehicle races all underwent significant reorganization at the beginning of the current century—explained in chapter 5.

The Bunkajin Neighborhood

One of the most problematic projects that the village office has ever undertaken is the *bunkajin* (literally, "culture people") project. In the early 1990s, when the council was totally controlled by compliant settlers loyal to Mayor Miyata, it passed a plan to build an area for people with special skills or talents on an unused block of land located on the southeast corner of "east section three" (Figures 3.7 and 3.8; see also Figure I.2). It was felt that these *bunkajin* would be able to mingle with the villagers and teach them something. Especially, they were expected to demonstrate their skills to the schoolchildren and somehow inspire them. The village

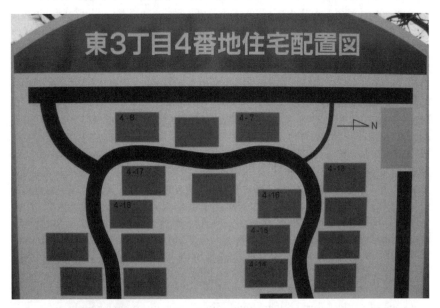

Figure 3.7: A street map of the *bunkajin* neighborhood, photographed in February of 2007, shows occupied houses (those with numbers).

Figure 3.8: The *bunkajin* neighborhood was looking less lonely in February of 2007 than it had looked ten years earlier.

government also hoped to attract individuals who could contribute their expertise in other ways.[9] The plan was to select people from among a number of applicants and pay the newcomers a salary of one hundred thousand yen per month for three years as well as to legally hand over the residential property to each person after he (or she) had built a house on it and resided there for seven years. Information about the project and how to apply was posted on the village website in Japanese and in English.

From the beginning, however, there were problems with the plan. Many villagers immediately complained about the use of their taxes for such a project. Another problem was the label *bunkajin*. This is a politically loaded expression that is frequently used to refer to people with special skills or knowledge, such as literary figures, scholars, or artists. Translated into English it could be "a cultural person," or perhaps even "a cultured person." When used on the national stage the term does not usually offend people, but using the term inside the village in this way made many farmers wonder: "If these people are 'cultured' then what are we—barbarians?"

Despite protests, the project went forward, and was reported on very positively by the local press as early as January of 1993, and even more positive coverage followed. As of April 1994, three people—a violin maker, a retired pilot and sky-sports instructor, and an engineer—had been accepted by the village government. In the end, the engineer backed out, so the other two *bunkajin* became the first to build homes in the new area. With only those two houses standing, the neighborhood seemed lonely and empty when I left the village in 1997. Upon my return in 2001, however, I was astonished to find that six more houses had been constructed—it was beginning to look like a real neighborhood. The first settlers had been joined by a chemist, a highly acclaimed professor of computer engineering, a professor emeritus of Akita University, a champion water skier, a sculptor, and an education specialist who served as the head of the village Board of Education for a time. The sculptor, Toshio Kamada, has taught at an Akita high school, but many years ago he was the art teacher at Ogata Junior High School. Yet although the neighborhood had shaped up, of the eight *bunkajin* who had built homes as of 2004, only the violin maker resided there all the time. The other seven continued to maintain homes elsewhere. There are a few more *bunkajin* houses in the neighborhood today, but the general residential situation has not changed much. The Ogata-mura house of Toshio Kamada, the sculptor, is actually a studio. Large logs and tall wooden figures in various stages of completion stand outside.

Despite some good signs, the *bunkajin* neighborhood has remained a fairly lonely place since its founding. Although some of the houses are architecturally interesting, and the layout of the neighborhood is aesthetically pleasing, neighborly relations between the residents—most of whom are usually absent—are rather thin. Local residents may also have made the professional newcomers feel unwelcome. One of the *bunkajin* confided in me that he could sense real discrimination against him in the village among some farmers—especially older ones. Several steps, however, have been taken in order to bring the residents of the neighborhood into the larger village community. One of these was the decision to add the *bunkajin* neighborhood to the *jūku* just to the west of it. This means that the *bunkajin* should always be invited to attend the end-of-the-year party by that group, and also that they are expected to participate in cleanup projects and the semiannual pan-village sports day as members of the *jūku*. In order to prove the usefulness of the *bunkajin* to the community, attention has been called to their local activities—especially to the guest lectures and demonstrations they have given in the schools. In the same spirit, the violin maker (Hiroki Sugawara) and the sculptor (Toshio Kamada) held their own concert and demonstration in the temporary exhibit gallery of the village's land reclamation museum on December 2, 2001. Sugawara played the classical guitar and Kamada spoke about his large carvings, many of which were displayed in the museum's gallery at the time, as well as his desire to reside permanently in his Ogata-mura studio after retirement. Both *bunkajin* spent much time talking with the other village residents who attended (about fifty) and fielded many questions. The event was more of an attempt at mixing with the farmers than a concert, which may not have satisfied everyone in the audience, but as an event it was fairly successful for the two hosts.

The other village residents' opinions of the project were generally negative between 1995 and 1997, when I worked as an English teacher in the village and had many opportunities to chat with them about it, especially at the community center. Many clearly resented the "uncultured"/"cultured" division between themselves and the *bunkajin* inherent to the very concept of the project, voicing the kinds of concerns mentioned above. Many also flatly rejected the plan, calling it a waste of their taxes. Others accused the Miyata administration of trying to raise the overall IQ level of the village—of compensating, in effect, for the (assumed) low IQ level of the villagers. I was never able to find a single adult in the village who had anything positive to say about the *bunkajin* project during those earlier years other than the *bunkajin* themselves (who were cautious anyway about sharing their opinions because they were fully aware of the general sentiment among farmers), the mayor, or others of the administration. In the interest of getting some quantifiable data on opinions about the *bunkajin* project among the younger villagers, I included some questions about it in the forms that were distributed to students of the junior high school in late 2001 to compare with the same questions I had asked of their forebears in 1997 (Table 3.2).

Table 3.2: Students' opinions about the *bunkajin* project, 1997 and 2001.

	I like it	I don't like it	I don't know	I don't know what it is
1997 (N=99)	10%	7%	20%	63%
2001 (N=94)	28%	5%	47%	19%

The greatest changes occurred in the categories "I like it," "I don't know," and "I don't know what it is." Whereas only 10 percent of the students reported that they liked the project in 1997, that number jumped to 28 percent in only four years. Only 19 percent of students responded that they did not know about the project in 2001, compared to 63 percent in 1997. From the data it seems clear that by 2001 students generally had at least learned about the project and the resident *bunkajin*, and that more of them eventually came to look upon the plan favorably. The main differences between 1997 and 2001 were that the number of *bunkajin* in the village had increased by six and that they had been giving demonstrations of their research and activities for the students. Many students reported that the demonstrations and guest lectures were interesting, but that some were hard to understand. A few were of the opinion that the project itself and the knowledge of the *bunkajin* would probably not be very useful to themselves or to the village in general. In the last ten years, since I asked the students their opinions, overall feelings about the project among the settlers seem to have settled somewhat. This is partly because of the increased visibility of the *bunkajin* but mainly because of structural changes made to the project by the village administration following the mayoral election of 2000.

The Land Reclamation Museum

The Polder Museum of Ogata-mura is located on the west side of the settlement, across the street from the JA gas station. The highway that runs between the gas station and the museum heads northward to Noshiro and takes one either to Oga (to the west) or Akita City (south). The structure is attached to the special products center. The building is of a rather unusual design—basically crescent-shaped from the air, but looking somewhat like a dome from the front or back (Figure 3.9). It occupies about 2,530 square meters of land, and cost over 1.5 billion yen to build, including the displays within. The village covered the entire cost alone, through loans of course, because the national and prefectural governments refused to help (see Wood 2005). Adults and college students pay three hundred yen to enter, and high school students, junior high school students, and children are charged only one hundred yen.

In the parking lot stands a bronze figure of Yūjirō Obata, governor of Akita Prefecture during the time of the reclamation. On either side of the governor's statue are bronze busts of Ryūnosuke Shimanuki, the first mayor of Ogata-mura, and the head of the Jigyōdan—the government agency that was responsible for filling in the lake and building and managing Ogata-mura. Upon entering the museum, to the left one sees six photographic portraits of men who played major roles in the reclamation. A shot of Professor Yansen from the Netherlands is included. To the right are three large satellite images of the Hachirōgata area that

Figure 3.9: The Polder Museum of Ogata-mura, with the attached "special products direct-marketing center" to the far left, cannot be missed by drivers on Highway 42.

show the lagoon in its original condition, during the reclamation process, and as it looks today. The main gallery of the museum stretches on to the right. The foyer itself is designed to impress upon visitors the fact that they are standing well below sea level. A stylized mock-up of an old wooden *utase* boat—complete with a wooden fisherman gazing out across the imaginary water surface—looms overhead, and embedded in the floor are small exhibits of whale and other aquatic animal bones that were found during the reclamation process (see Figure 3.10).

Along the back wall of the main gallery is a brief photographic summary of the reclamation. There is a small theater with wide panoramic displays on the walls and smaller screens set in the floor, which broadcasts video presentations of the village's history, special places of interest, and scenes from the four seasons. Behind the theater is a large, circular diorama of the region. Next to the diorama is probably the most notable exhibit—the *ocha-no-ma gekijō*—a scene in the living room of one of the old peaked-roof houses reenacted by three life-size models of fictional first-wave settlers. The room is set in its actual position within the plan of the old house, which is outlined on the museum floor, and is complete with an old television, toys, and magazines from the period, kitchen implements, pots and pans, and food, beer, and sake on the table. Originally, when a button was pushed, the room lit up and the figures sang and shouted to one another, and were even scolded by the mother of the house for being too loud. Their conversation focused on the troubles that they had in farming the new lands, and mentioned the failed attempt at spreading seeds by helicopter as well as the introduction of mechanical planters. Even an old newsreel from the first settlement of the village aired on the television. This display, however, was later changed in accordance with the requests of numerous villagers, who were sharply critical of the exhibit—branding it inaccurate, inauthentic, and just plain silly (see Wood 2005 for more on this). Many felt embarrassed by the rowdiness of the settler-figures in the display. They came across like classic country bumpkins (*inaka-mono*), speaking in strong Akita dialects. Few settlers or their wives or children could relate to these figures, and even fewer cared to be associated with them (in the minds of visitors) or, especially, to be represented by them. Fortunately for those who felt this way, the museum operating committee took their complaints seriously and made some changes rather early on. Today, visitors can view a variety of presentations on the back wall of the small theater. These cover the history of the reclamation and the local Hachirō Tarō dragon legend, and include actual newsreels of the early settlement period. The displays also change from time to time. It is a significant improvement. Filling out the rest of the gallery is a life-size diorama of a period tractor mired deep in the mud as several farmers struggle to free it, workstations for reading, and several video-game stations. Along the front wall of the gallery are a number of small dioramas that depict different aspects of the village's agricultural cycle as well as some stages of the reclamation process.

Figure 3.10: An artistic rendition of an *utase* boat and fisherman placed at the pre-reclamation water-line of Hachirōgata greets visitors to the land reclamation museum. Beyond are large photographs of the lagoon before, during, and after the reclamation.

There is also some gallery space in the building for temporary exhibits. Collections of sculptures by Toshio Kamada have been displayed, and works by resident groups are occasionally shown as well. Beyond the smaller galleries are offices and storage rooms, and the hallway that runs along the back of the building, overlooking local farmers' rice fields, serves as a lounge area with a small display on new developments in ecofriendly agriculture—always a popular topic in the village. On the walls of the south end of the hallway is a collection of photographs that introduce visitors to the town of Dronten in the Netherlands, which was also built on reclaimed land.[10] The museum is considered an educational facility by the village, and falls under the auspices of the Board of Education office. Therefore, the head of that office at any given time is also the head of the museum. Although ultimately responsible for the facility, the education head generally stays in his office in the center of the village, and leaves the daily management of the museum to the assistant director.

The museum opened its doors on April 29, 2000, but it was not a happy occasion for the many Ogata-mura residents who had opposed the mayor's plan from the beginning. They had even asked for a referendum—a chance to vote against it—but were refused this by the village assembly, which was packed with Miyata's supporters. Theirs was a valiant struggle, but they were repeatedly snubbed by Miyata and his cohorts—both those on the village council and those in other positions of influence. Although the administration had ostensibly expected 150,000 visitors to the museum during its first year, this number was not attained until about three years after the grand opening. Visitor number 200,000 walked in the door in October of 2004, bringing the total income from ticket sales to about 25 million yen—still a far cry from the 1.5 billion that the village spent to build it. The museum's failure to generate a profit—indeed, the impossibility of it ever doing so—has been a major point of contention for anti-Miyata villagers. Even two or three years after its opening, it was not hard to find adults in the community who had yet to set foot inside it. This partly reflected the fact that the facility never related very much to the actual lives of the farmers. For example, the museum focuses on the reclamation and the earliest years—a theme to which only the first settlers can relate very well. Those who came in the fifth wave had different experiences. Also, for most village farmers, problems with rice production and marketing have dominated their lives since the mid-1970s, and this entire aspect of the village's history was intentionally glossed over by the museum at the beginning.

Basically, therefore, what the museum offered was a fairly sterile, if interesting, textbook version of the creation of the land and the construction of the farming community, not too unlike the early books put out by government agencies covering the reclamation and village-building. The facility stands out among the big projects of the Miyata administration as the ultimate attempt by it to whitewash the past, usurp the "real" history of the village and redefine its identity—the centerpiece of the second reclamation. Moreover, it is also a good example of the "if we build it they will come" mentality regarding regional development that became very deeply ingrained in Japanese politics during the bubble economy years (see Matanle et al. 2011: ch. 9). From the time of the project's birth the majority of villagers were displeased at best about the prospect of their tax revenues being used for such an endeavor, and although this sentiment has tapered off somewhat over the years it has never completely vanished. Dissatisfied villagers succeeded in partially reclaiming the identity of the village as defined by the museum not only by ensuring that the *ocha-no-ma gekijō* was changed but also by prompting the museum to begin displaying old photographs from the first years of farming in the village, such as local women arriving by bus to help with the hand-planting or settlers counting out bills to pay them, etcetera. These straightforward, still shots contrast with the somewhat over-dramatized video presentations in the museum's small theater. More recently, though, the museum has made significant improvements to its homepage, giving more balance to its overall portrayal of the village's history. Today, firsthand accounts of early experiences in the village written by settlers can be read, and many photographs are now available as well. All the same, though, the black market rice and police barricade incidents have never featured prominently in the museum's total package.

I included questions about the museum in a questionnaire that the elementary school administration distributed to parents on my behalf in March of 2002 in order to obtain quantifiable data on public opinion at the time. Out of 155 forms sent out, 111 completed forms came back. Twenty-nine percent of the parents had yet to visit the museum, and the number of visits for those who had been there ranged from one to six. Twenty-two percent answered that they would not recommend the museum to friends or other visitors, but the main reasons for this were fairly vague. That the museum was simply not interesting was the main reason, and a few people pointed to the absence of the rice quarrels in the museum's version of Ogata-mura's history. Some respondents, and others with whom I spoke personally, complained about the use of such a great amount of money for the facility, whereas new school buildings could have been built instead. In general, the museum still appeals more to public officials and first-time visitors to Ogata-mura than to local residents. Nevertheless, if some village residents can have their works displayed in the temporary gallery, and if the facility can serve as a place for communication and social interactions between locals—*bunkajin* and farmers, for example—then perhaps the museum will prove to have been worth the cost eventually. In fact, in order to inject more life and authenticity into the museum, and to make more opportunities for visitors and villagers to interact, the museum started up a volunteer guide program not long after it opened (Wood 2005: 44–47). Today, there are at least one dozen guides (all settlers). These guides undergo some training in advance, and they not only escort groups through the museum itself but also travel in their vehicle with them on one of several set routes through the reclaimed land area, providing explanations, anecdotes, and stories to place the museum exhibits in their cultural and geographic context. This program, which was begun by the assistant director, has been a very positive development for both the museum and the village itself. However, the museum has always had to make certain that only accredited farmers (*nintei nōgyōsha*) were assigned to guide agriculture-related groups, for at the beginning complaints came from some visiting groups of farmers about comments made by noncompliant settlers who guided them. Although the museum has been a very problematic venture from the beginning, it does seem worthwhile to educate not only visitors but also children of the area about the largest Japanese land reclamation project ever—and the great farms that lie below sea level—right in their backyards.[11] Local schoolchildren may become more sensitive about the effects of such gigantic engineering projects.

The Nanohana Festival

Since 1995 the Nanohana[12] Festival has taken place every year at the beginning of May in the 3.7 hectare *nanohana* field at the north end of the village, across the street from the hotel, when the field dazzles with the yellow flowers. The festival differs from the vehicle races both in its smaller scale and in the fact that it was conceived by the village office rather than being imported from the outside. The 1996 event centered on the opening of the hotel, Sun Rural Ogata. Professional models were flown in by helicopter and they posed for photos among the flowers. Prizes were offered to participants for the best portraits resulting from these free sessions (Figure 3.11).

Concerts, games, and food were also part of the entertainment. Since 1997 a miniature steam-driven locomotive has taken paying riders along a track running through the field. The festival has become heavily commercialized and has come to resemble special occasions that take place in city parks every spring. This is especially noticeable in the food available, which includes chocolate-covered bananas, cotton candy, and fried potatoes. The games also attracted much attention due to the number of prizes offered at the beginning. But there were very few Ogata-mura children among the one or two hundred that were there for the event in 1996 (see Figure 3.12). I was unable, of course, to find any local farmers at that event. The only adults there associated with Ogata-mura were the village employees who were required to work the event and several families of the junior college faculty members. In contrast to the solar events, the timing of

Figure 3.11: An advertisement for the 1996 Nanohana Festival featured the models who were to be flown in and the hotel, Sun Rural Ogata.

Figure 3.12: Crowds filled the entrance to the *nanohana* field on the day of the 1996 Nanohana Festival.

the Nanohana Festival (and the World Econo Move, which takes place at about the same time) is bad for farmers. They are always far too busy planting their fields in May to engage in such activities. Moreover, since all able-bodied members of the village farming households help during this crucial time, mothers are generally unable to take their smaller children to the festival. This was one of the main complaints about the event. Many asked, "Why do our taxes go to support an event that our own families can't enjoy?" The way of holding the event was held up as a problem in need of attention in Tōru Wakui's 1996 campaign for the office of mayor. Of all special events planned by the Miyata administration, the Nanohana Festival was probably the one that was most obviously not for the residents.

The Sociopolitical Costs of Cosmetic Surgery

If the 1970s could be characterized as a period of necessary infrastructural development in Ogata-mura, then the following two decades can be understood as a time of beautification that occurred in response to disasters—calamities caused by Mother Nature and by policymakers in Tokyo. Although the Miyata administration did not actually unleash the torrent, it lent force to the current by siding firmly with the national government and pointing the finger at lawbreakers. It then began to systematically shut them out of the political process. With the village council firmly under the control of the compliant faction of settlers, which supported Miyata unquestionably on most issues (at least at the beginning), he was able to accomplish nearly anything he wanted to do.

The paternalistic attitude of the mayor and the often smug demeanor of his administration aggravated the opposition settlers almost beyond description. In fact, according to the English side of Miyata's business card (*meishi*) his position was not "mayor" but "master." This was probably a simple error in translation, but it was actually very accurate. As the administration's beautification campaign intensified, and as the Rurec Plan slowly came to fruition, the noncompliant settlers grew more and more upset. They tried when possible to stop this second reclamation, or to at least slow it, but failed again and again. They failed because Miyata's support base was too strong, and because the lines determining who voted for whom had been set by the simple matter of how one marketed one's rice. Villagers on opposite sides of the rice-fight dividing line became unable to discuss with each other not only farming and rice marketing, but also village politics in general. Some noncompliant settlers even began to feel uncomfortable walking through the doors of the administration building. But public opposition to the village's big projects not only fed into the "bad farmer"/"good farmer" dichotomy; it slowly came to cut across this division and eventually backfired against the mayor and resulted in a political revolution.

Notes

1. Sanger (1991).
2. Of this, he said: "The rice was piling up, so they told us to reduce our crops to a certain level, but we rejected it. We said we didn't want to do it. So then, the officials from the government office came and said, 'If you're not going to cooperate on the crop reduction, then you people just get out of Ogata-mura.' They threatened us like that. They set a time limit, and they set an amount, too. Well, there was no way we were going to just pick up and return to our hometowns. We didn't want to leave, so even though it was just awful we followed orders and cut it. Yeah, but the 'country' [the national government] was really the bad one then."
3. See Moore (1993) for more on this.
4. *Yami* indicates something done in darkness or under cover and *gome* and *mai* are other ways to pronounce *kome*, or uncooked rice.
5. Interested readers are encouraged to see an exchange between Kurose and a MAFF bureaucrat that played out in the pages of the magazine Chūō Kōron in 1988 (Kishi 1988, Kurose, 1988a, b).
6. Moore (1990: 96) explains how postwar occupation policies (initiated under the auspices of the U.S. government), encouraged conservatism among the farmers of Japan. For example, villages of less than five thousand residents showed a 17 percent drop in the number of nonconservative votes from 1947 to 1955—just after the land reform.
7. The fact that the country's first space rocket launching site was on the shore of Akita Prefecture explains why the idea of building a launch pad in the village was not as outlandish as it might seem.
8. I targeted the students because they represented the future of the village and also because they were very accessible to me, as an English teacher in the public school in the mid 1990s.
9. It was thought at one point that engineers, for example, could become involved in the solar events.
10. The Ogata-mura government forged a sister-city relationship with Dronten in 1992, held a "Holland Festival," and planted many tulips around the settlement to commemorate the occasion.
11. This seems especially true today in light of the many local environmental and economic problems which arose due to closing off Isahaya Bay in Nagasaki Prefecture.
12. *Nanohana* (Brassica napus) are rapeseed plants, or rape blossoms, from which the oil commonly known as "canola" is derived.

4

RICE: ALLIANCES, INSTITUTIONS, FRICTIONS

If a farmer doesn't build something that can be passed down, he can't really expect his son to take over.

–Nobuhiro Machida

Farming in Ogata-mura is big. With the exception of Hokkaido, where rice is of minimal importance, the Hachirōgata reclaimed land area probably has the greatest concentration of large-scale farms in all of Japan. According to village office data, 271 of the 523 farming households in Ogata-mura still owned exactly fifteen hectares of land in 2010; about one-half had neglected to increase their holdings beyond the original allocation. One-hundred and ninety-four households owned more than fifteen hectares but less than thirty hectares, and 26 had more than thirty hectares. Two households (one of them being Tōru Wakui's) now possess over fifty hectares.[1] On the lower end of the scale, 22 are reported to own less than fifteen hectares. These households have sold significant portions of their landholdings to their neighbors and scaled down their operations for various reasons, such as having no heir or ill health.

In other words, farms have not shrunk in size due to partitioning—dividing land between heirs and creating "branch households" (*bunke*) in the old style.[2] This is something that the settlers never needed to be officially restricted from doing by the Jigyōdan, which built and managed the village. Despite the large size of the farms, it has been clear to them and to their heirs that while "expand and divide" might be an acceptable strategy, simply dividing a fifteen hectare farm between two siblings would not.[3] Rather, they have sought to secure a single heir—either their own son or the husband of a daughter. In one case, a childless settler couple adopted a daughter, raised her, and then later made her husband their heir. He took up residence in his wife's family home and changed his surname to

Endnotes for this chapter begin on page 160.

hers. Such a man is typically referred to as a *muko-san*. Sons were born to this couple, so in this way the continuation of the household was basically guaranteed (see also Beardsley et al. 1959: 236–238, and Embree 1939: 61–64).

Yet even though Ogata-mura settlers do of course hope to secure an heir, they did buy their land after all, so most have not been terribly worried about having someone to pass it on to. Where sons exist, an heir is usually secured because of the size of the landholdings (and the business potential). Ogata-mura farmers also have many opportunities to buy more fields—something that most Japanese farmers cannot easily do simply because land is not so readily available. In addition, the majority of settlers have been somewhat against forcing a son or son-in-law to inherit their farmland. They may say, "I made my decision to come to Ogata-mura, so my son can decide for himself whether he wants to farm." Some (but not all) of these settlers think that for their children to have a sense of being bound to the land simply due to so many generations of farming, as many small-scale farmers feel, is too "feudal"—a term often applied to anything that appears culturally antiquated. For them, one way that Ogata-mura can be a model for a new kind of Japanese agriculture is for all of their sons and daughters to truly be free regarding decisions about their own futures.

Although some Ogata-mura farmers grow wheat, soybeans, pumpkins, melons, and garlic, rice is still the king of the crops in the village. It is one of the biggest rice producing communities in the country; in November of 2005, Ogata-mura ranked eleventh among all municipalities in the nation in terms of total monetary value of rice produced, with a figure of 11.6 billion yen (MAFF 2006: 21). In the early 1990s, rice produced by village farmers amounted to nearly five thousand tons, while wheat weighed in at thirty-four hundred tons and soybeans finished third with a total of just over one thousand tons (Ogata-mura 1994). According to a village survey published in 2001, the amount of rice produced had risen at the expense of wheat, now coming in third after soybeans (Ogata-mura 2001). Table 4.1 compares land area in the village devoted to the three main crops—rice, wheat, and soybeans—in selected years between 1975 and 2009.

Table 4.1: Ogata-mura land area devoted to rice, wheat, and soybeans.

Year	Rice (hectares)	Wheat (hectares)	Soybeans (hectares)
1975	5,185	937	33
1980	4,652	3,534	482
1985	5,957	2,310	791
1993	7,936	615	469
1998	8,073	169	510
2000	8,582	143	486
2005	8,394	74	389
2009	8,299	229	603

Source: Ogata-mura village data (Ogata-mura 2007: 9, 2011a: 38).

Production levels per area of land under cultivation have risen since the early 1990s. In 1991 a one-thousand square meter (ten are) plot yielded an average of 532 kilograms of rice, and the same area of land produced 580 kilograms six years later (Ogata-mura 1998). In 2009 the village posted an average of 599 kilograms of rice for that land area (Ogata-mura 2011a: 38). Ogata-mura's rice production system is quite efficient. This is easily illustrated by comparing production cost for the village, the prefecture, and the nation for select years between 1971 and 2004 (Table 4.2).

Table 4.2: Average rice production cost (in yen) for the village, the prefecture, and the nation for select years between 1971 and 2004 on 10 ares of land.

	1971	1980	1989	1996	2000	2004
Ogata-mura	29,800	93,096	82,009	112,777	98,575	99,159
Akita Prefecture	42,738	118,767	122,688	118,581	111,590	105,753
Japan	45,427	131,714	134,248	133,346	129,029	119,558

Source: Ogata-mura village data (Ogata-mura 2007: 11).

The Business of Growing Rice

As mentioned in the previous chapter, most Ogata-mura rice farmers grow Akita Komachi rice, which was developed by Akita Prefecture in the early 1980s. Some grow other types, such as Hitome-bore and Koshi-hikari as well. Regardless of the type, however, the main work begins in late March or early April, depending on the year. The general pattern is as follows: as soon as the weather allows, they stretch large, transparent, plastic sheets over the metal frames that form their long greenhouses—often while snow still falls. A fifteen-hectare farm requires four or five of these so-called "vinyl houses" (or polytunnels). Once these are ready, each household prepares hundreds of plastic trays in its workshop and sets up a conveyor-belt system that sprinkles soil and then seeds into the trays, which are then loaded onto trucks and carried to the greenhouses. The seeded trays are placed on the ground tightly together, leaving only a narrow aisle for walking. Within one week or so the seedlings appear, and plenty of water is given to them for the next five or six weeks. During this time the fields are dry-plowed, and then flooded before being wet-plowed. Finally, the trays are taken to the fields by truck—usually in early May (Figure 4.1). By this time, the seedlings have formed strong root systems and can be removed from the trays in the form of mats, and these are loaded onto a planting tractor that can hold eight to ten of them lined upon the back. As the machine is driven up and down a field, the small arms on its tail end stick the seedlings into the soggy ground, planting eight or ten rows at a time (Figure 4.2). As the seedlings are planted, the mats slide down the back of

Figure 4.1: A truck loaded with seedling trays stands unattended between flooded paddies

Figure 4.2: The mechanical planting arms of a rice-planting tractor, ready for another run. The mats of seedlings gradually disappear as the individual plants are deftly inserted into the mud by the arms in neat rows.

the machine. Usually the household head (or his heir) drives while his wife and other family members load the tractor with seedling mats each time they run out. The job of planting is of the utmost importance to the farmers, and generally all who are able help, but a team of three can handle the job easily, and even two can manage it well enough.

Once the mechanized planting process is complete, the leftover seedlings are hand planted along the edges and corners of the fields, and wherever the machine missed a spot. The entire process is usually over in about two weeks, but may take longer if the weather has turned bad or if a household possesses more than fifteen hectares of rice paddies. June is generally the most crucial time for the plants' growth. Weeds around the edges of the fields must be cut down and smaller ones that spring up have to be pulled out. Chemicals can be applied to destroy weeds and pests, but most farmers prefer to limit the use of these in order to grow more valuable rice. Problems sometimes arise, though, when one farmer works hard to grow rice that is essentially chemical-free, and his neighbor uses pesticides and chemical fertilizers more liberally, because then the first farmer's rice will not really be free of chemicals, either. His rice will probably not pass the test to be labeled as highest-grade, clean rice. This is a real source of friction between some Ogata-mura farmers. A number shun chemicals in favor of ducks, which provide natural fertilizer while eating pests (Ikebata 2007). Nobuhiro Machida has been using ducks in some of his fields for years. Fish are also used in the same way by a number of village producers. Other farmers follow an even purer growing method, putting only materials fit for human consumption into their fields. Each year they process rice straw and husks from the previous autumn and return them, finely ground, to the soil. Another method involves using the same field for rice one year and then for vegetables the next. Certain dry crops will actually help return nutrients that are especially beneficial for rice to the soil.[4] Some Ogata-mura farmers are now experimenting with more radical approaches. For example, a few now skip the process of growing seedlings in greenhouses and simply use machines to spread seeds directly over the fields. Also, a small number have been trying a technique that involves not only no application of chemical fertilizers or pesticides but also no plowing either (*fukōki saibai*—see Ichinoseki 2007, Kaneda 2007).

During July the rice plants grow quickly as the fields slowly dry out beneath them. To help the water drain away and let the ground harden well before harvest time, small holes are usually dug among the stem bunches. In early August— about three months after the seedlings were put in the fields—the tall plants bloom with tiny flowers and then begin to change from green to brown as the soil beneath continues to dry. By September, the symmetrical pools of water that had so well reflected the blue sky of early May have transformed into a great, unbroken sea of rustling, golden rice plants. In years when the weather allows planting to be done early, harvesting might begin before mid-September, but usually the farmers start driving their harvesters back and forth through the fields and cutting down the plants by the end of that month. Barring any serious mechanical problems, harvesting usually progresses quickly and is complete by October. Farmers must then either deliver their rice to a facility for drying, polishing, and storing or use their own equipment. Once the rice has been properly processed, there is the task of marketing it. This is a fairly simple matter for those who use the Country Elevator or the Akita Komachi Corporation, or belong to a smaller marketing association, but the issue is loaded with political and ideological meanings in Ogata-mura.

Rice Marketing in the Village

In 1990 Tokyo raised the amount of farmland that could legally be devoted to producing rice to fifteen hectares, but initiated new crop-diversion (*tensaku*) policies that offered cash rewards to farmers for limiting rice production to a certain amount, which constantly fluctuated. These policies continued to create friction between strict Country Elevator loyalists and others. Even though Ogata-mura farmers could begin planting rice more freely from 1990, marketing it through any channels other than those controlled by the government remained illegal until the passage of the New Food Control Act (Shin Shokuryō Kanri Hō) five years later. The passage of this act may have contributed to an increase in the number of overproducing settlers; figures indicate that by the end of the twentieth century the number of village farming households not observing *tensaku* guidelines had surpassed the number of households remaining obedient, with 302 falling into the former category and 249 into the latter (Yamano 2003: 125).

Perhaps somewhere between 5 and 10 percent of Ogata-mura settlers do not grow rice—either because they have given up on commercial farming altogether or because they now grow other crops instead. Those who no longer farm either retain ownership of their fields and allow another person to tend them for a large cut of the profits, or they have sold their fields to other village producers. Once their rice has been harvested, they then market it in one or more ways, and rice marketing says everything about their identities as Ogata-mura rice farmers and their political and economic ideologies and alliances. The six main categories of Ogata-mura rice farmers, according to their marketing means, are: (1) those who exclusively or mostly use the Country Elevator; (2) those who exclusively or mostly use the Akita Komachi Corporation; (3) those who divide their rice between the two (and possibly other marketing firms); (4) those who belong to mid- or small-scale marketing organizations such as the Dōyūkai or Nōyū (see below); (5) those who operate their own small-scale marketing firms; and (6) those who sell only their own rice directly to their customers by themselves.

The Country Elevator

Although a great many Ogata-mura farmers no longer use the Country Elevator, it has continued to be the largest corporation in the village in terms of facilities and overall volume. About 270 farmers in the area sell their rice to the company, which claims to be the largest single handler of organically grown rice in the country (with total annual rice sales of 18 thousand tons), employs about sixty people on a full-time basis, and has over 340 million yen in capital investments today (see Figure 2.4). The village itself, the village agricultural cooperative (JA), and Akita Prefecture were once the primary shareholders, but the Akita government rid itself of its shares sometime in the 1990s. The JA also holds far fewer shares today than it once did, amounting to less than 15 percent of the total.[5] Currently, the village government, various prefectural agricultural financing organizations, and individual users own most of the elevator's stocks. The company differs from other regional country elevators in that it was never completely under the control of the village JA. Normally, a JA would be established first and then it would build a grain elevator facility for local farmers. In Ogata-mura, the Jigyōdan built the grain facility first and then the agricultural cooperative was established later. For legal and financial reasons it was too difficult for the latter to completely take over the giant facility, so it was made a joint-stock corporation, with nearly all shares owned by the Ogata-mura JA.

Many of the 270 producers who use the company now live outside of the village. Some of these farmers own fields within the reclaimed territory—they (or their fathers) once relied on fishing the waters of Hachirōgata and therefore received land as part of their compensation from the government. As for Ogata-mura settler households, many in the village sell to both the Country Elevator and other companies as well. Much of the rice sold by the company goes to hospitals, hotels, and retail outlets across Akita Prefecture and in the Tokyo area, but it also sells rice and other products directly to consumers through a mail-order service. In order to remain competitive with other rice marketing corporations that have sprung up in the village over the last twenty-five years or so, the company has begun handling a large variety of rice—mostly Akita Komachi, and including regular, chemically grown rice, reduced-chemical rice, and rice which is certified chemical-free, or organic. It also markets unpolished rice, or *genmai*, and has a facility that produces natural, nonfecal fertilizer, or *yūki hiryō*, using the organic materials left over from processing rice, wheat, and soybeans. The Country Elevator also operates an outlet store in a small shopping mall, Bay Paradise, near the Akita City seaport of Tsuchizaki. This store carries Country Elevator rice, an array of general village products, and some fresh vegetables grown by Country Elevator clients—shipped straight from the village daily. Yet, this store closes early in the evenings, and visitors to Bay Paradise, despite its utopian name, are generally few—especially in the colder months.

One problem that the Country Elevator faces today is that its facilities are aging. Over the next ten to fifteen years some major repairs or purchases may have to be made. Another problem is that the facilities are too large—reportedly the largest in Asia. With eight giant elevators, a number of smaller ones, and five spacious warehouses, the corporation can store nearly sixty thousand tons of dried, market-ready cereals and legumes, but since the late 1980s it has been operating at half capacity or less, which has resulted in higher usage rates for the farmers. Producers report that they must pay approximately one million yen to use the elevator's processing facilities and distribution network for twelve to fourteen hectares' worth of rice—three to five times the cost of using a smaller company. On the other hand, even if a farmer has to pay such a great amount per year to get his crop to market by way of the Country Elevator, it would take many years for his annual processing expenditures to amount to the total cost of buying all of the machines himself. Furthermore, if a farmer has his own machines he must cover maintenance, repairs, and electricity as well. Machines for processing the highest-grade chemical-free rice and *musenmai*—ready-to-cook rice that needs no washing—are reported to cost seventy million to ninety million yen. The prohibitive cost of such machines has been a factor in the tendency for noncompliant farmers either to band together to form corporations or to found private ones on their own and invite others to utilize them. These newer marketing associations have now become more competitive than the Country Elevator.[6]

For its part, the Country Elevator is trying to encourage as many farmers as possible to bring their rice in for processing, storage, and sale. The problem is that there are a number of other similar grain elevators owned and operated by local agricultural cooperatives surrounding the Hachirōgata reclaimed land area. Therefore, the company is attempting to forge relationships with other JAs in the region to encourage them to utilize the facilities in Ogata-mura. Also, in particular, it is targeting farmers who live in surrounding communities but own fields inside the polder dam.

The Akita Komachi Corporation

In 1987 Tōru Wakui—the previously mentioned settler of the fourth wave, a strong advocate of producers' rights to freely market the fruits of their labor—founded the Akita Komachi Corporation (Akita Komachi Seisansha Kyōkai), a joint-stock company dedicated to selling Akita Komachi rice grown in the soils of Hachirōgata to consumers across the nation. He did this with the cooperation of a number of Ogata-mura rice growers who also had defied the government's *gentan* policies (Mizuki 2002: 147). His two main business partners, however, eventually backed out of the operation and went independent. By 1989 Wakui had built a 330-square-meter low-temperature storage facility for market-ready rice, and the company steadily expanded to become the Country Elevator's main rival, with nearly four billion yen in annual sales.

Roughly one-third of Ogata-mura farmers now sell at least some of their rice to the Akita Komachi Corporation, if not more. In 1995, the corporation was proud to appear in a textbook used by the Harvard University Graduate School of Business Administration. In July of that year, along with two other village rice marketing companies, it established a small joint-stock corporation, Yūki, to produce nonfecal, "all-natural" fertilizer. Today Wakui's company sports a state of the art facility for processing and storing a variety of rice types, including *musenmai*. Ogata-mura farmers generally agree that in recent years prices offered by the Akita Komachi Corporation for rice coming in straight from the field are roughly equal to, if not slightly higher than, what the Country Elevator pays, although it has at times offered significantly more than the Elevator. Rice that passes a very strict test can fetch a much higher price for the producer and be marketed by the company as top-grade chemical-free rice. The company also offers all of the types of rice that the Country Elevator sells, and more, including unpolished rice that has been allowed to begin to sprout before being dried (*hatsuga genmai*).

In 1997, the corporation began producing "all-natural" ham, sausages, and bread. The following year saw the opening of a brewery, and in 1999 a large greenhouse and a glassworks facility were completed. Visitors were able to make their own sausages, bread, and pasta, and then enjoy eating them while drinking beer produced on site. This extra endeavor—Wakui's own version of *mura-okoshi* (village revitalization) work—attracted much attention and greatly impressed the multitude of noncompliant village farmers who had drawn inspiration and moral strength from his entrepreneurial leadership over the years. It was a down-to-earth, alternative version of Mayor Miyata's high-profile, high-cost, nonagricultural endeavors. However, after a few years the corporation decided to discontinue this touristic enterprise and close the entire operation, ostensibly because it was deemed too dangerous to have visitors (including many children) walking about inside the complex, through which large trucks and loaders constantly travel.

Wakui has also created his own version of Ogata-mura's history in opposition to the official one presented by the village government. For example, the historical overview of the reclamation and the village's development in his company's very sophisticated brochure covers major developments in the Ogata-mura farmers' ongoing struggle to sell their products as they please, including detailed notes on matters such as *aogari* (the forced destruction of rice plants in the 1970s), the *kenmon jiken* (the police checkpoint episode of 1985), and the seizure of settlers' land by the government, which have (not surprisingly) been glossed over in the official village version. Furthermore, in January of 2000 he opened a small Ogata-mura historical photograph museum, inside his company headquarters, as an alternative to the land reclamation museum that was in its final stages of completion. In addition, Wakui has been a major figure in village politics since he ran against Mayor Miyata in the 1992 election, which the mayor won by a comfortable margin. He entered the race again in 1996 and lost by a much smaller number of votes. Following the election he spoke about his own political aspirations, admitting that he did not especially want to be mayor, but rather wanted to prove that Miyata could be defeated. A couple of years later Wakui said that he probably would not run again because he expected that someone else would enter the race in 2000, which is exactly what happened.

The Ogata-mura Dōyūkai

The story of the founding of the Ogata-mura Dōyūkai goes back to the early 1970s, when the cooperative farming groups were breaking down. The third-wave settler Takeru Isono from Niigata was instrumental in the creation of the company. Around the time of the first *aogari* episode, Takeru—having grown weary of the six-man joint-farming arrangement—convinced two like-minded members of Essa Farm (his cooperative farming group) to join him in purchasing two top-of-the-line, mid-sized rice harvesters equipped with autoloading receptacles for catching grains—machines that no one settler could afford to buy on his own. They operated the machines in two teams, with help from their wives, moving from one field of one man's holdings to one of another man's holdings, and so on, day by day, until all harvesting was done. In this way, they were able to complete the critical autumn task of bringing the rice grains in for processing and storage in record time, and fairly cheaply. In fact, once the three men had finished harvesting their own crops, other settlers asked them to bring the machines over to their fields and help them harvest, which they did for a fee. The men achieved great success with their enterprise. All three of them switched to overproduction soon after the *aogari* episode, and all three succeeded in increasing their landholdings well beyond the original fifteen hectares they had bought on loan from the government.

In 1988 Takeru and his two entrepreneurial colleagues banded together with seventeen other noncompliant Ogata-mura farmers, and assembled 21 million yen in capital to form the Akita Komachi Seisansha Dōyūkai—with the goal of shipping rice directly to consumers across the nation. By the end of the following year the number of members had increased by four, the association's capital investments had more than doubled, and they had built a 165 square meter low-temperature storage facility. Incorporation came in 1992, from which point it was known as the Ogata-mura Dōyūkai. The company is located on the south side of the village, just down the road from the Country Elevator. Since selling rice directly to consumers was technically illegal when the Dōyūkai was founded, the government often sent agents to pressure the members to cease their operations during the first five or six years. By that time, however, Tokyo was actually starting to give up on seriously enforcing the law, which was finally repealed by passage of the Shin Shokuryō Kanrihō in 1995.

Today the Dōyūkai remains a private corporation—it does not issue stocks—but maintains an unusually high total capital of ninety-six million yen. The members' combined land area devoted to rice production amounts to nearly four hundred hectares because a few members possess twenty hectares or more. The company generally lists about one dozen people on its payroll. It has a very efficient processing and storage system only for the use of its members, but there is also a small branch company, Mizuho (est. 1994), that can be used by any producer who wants to market his rice through the Dōyūkai. In addition to shipping rice directly to consumers, the Dōyūkai sends rice to hotels, traditional Japanese inns (*ryokan*), hospitals, supermarkets, and rice merchants. The company has also begun marketing its own special brand of Akita Komachi rice, called Hachirōgata Komachi. In 1995 the company helped to establish the Yūki natural fertilizer corporation with the Akita Komachi Company and one other small marketing organization, Nōyū. The corporation's administration is composed of members who are elected to their positions through group meetings. Officially, the president serves for three years, but may hold the position for longer if the members are in agreement. There are six officers who fulfill general roles, and two of these are auditors. Most of these are the sons of the settlers who founded the company.

The Akita Nōyūkai (Nōyū)

In March of 1989—one year after the founding of the Dōyūkai—the farmers who had formed the SKK (Seiji Keizai Kenkyūkai) around 1980 dropped that name and assembled 12.5 million yen in capital to start a new joint-stock corporation, which they called the Akita Nōyūkai, or simply Nōyū. Although the company is still technically a public corporation today, the stocks are all in the hands of the remaining founders and their family members. Nōyū quickly set up a business office and processing facility on the east side of the village, in the area that had been prepared by the Jigyōdan for cooperative farming groups' communal warehouses. Nobuhiro Machida, a fifth wave settler from Toyama, not only was a founding member of the SKK, but also served as CEO of Nōyū before later breaking away and going independent. By 1991 the company's total capital had grown to the current level of 49.7 million yen. Like in the Dōyūkai, officers are appointed by members in general meetings. There are seven officers, two of whom serve as auditors, and also like in the Dōyūkai these officers are the sons of founding settlers.

Unlike the Dōyūkai, however, Nōyū today concentrates primarily on marketing *musenmai*. The customer list looks nearly like that of the Dōyūkai. Much of Nōyū's rice goes to consumers and institutions in the Tokyo area. The first time I went to the business office to meet the president, he told me that he had spent the previous week running around Tokyo greeting major customers and attempting to recruit more. Official company ties with its two main allies in the village, the Akita Komachi Corporation and the Dōyūkai—which are also its competitors as well—include the joint founding of Yūki in 1995. Furthermore, in an attempt at smoothing relations and easing some of the bad feelings between noncompliant farmers (Nōyū members included) and compliant farmers, Nōyū purchases tulip bulbs from a group of farmers who have always remained loyal to the Country Elevator and includes two in each of its rice shipments to consumers.

The Dōyūkai and Nōyū Compared

A brief comparison of the Dōyūkai and Nōyū reveals much about the nature of rice production, marketing, and social relations in Ogata-mura. It also helps shine a light on the role that the old cooperative groups have played in the development of the village's agriculture, and better illustrates the impact that the separation of political and economic relations from social ones in the village has had on the community.

Both companies have nearly the same number of members. It seems that a group of twenty to thirty like-minded farmers can function rather well together—finding ways to agree on business management and choosing their officers quickly and efficiently—as long as each member retains total control of his own production. It also seems to be a good number of producers for competitively marketing their products.[7] Although Nōyū is a joint-stock corporation, both companies remain under the complete control of their members, since only Nōyū's founding households hold the company's stocks.

But even though they are quite similar on the surface, the Dōyūkai and Nōyū each has its own character. Nōyū seems to be more like a business, while the Dōyūkai is a little more like a private club. Since Nōyū is identified as a joint-stock corporation, it can get a little more recognition from potential customers in general.[8] Furthermore, Nōyū has always carefully maintained its level of capital at a point just below the fifty-million yen level requiring a company to hire a licensed tax accountant to handle its tax reports each year, while the Dōyūkai has not. I realized how different the two companies actually are when I tried to distribute questionnaires to their respective members. I went to the Dōyūkai office in late January of 2002 and met the president, a settler by the name of Sugisawa, who agreed without hesitation to help me. I told him that it would take me a little time to prepare the form, and that I would show him a copy when I was finished. I wanted to meet Mr. Kawabuchi, the president of Nōyū, first and get some information so that I would be able to prepare a comprehensive questionnaire—nearly identical for the members of each company. However, problems with his schedule, and my coming down with the flu in February, prevented me from visiting the Nōyū office until March. Once I had Mr. Kawabuchi's permission, I made the questionnaire and contacted the presidents of each company. I had no trouble with Nōyū—without even asking to see the questionnaires first, Mr. Kawabuchi requested that I send the forms and accompanying letters of explanation in individual envelopes to him before a weekend general meeting at which he promised to distribute them to the members. In the end, I received fifteen out of twenty-nine forms—a fair return.

Unfortunately, Mr. Sugisawa of the Dōyūkai was not available by the time I had my forms ready, and a young officer of the company called me back about my plan. When I explained what I wanted to do, he surprised me by immediately refusing. I said that the president had previously agreed to help, after which he changed his tone and asked to see the forms. I sent a copy by fax and awaited his response. To my dismay, when he called me back his tone was more negative than it had been the first time. He implied that he had checked with the president and that they had agreed that most of my questions—especially the ones asking members to rate the profitability and efficiency of various rice marketing organizations and to give their opinions on the future of the Country Elevator—were unacceptable. Surprised, I offered to omit the offending questions from the forms and perhaps even send them directly to members without involving the company itself. This, I hoped, would not ruffle any feathers. Sadly, the young officer objected to that as well, saying that asking their members such questions would be "very problematic," and I was left to decide what to do. I considered mailing forms only to those members who had personally told me about their rice marketing arrangements, and not to the ones whose membership in the company had been revealed to me by the president. But in the end, not wanting to make any enemies in the company, I gave up.

Later, I received a telephone call from the Dōyūkai president, who told me that he had only just seen my questionnaire, but that he was in agreement with the young officer who had foiled my plan. He apologized for the confusion, and offered to answer the questions on my form himself in proxy. He explained to me that he and the other members were simply brought into the company by friends, and that, to him, my interest in having the members rate their own company against others in terms of profitability and efficiency of operations was moot—for they were all simply trying their best to survive in the current environment within the boundaries that they had set by their own actions years before. There was also some suspicion on the part of Mr. Sugisawa and the young officer that what I wanted to do was to establish a scale by which to objectively rate the different companies—to determine which was the "best" and which was the "worst." They did not want their members to be involved in anything of that nature. My impression was that the Dōyūkai executives were protecting their members from outside intrusions.

That the Nōyū president distributed the same forms to the members of his company, and that I got over 50 percent of them back, says something about the emphasis on business among Nōyū management and the general "private club" or "extended family" attitude within the Dōyūkai. Members of the latter know each other fairly well and many of them associate with each other frequently. Members of Nōyū, on the other hand, tend to keep business a little more separate from their private lives, and business is handled by the men—most of the wives, in fact, do not seem to know each other very well. Comparing the composition of each corporation's membership reveals some of the ways in which the original social arrangements of the village community—influenced by settler wave, cooperative groups, and farmers' places of origin—have contributed to the current situation (Figure 4.3, Table 4.3).

Table 4.3: Membership of the Dōyūkai and Nōyū according to settler wave.

Settler wave	First	Second	Third	Fourth	Fifth
Dōyūkai (24 members)	11	3	9	1	0
Nōyū (29 members)	2	11	4	3	9

Of the twenty-four members of the Dōyūkai, eleven are first-wave settlers and seventeen live in section two of the west side of the village (*nishi nichōme*). No fifth-wave settlers belong to the company, and only one is from the fourth wave; it is largely an association of early settlers. Considering those who live in *nishi nichōme*, it is easy to see that most of them got involved through relationships within their old cooperative farming groups (Figure 4.4). As for the eleven first-wave settlers in the company, three are members of Tarō Farm, three are members of H-18 Farm, two are members of Tony Farm, and the other three are from different groups. There are three second-wave members of the Dōyūkai, of which two are from the same cooperative group. Three of the third-wave members of the Dōyūkai live in *nishi nichōme*, all of whom belong to the same cooperative group, Essa Farm of Niigata Prefecture. This pattern may very well be the root of the company's family-type attitude. The situation for Nōyū differs somewhat from that of the Dōyūkai—its business competitor and political ally. Ten of the members of Nōyū are clustered in the second-wave settlers' neighborhood on the east side of the village. Of these, three belong to Chōkai Farm, and two each to Hachirō Farm, Seishū Farm, and Mizuho Farm. Only one belongs to a different group. The other members of Nōyū—including three fourth-wave settlers and nine fifth-wave settlers—are scattered across the village. No pattern relating to cooperative group membership seems apparent; only two of the fifth-wave Nōyū members belong to the same cooperative group.

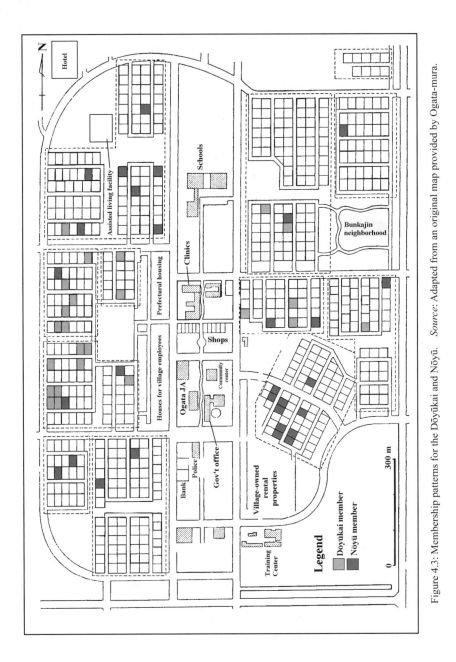

Figure 4.3: Membership patterns for the Dōyūkai and Nōyū. *Source*: Adapted from an original map provided by Ogata-mura.

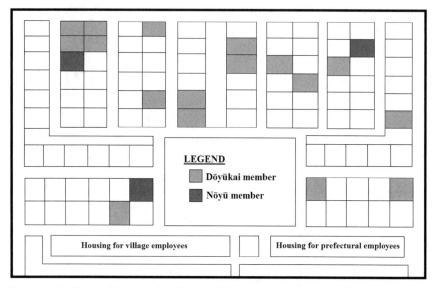

Figure 4.4: Dōyūkai and Nōyū members' households in *nishi nichōme*.

Whereas the Dōyūkai is largely controlled by first-wave settlers who pioneered Ogata-mura agriculture, Nōyū has a widely scattered assortment of members who entered the village later that gives balance to its core of second-wave settlers (Figure 4.3, Table 4.3). It may be that when I tried to distribute questionnaires to both groups I inadvertently exposed some major differences in attitude between earlier and later settlers. For example, many Ogata-mura farmers agree that since first- and second-wave settlers were the earliest to farm the new fields, and that because they were already fairly well established in the village when the rice-limit problems and the first *aogari* episode occurred, they were more concerned about farming and community building than the members of the fifth wave, who entered the village much later and were still only just getting started when the political problems arose. Some people have suggested that fifth-wave farmers—especially the noncompliant ones—and many members of the fourth wave, as well, had to be more concerned about the business of farming early on in order to survive.

It may not be a coincidence, after all, that the leaders of the Dōyūkai and Nōyū at the beginning of this century were fourth-wave and fifth-wave settlers, respectively, and that Wakui of the Akita Komachi Corporation—perhaps the most ambitious and successful entrepreneur in the village—is a fourth-wave settler as well. In addition, Sadayoshi Miyazaki, who has been an important, behind-the-scenes prime mover in Ogata-mura opposition politics and who also headed the village agricultural cooperative, is a fourth-wave settler. This is not to say that the earliest migrants are not entrepreneurial or business-minded at all, but rather simply that their first experience in the village centered on survival by hard labor, while the last settlers' survival depended more on making the right business decisions at the right time. It seems that the basic differences between the Dōyūkai and Nōyū, therefore, are at least partially due to the government's handling of the Hachirōgata settlement and farming project.

Other Means of Marketing Rice

Ogata-mura rice farmers who do not market their rice in any of these ways do so by various other means. Many simply began shipping their own rice directly to consumers using private transport companies such as Yamato and Pelican over twenty years ago when agents began scouring the village to help set up such relationships between producers and consumers who were willing to pay high prices for rice which they could trust. Many Ogata-mura farmers who started marketing their rice in this manner eventually formed small private companies so that they could also sell other farmers' rice with their own; household tax returns become considerably more complicated if they sell any rice that they do not produce themselves, so dividing household taxes and business taxes through incorporation made life easier. Nobuhiro Machida is one settler who established his own business—after leaving Nōyū, in his case. Of his decision to go independent, he said, "Of course, in a joint-stock corporation all the stockholders hold shares, right? They all held equal shares. That means that as long as everything's going well, as expected, they're all happy, and that's fine. But if things are going badly, it's the boss who's to blame. That's how it was." By the time of the police blockades of late 1985, Nobuhiro had formed his own personal company, Rice Akita, Ltd., which he still operates today. "Only the name is big!" Nobuhiro exclaimed in 1997. "A few years ago when there was a shortage of rice I got a bunch of calls from all across the country—everyone wanted to order tons of rice from me—but I had to explain that I didn't have that much to sell! People seemed to think I was a major wholesaler."

Other farmers began banding together to form small companies, and still others formed noncorporate marketing groups that save themselves trouble, but sacrifice potential overall profits—while keeping overheads down—by simply selling their rice in an unpolished state (*genmai*) to retailers and large wholesalers. Isao Satake is one of these farmers. In the mid-1980s Isao joined a marketing group that was selling its rice as *genmai* in bulk to various buyers across the country, including hospitals, hotels, and other large institutions, and he still belongs to this company today. The personal financial risks are limited, but there is also a lower chance of great profits. There is much less work during the off-season, for agricultural down-time is not taken up with various business matters. The arrangement suits him well, for he cherishes the farming lifestyle more than he values maximizing profits. "It's just the two of us," he has said, "so it's always been better to be free in the winter so we can travel." Of his choice to defy the government in the first place, and speaking the final sentence in English for effect, he explained:

> I went independent because I couldn't grow my rice as I pleased. You see? I came here to farm freely—as I wanted to. But, the government said difficult things, so I didn't want to sell to the government. If you sell to the government, there are a lot of promises [you have to make] and troublesome matters. I don't like troublesome matters. *I have to be a pure farmer!*

But for Isao this was no simple matter, because his father and an elder brother held public positions. In fact, his brother was an instructor at the training center, and so had taught many Ogata-mura settlers about large-scale farming. Because of Isao's illegal activities, his father and brother were threatened with dismissal by prefectural representatives. But Isao, like so many others, had already been shut out by the Country Elevator and branded as a "bad" settler by the Miyata administration. The situation troubled him greatly. His wife, Hiroko, later reflected on her husband's anxiety: "I really was afraid that he might have a nervous breakdown for a while there . . . This was no 'home' for us, then. We even talked about getting out of Ogata-mura and going to the U.S.A. or Canada." During this period one of their close neighbors committed suicide, probably partly due to the conflicts and social tension.

Finally, in addition to these different ways of selling rice, a small amount of it is marketed through the Ogata JA. As stated above, there was a time when the cooperative owned the majority of the Country Elevator's shares, and therefore largely controlled rice marketing in the village from backstage, but today it is a minor player in the rice business. Like other JA associations across the country, it offers banking services; carries out repair work on cars, bicycles, and agricultural machines under contract from the makers; and sells various farming supplies such as fertilizers, pesticides, and even seeds—but unlike other JAs, with the exception of a few notable specialty items such as its locally famous pumpkin pies it largely stays out of the buying and selling of farm products.

Profitability

As for profits, succeeding in growing chemical-free rice of a quality high enough to be purchased by Wakui's Akita Komachi Corporation as top-grade rice probably yields the highest overall returns. This does not require any investments in processing or storage facilities on the part of the producer, but it does require much effort. Members of the Dōyūkai and Nōyū seem to be faring well, too. Those who send their rice directly to consumers on their own tend to have rather impressive houses—although not everything can be seen by simply judging from house types today. The Country Elevator generally appears to offer the lowest overall profits for farmers. One problem might be the high cost of using the corporation's processing and storage facilities.

As mentioned in chapter 3, during the village's "golden era"—the 1980s and early to mid-1990s—when rice prices were at their highest, Ogata-mura farming households holding only the standard fifteen hectares could bring in thirty to fifty million yen (roughly U.S. $210,000 to U.S. $350,000 at the January 1990 exchange rate) per annum simply by planting all that the rice that they could and not complying with the government. But because of the drop in rice prices following the passing of the New Food Control Act in 1995, the situation is not quite so favorable now. Today, an Ogata-mura farmer with fifteen hectares might earn about fifteen to twenty million yen per year (and possibly more). However, it costs most of them about thirteen million yen to produce a crop. The profit margin, therefore, has become quite small, which hurts everybody—whether they use the Country Elevator or not. Thus, they have been encouraged by the political and economic situation to expand their farms, as is evidenced by the fact that over two-hundred of Ogata-mura's farming households now own more than 15 hectares of farmland. In addition, the number of large farms is steadily growing.

Closely related to profitability and marketing is the issue of farmers' decisions on whether to maximize rice production or to comply with government guidelines and divert some land to other crops. The latter option includes a choice about participating in the government's accredited farmer (*nintei nōgyōsha*) scheme. Not surprisingly, the program is not viewed on the same level by all Ogata-mura farmers. In general, those who have remained loyal to the Country Elevator and supported Mayor Miyata have had the accreditation since the mid-1990s, when the village began participating in the system. These producers tend to exhibit a sense of pride in their status and in the length of time they have had it—to wear the label as a badge of their having always been on the "good" side and not having been one of the "bad" ones: "We've had that from the beginning. No—we're not like those opportunists who just got the status recently," said the elderly wife of an original settler one afternoon while entertaining my curiosity on the front steps. This, of course, is not so for all users of the Country Elevator, but there is a noticeable trend.

On the other hand, some farmers clearly express their rejection of the *nintei* designation, and take pride in this, saying, "If you don't need financial help from the government, you don't need to bother." Some of these villagers call the designation scheme a ploy to saddle the nation's farmers with debts and drive them into insolvency so that they will be forced to give up their land and make way for a larger, more efficient, industrial agriculture that is disconnected from the concept of farming as a lifestyle. Isao Satake is highly suspicious of the *nintei* program: "I don't need the government to declare that I am a farmer—I give myself my own accreditation as a farmer!" Unlike Isao, who has remained consistent in his rejection of government offers and support, there are some Ogata-mura farmers who have gained the *nintei* distinction only to drop it later, or not reapply for it at the five-year point, because they did not feel any need to borrow money or ask for assistance from the government. Some who have carried the *nintei* label for many years and always remained loyal to the Country Elevator view these settlers (or heirs) with suspicion—even derision—accusing them behind their backs of skipping in and out of *nintei* status only for the purpose of borrowing money. In other words, there is a feeling that some village farmers have complied with *tensaku* guidelines, obtained the *nintei* status, borrowed money to buy more land or build facilities, and then shifted back to maximum production of rice, thereby dropping the status and any claim to nonloan support from the government. Whether this has actually been done deliberately by any Ogata-mura farmers is unclear, but the feeling that it has been done exists nonetheless. As of spring 2010 there were approximately 230 accredited producers in Ogata-mura (out of about 523 farming households), fewer than ten of which were corporations.

Total or partial rejection of the *nintei* status aside, there are some especially pragmatic, entrepreneurial farmers who have made good use of the designation and the opportunities that accompany it. Nobuhiro Machida is one of these. At one point he decided to expand his landholdings beyond the standard fifteen hectares by an extra ten. To do this, he decided, it was best to apply for accreditation and take advantage of the government's low-interest "Super L" loan. Technically, it is actually his company—Rice Akita—that is the accredited farmer (accredited farming entity in this case) but as the head of the company the status was granted to Nobuhiro. Also, he did not buy extra farmland for his own private possession, as Takeru Isono has done. Rather, it is the company that purchased the extra ten hectares, yet Nobuhiro tends to this property as well as his own fifteen hectare farm. Since he is now a *nintei nōgyōsha*, he must comply with *tensaku* guidelines: he must utilize a certain percentage of the total area (generally hovering around 25 percent but fluctuating annually) for crops other than rice. But Nobuhiro, like many other accredited farmers, takes advantage of the legal loophole allowing the growth of a certain (also fluctuating) amount of rice in excess of the guideline if that extra amount is designated as *kakōyōmai*. This rice, therefore, is not to be sold in the form of dry, raw grains to be cooked and eaten as they are. In recent years, according to Nobuhiro, it has been better economically to become accredited, increase farm size (even if through a loan) and take advantage of the *kakōyōmai* allowance to produce as much rice as possible in accordance with *tensaku* policies. That he has shifted from defiance to compliance illustrates Nobuhiro's ability to place practical matters such as success in business over personal ideals. Also, in 2010 many others like him did the same (see chapter 6).

However, Nobuhiro's rice business has not been expanding in all directions lately. Like the other marketing associations in the village, Rice Akita has in recent years begun offering a wide array of high-end rice products, including chemical-free organic rice, *musenmai*, *hatsuga genmai*, and others. But the market for these has been contracting. While explaining his product list in the autumn of 2006, Nobuhiro pointed at the higher-end products, which tend to yield greater profit margins, and lamented, "I just can't sell as much of this now as I used to." He pointed at the photos of the bags of lower-end, standard, polished rice, adding, "You see these? If I can't offer rice like this at a competitive price, I really can't stay in business. These days, you've got to be able to sell basic rice cheaply or people won't buy it. They'll still pay a little more for the security of knowing exactly who grew it and where, but they want cheaper deals." The problem is that it is more difficult to sell such rice for the kind of profits that higher-end products afford. The basic production costs remain steady while the prices continue to drop. Despite this situation, though, Nobuhiro acknowledges that he must work to produce and offer what will sell not only to survive but also to cultivate a healthy business, in opposition to the philosophy of fellow settler Shinichirō Sakamoto. "I'd love to live the kind of farm life that Sakamoto-san envisions," said Nobuhiro. "We producers grow high quality products while not worrying about markets and prices, and the consumers pay well for them, and everyone is happy. I'd love to live that kind of ideal farm life. But that isn't reality. Consumers won't just continue to support us if we can't offer them what they want at prices they can accept." His wife, Takako, joined in, saying, "Look at Sakamoto-san's situation. He doesn't have a farm that can be passed down to the next generation. His son isn't taking over as his heir." "If a farmer doesn't build something that can be passed down," added Nobuhiro, "he can't really expect his son to take over."

Business and Politics in an Ogata-mura Neighborhood

The village is divided into east (*higashi*) and west (*nishi*) sides. The west side is divided into sections one (*ichōme*), two (*nichōme*), and three (*sanchōme*). West section two (*nishi nichōme*) is especially interesting because it contains the homes of families belonging to each of the first three migrant waves. As a matter of fact, all first-wave settlers live in the area. From September of 2001 to February of the following year I conducted a study of the neighborhood by visiting each of the households within it whose head or former head had migrated to Ogata-mura as part of the national settlement program.[9] Studying the neighborhood carefully helped clarify the interactions between the two social arrangements that initially shaped the village society—the "old social order" from the earlier period based on cooperative group membership and place of origin, and the "new social order" from the later period based on rice marketing strategies and individual ties.

In the *nishi nichōme* area, there were 104 households belonging to families that settled in the village under the national settlement program at the time of

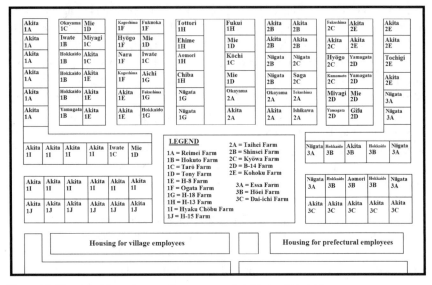

Figure 4.5: Place of origin and cooperative group membership in *nishi nichōme*.

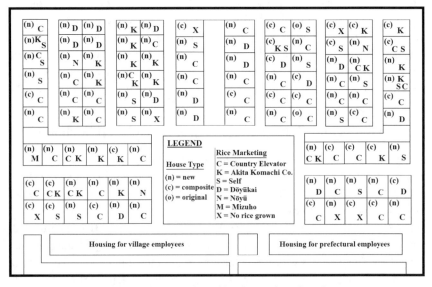

Figure 4.6: Household rice marketing strategies and house types in *nishi nichōme*.

the survey (Figure 4.5). Five of them no longer grew rice, and several of these had even ceased all farming activities. The houses of the neighborhood could be divided into three house types—"new" (n), "composite" or "integrated" (c), and "original" (o) (Figure 4.6). Homes of the first category showed no sign of the original triangular structure built by the Jigyōdan, while those of the second still contained the original part, and those of the final category had been altered only minimally since initial construction (these were already rare in the 1990s).

Cooperative Farming Groups of Nishi Nichōme

There are eighteen cooperative farming groups in *nishi nichōme*. Seven of them originally had only 5 members each, ten had 6 members, and one (Hyaku-chōbu Nōjō—the Hundred Hectare Farm) had 10 members. The households are divided into four different blocks, or *jūku*. First-wave settlers fill the south side, while members of the second and third waves dwell in the northern half (Figure 4.5).

Block one (the lower-left quadrant of Figure 4.5) consists of eighteen settler households and also the homes of village employees. One of the first-wave groups, H-15 Farm, experienced a split between its members very early in the community's history. At the first house I visited on the street I was told by the wife of the settler's son (the *yome-san*) that she had no idea which group her family belonged to. An older member of another household said that the group was called Chūō Farm. However, a settler on the other end of the street identified his group's name as H-15 Farm. He invited me in and explained the situation over copious amounts of green tea made with delicious water he had traveled some distance to obtain from a natural spring. He had lived in Manchuria as a teenager during the Japanese occupation, and had watched his own father and other migrants attempt to farm there under cooperative conditions similar to those originally planned for Ogata-mura. But the system collapsed. "There were a lot of fights," he said. "It just didn't work at all." When he participated in the Hachirōgata training program and heard of the cooperative farming plan, he told his group members that it would not work and that he wanted no part in communal group farming—only in group ownership of equipment. Two or three other settlers near him agreed and followed his example, while the others decided to use the name Chūō Farm and attempted to keep up a total communal system for a couple of years. This left everyone divided roughly along the center of the street, and resulted in some confusion over the name of the entire group.

Today, only the name H-15 Farm will generally be recognized, but at least two of the settlers on the north end of the street were listed as belonging to Chūō Farm in the official settler guide published by the village just after the end of the national settlement program in the mid-1970s. Although the group experienced this split early on, there seemed to be little difference, if any, between social relations among the members and those among the members of other groups that did not experience such splits as of 2002. The group members no longer met regularly. One had quit farming and sold his fields. Of the other five, two were still marketing all or most of their rice through the Country Elevator, one was a member of the Dōyūkai, and two marketed their own rice independently. But as with all groups, the original settlers were already beginning to disappear—a major factor in the thinning of social relations within groups.

Hyaku-chōbu Farm is a group of ten settlers that banded together to form an especially large group. Five members migrated from Yuri County in the southern part of Akita Prefecture and the other five from the immediate Hachirōgata region. *Hyaku-chōbu* literally means "one hundred hectares," for the total size of the cooperative farm they originally created by combining their ten-hectare plots. Most members of the group (the men) still jointly owned some seldom-used machines, and so they would meet one or two times each year in order to discuss matters relating to their maintenance and repair, but even in 2002 this was slowly fading as the second generation took over. Costs were always shared equally by all. They also still got together once each spring to repair roads and cut weeds around their rice fields. No regular socializing occurred between the wives along the street anymore. Five of the ten member households of Hyaku-chōbu Farm were selling at least some of their rice to the Akita Komachi Corporation. Being close neighbors as well as members of the same group, they decided years ago to try the company together. Several members of the group had chosen to stick with the Country Elevator, one belonged to Nōyū, and one sold rice exclusively to Mizuho, the child corporation of the Dōyūkai. The members of this group maintained some ties through continued collective ownership of equipment, but, as in all other cases, marketing strategies eventually came to take precedence over the older neighborhood relations.

Block two (the upper-left quadrant of Figure 4.5) is a collection of thirty-six settler households that form a complete *jūku*. The residents are divided into eight cooperative groups, but three of the groups have members in the neighboring *jūku*. Two of these are Tarō Farm and Tony Farm. One member of Tony Farm is located in block one, to the east, with members of the Hundred-Hectare Farm.[10] Even though the members of Tony Farm were bound by strong geographical ties (since all came from Mie Prefecture) and by the shared experience of studying in California, they were no different from members of other groups in that there was little socialization among them when I surveyed their neighborhood. Two had joined the Dōyūkai, and the other three continued to use the Country Elevator (one member's son was the president in 2002). All members of Tarō Farm had broken away from the Country Elevator, and were evenly divided between the Dōyūkai and the Akita Komachi Corporation. The members of this group generally had rather large and new houses, even in 2002.

Covering one side of the southernmost street in the block is the all-Akita group, Reimei Farm. Although the members were previously very tight, they also grew apart with time, with changes in rice marketing strategies, and with the gradual loss of the original settlers. No regular meetings occurred between the members in 2002, but some of them still owned a few small machines on a communal basis. As in other groups, the members marketed their rice differently, but simply did not discuss the details with each other. Across the street is Hokuto Farm, also divided regarding marketing strategies. No regular meetings occurred between residents of the street, known by people of the entire block as *minami dōri* ("South Street").[11]

On the next street to the north, *naka dōri* ("Central Street"), there is H-8 Farm and Ogata Farm. Although the five members of H-8 all hail from Akita, strong divisions existed among them relating to rice marketing. Of the two who still used the Country Elevator ten years ago, the house of one—on the corner—was quite small, while that of the other was very large.[12] One of the other three members sold his rice to the Akita Komachi Corporation, and the other two had gone independent. No regular meetings took place between members of the group, as was the case for members of Ogata Farm. In contrast, however, the latter were still somewhat closer to one another than those of H-8 Farm. The grandmothers of the group occasionally got together to socialize, and they had only stopped taking yearly trips together around the time I surveyed the entire neighborhood in 2002. One member thought this closeness might have been due to the fact that all of them were from places other than Akita—either because they had to try harder to get along in the beginning due to their different customs and dialects, or because they felt more unity since they were all complete outsiders.

Although the grandmothers of Ogata Farm still associated with each other on occasion, there were no regular meetings between residents of *naka dōri* as a street association, which might have been due to divisions between members of different groups, neighbors in general, or members of H-8 Farm. I was warned by a resident of one street not to ask anyone on *naka dōri* about regular meetings such as those which occur on the next street to the north. The word on residents of *naka dōri* was that there had been a period of much conflict between them over an unknown matter—probably relating to rice marketing—and I was told that asking questions might encourage backbiting. I did test the waters of the street, with caution, but found no signs of trouble.

Kita dōri ("North Street") has one member of Ogata Farm, one of Tony Farm, one of Tarō Farm, the five members of H-18 Farm, and four of the five members of H-13 Farm. One of the households of H-13 Farm consisted only of the older couple in 2002. Since their only child—a daughter—had married out and moved to Osaka, they no longer farmed but rather paid another farmer a percentage of the profits to work the fields and market their rice for them. They did not know how he sold the rice—they simply awaited the deposit he made for them each year after the harvest. It is interesting to note that, while no regular meetings occurred between any residents and their respective group members, this street alone had a healthy get-together (*ocha no kai*) group among the grandmothers for many years. They normally met one afternoon each month at one member's home for tea and food—provided by the host for that month. There they would while away a few hours, eating, drinking, and, most importantly, chatting. This included a fair amount of gossip and storytelling. Sometimes daughters-in-law (*yome*) were present for these parties, but usually not—the difference in age made for unappealing topics. Besides, some of the stories told at the parties were about the younger wives anyway (see also Miyamoto 2008:42–44, 2010:230–233). But avoiding involvement was not always possible; one younger mother of *kita dōri* complained that she had always ended up spending many hours in the kitchen helping her mother-in-law prepare food when her turn to host came around. Even though the earlier, communal-type social relations between members of the same groups had largely broken down by the start of this century, enduring connections between residents of the same street, such those on *kita dōri*, have helped maintain a strong sense of community between some people.

Exactly why the grandmothers of *kita dōri* were able to continue the regular get-togethers for so long is unclear. One member suggested that it was because no settlers from Akita live on the street—the same reason given for the continued social interactions between the grandmothers of Ogata farm. Somehow, she felt, the fact that all of them were complete outsiders—total strangers to Akita as well as to each other—also helped them bond well. Perhaps, having no relatives anywhere in the area, they ended up forming tight relations with neighbors in addition to the strong cooperative group ties that everyone initially formed. One problem with maintaining these bonds in the village has been that the cooperative groups were originally created for a type of production that left the farmers unfulfilled and that changed dramatically. It is no surprise, therefore, that the corresponding social relations changed as well. Furthermore, since the members relied on each other like relatives from the beginning, always staying within one's group for socializing was like never going beyond the boundaries of kinship for making friends. Finally, the old groups were small, making it hard to maintain close relations among the members if two of them did not get along well, or if several of them preferred to stay out of group matters in general. An entire street, on the other hand, provides a greater number and variety of people with which to associate. It could be that freedom from tight group relations has helped allow village residents to associate with others more easily. For example, the grandmother who lives on the corner of *kita dōri* and belongs to Ogata Farm said that when her family first settled in the village she was a bit lonely, being on a different street from the other members of her group and therefore unable to greet them in front of the house regularly. But, later, after some time had passed, she came to appreciate the freedom accompanying separation from the others, who were originally nearly as close as blood relatives.[13]

In the next *jūku* to the north there are another thirty-six houses. Four households on the south side belong to the first wave of settlers, and two on the north end belong to the third wave. The others, save one, came with the second settlement wave. No regular street meetings occurred between residents of this *jūku* in 2002. A few groups, however, were still holding one small party per year. In particular, members of Taihei Farm usually assembled one day every summer, normally involving all members of each of the six households. It is interesting to note that this is the only one of the old cooperative farming groups in the area whose members were all still marketing their rice through the Country Elevator in 2002, despite the fact that the second generation was beginning to take over. Being among the overcompliant settlers who rallied around Shinichirō Sakamoto, their homes were always some of the least altered in the neighborhood. Only two of the six no longer had the old peaked-roof section, and one of the older houses was actually nearly all original, with only a garage and a few minimal additions to the house itself, as of the survey period.

Kyōwa Farm had one non-settler member in the group. Over twenty years ago, after enlarging the house, the original settler who lived in the westernmost plot on the end of the street quit farming and returned to his home area in Fukushima Prefecture. The owner of the house in 2002 had previously been married to the proprietor of a beauty salon in the village, but was alone at the time—mostly doing odd jobs and taking occasional part-time work. The members of Kyōwa Farm brought him into their group in place of the former resident, so he did perform his duties to other group members when the need arose. In this way, the group's members helped ensure that their support network would not weaken too much due to the loss of a member (and ensure that the new member would not be isolated). Group B-14 did not hold regular social gatherings, but the members still owned some equipment cooperatively, and therefore met at least twice a year to discuss matters of usage, maintenance, and repair. Certain members—especially those who had formed their own private corporations—participated less in the use of such machines. Continued reliance on the Country Elevator appears to have encouraged joint ownership of farm equipment, and it may also be connected to the maintenance of ties among group members, as the case of Taihei Farm suggests. Finally, at the east end of the northernmost street of the *jūku* are the homes of two members of the third-wave all-Niigata settler group, Essa Farm. One of these belongs to Tarō Omori, who taught fellow group member Takeru Isono to ski.

The fourth quadrant of *nishi nichōme* (lower-right on Figure 4.5) consists of fifteen settler houses and the cluster of prefecture-owned duplexes for employees of the agricultural junior college (now a part of the prefectural university system). These were always significantly smaller and less impressive than even the oldest and simplest of the farmers' houses, and they are in especially bad shape today (and mostly empty). Takeru Isono and three other members of Essa Farm live in this *jūku*, and surrounded by their homes are the six members of Hōei Farm, four of whom hail from Hokkaido. The other two are from Aomori and Akita. Some members reported joint ownership of equipment in 2002, but no regular social meetings occurred between them anymore. In contrast, the members of the last cooperative group in the *jūku*, Daiichi Farm, still did gather socially at least twice a year, either for an end-of-year party in December or for a new year's party in January, and for a post-planting party (*sanaburi*) in the late spring once the crops were safely in the ground. Two households of the group, however, had already quit farming and had sold their fields to others. One of these did so because their only son moved away and decided not to return to Ogata-mura. The two households that no longer owned farmland did not always participate in the group's social gatherings. Rather, when a gathering took place, one household or the other would generally send a representative. One member of the group, living on the far north end of the *jūku*, is Seiki Miyata—mayor of the village for over twenty years. One reason for the group's continued solidarity is probably the fact that they were once all neighbors in the same hamlet in the old town of Hachiryū, just to the north of the reclaimed land. It was not particularly difficult for them, therefore, to work together in the beginning, although they discontinued their communal farming activities early on as did everyone else. Socializing between the farmers of the *jūku* and the residents of the prefectural housing was never particularly notable, with interactions normally occurring only at the regular *jūku* parties.

In sum, a close look at this neighborhood shows again that belonging to a particular cooperative group was very important for most Ogata-mura settlers in the beginning. Membership helped reinforce their identities as migrant-settlers, and as pioneers. Despite the inherent problems, having collective farms with names probably inspired many to work hard at preparing the virgin fields for agriculture and establishing a new, efficient farming system. According to some settlers, certain groups (farms) were known at the start for the speed with which they had prepared their fields for planting, and early parties between the member households of many groups are still remembered with nostalgia and fondness. As members of the same group—often from the same place of origin—they enjoyed reminiscing about their homelands, or at least about their neighboring homelands, and finding more things in common. Those who hailed from completely different areas adjusted to Ogata-mura life more smoothly by comparing memories of their respective *furusatos*.

Even though cooperative group membership is of little importance today, at the beginning it connected Ogata-mura farmers to their pasts, as well as to each other. Belonging to a group symbolized the common experiences of migrating, studying, and working together. A settler's identity as a pioneer was reinforced by being part of a smaller group with which he could identify, rather than simply being a first-wave settler, or a person from a certain place. Perhaps not unlike representatives in the Japanese parliament (the Diet), who are divided into various factions within their own parties, the Ogata-mura settlers' identities and support networks were clearly defined by membership in cooperative farming groups. This helped give them strong foundations upon which to build their futures in the new village.

There are also institutions at the *jūku* level that help maintain neighborhood solidarity and a sense of identity. Times of great need require help from other members of the same *jūku*. The most obvious, and serious, of these are funerals, as explained in chapter 2. When a death occurs, a household can expect help from their *jūku*, from other residents of their street, and from members of their cooperative group, although not necessarily in that order. While most individual groups no longer hold regular social gatherings, all *jūku* do. Every block in the village has either an end-of-year party or a new year's party for all households, and members of each generally attend—from the most aged seniors to the smallest babies. Newcomers to the village, such as women who have married in, are typically introduced to the entire *jūku*. Friendships often start at that level. The *jūku* will also sometimes organize *sanaburi* or occasional trips for its members, but not all need participate. Therefore, members of especially tight and active groups will have several parties to attend at the beginning or the end of each year, and a number of possible trips and excursions to choose from during the less busy months. There are also the parties and trips planned by social groups that center on hobbies, such as the pan-village singing, dancing, or sports associations. Especially for the younger generations, it is these that have clearly begun to take precedence over most of the older associations that the government planners and original settlers—their parents and grandparents—started. But thanks to this web of social relations in which each household is invariably enmeshed, no job goes undone in times of need. Fields will be tended to and legal matters taken care of. This is an important system that provides security and solidarity for the residents of Ogata-mura, even if they are not farmers, and even if they market rice differently from one another.

Households of Nishi Nichōme and Rice Marketing Strategies

There has been in place a complex social network made up of different webs linking residents of Ogata-mura together in various ways since the community's founding. This was based on the plans that were laid out by the government agents who designed the settlement and on the networks that the original migrants made. Also, given what has happened since the founding of the village, the current situation is best understood after obtaining a grasp on the range and types of rice marketing strategies that exist in the village today. This new system, as well as that which individuals are creating all the time through participation in other social circles, has contributed to a weakening of some of the original networks. It is difficult to deeply explore individual social activities and their effects on the older arrangements, but it is quite possible, and beneficial, to consider the ways in which rice marketing strategies have changed the lives of the villagers and increased the divisions between them—divisions based on personal differences that appeared very early on and contributed to the disbanding of the old cooperative groups.

One way to do this is to look at houses in relation to rice marketing strategies. I did find that the members of the Dōyūkai and of Nōyū differ somewhat according to settler wave and cooperative-group membership, and (again) it is generally known that settlers who marketed their rice illegally during the village's "golden era" of high rice prices earned much more money annually than their loyalist counterparts, and therefore were able to replace their original village houses with much larger ones early on (as reflected in occasional comments of villagers, also see Moore 1993: 290). There was, in fact, considerable variation among the houses of *nishi nichōme* even as of early 2002 (and there still is at the time of this writing). A small number were rather old and dilapidated, exhibiting minimal alteration (Figure 4.7). These tended to have a lot of open space in their residential plots because the houses themselves were still so small. Others were only slightly altered, with an extra wing that was obviously added by the settler and perhaps a large garage or storage shed (Figure 4.8). Both of these types of settler homes were still dominated by the original peaked-roof part, forming the central section of the abode. Houses of these two types were primarily concentrated in the northern part of the neighborhood, in the second-wave settler area.

In other homes the original peaked-rook section was prominent, but had become somewhat lost in the overall form—it remained but was no longer the dominant part of the house (Figure 4.9). Such homes were very common across the village in 2002 (and they can easily be found today). In many cases the original peaked-roof section no longer existed at all, having been demolished by the owner and replaced with a new structure at some point. This might have been achieved by first adding a wing to the original house and then having the latter destroyed (while living in the former) and a new, larger section added to the wing. Many homes also clearly showed that the family must have simply relocated for a time in order to have the entire thing replaced at once with a totally new structure showing no trace of the original house layout within the plot. These were common ten years ago and they are even more common today. Such houses can easily be divided into two general categories—relatively large and comfortable-looking homes that might be found in neighborhoods of larger towns and cities (Figure 4.10), and massive structures filling their lots and towering over the street, larger than most houses in towns and cities (Figure 4.11).

Figure 4.7: An older village house, little altered.

Figure 4.8: A village house with a large addition but showing little alteration of the original section (note that the original section—heavily altered—is still visible in the house behind it).

Figure 4.9: The original part of this house is noticeable but it is not dominant.

Figure 4.10: A relatively new and large house in the neighborhood.

Figure 4.11: The home of a first-wave settler—one of the largest houses in the village.

Comparing 2001–2002 data on rice marketing and house type in the neighborhood did not reveal any outstanding correlation—the biggest, newest houses were not necessarily owned by settlers who defied the government and sold black-market rice, and the smallest and least altered ones were not in all cases the homes of loyalists who always obeyed the law and exclusively used the Country Elevator. Although the overcompliant loyalists' simple homes did stand out, it was quite easy to find exceptions in all cases—mainly a reflection of the passage of time. However, the majority of the houses owned by the six families that no longer grew rice were on the lower end of the scale (represented by Figures 4.7 and 4.8) and comparing the forty-eight houses owned by settlers who still sold all or some of their rice to the Country Elevator with the fifty-one houses of those who sold none to it showed that the latter tended to be slightly more modified and larger than the former. Also, more of the least modified houses were owned by compliant settlers' families than were owned by those of opposition settlers (there were almost none of this type owned by them, in fact).[14] This difference was even greater in the past; in the early 1990s it was possible to tour neighborhoods in Ogata-mura and pick out the houses of those who had defied the government and maximized rice production throughout the 1980s quite easily, as their homes contrasted so strongly with the older and smaller homes of the loyalists.[15] Overall, though, this situation is fading. As a community, Ogata-mura will benefit if memories and feelings can fade as quickly.

Nishi Nichōme: Reflections

The residents of *nishi nichōme* are embedded in complex webs of social and business relations that are derived partly from the earlier structures and partly from more recent structures they have created themselves. Although they still see their fellow cooperative-group members often, and are especially close to some, they usually enjoy branching out and making connections with others whenever possible. Discussions with younger people and data from the questionnaires I distributed to certain groups indicate that many of the relations with other group members and neighbors are kept alive by the older generation—especially the grandmothers—like the regular tea party held on one street. It might be that these relations will break down significantly in the future as the generations change, and as networks of kin relations in the village increase in size and strength. Furthermore, there is the general belief among most villagers that the number of farm households will continue to decrease as those who are already in debt and those who cannot secure heirs give up, and possibly move away.

Differences in rice marketing strategies have brought about greater divisions between village farmers. While the grandness of a particular house may not necessarily relate to this today, the erection of large, fine houses by law-breaking settlers during the 1980s and 1990s worsened the bad feelings that their law-abiding neighbors had for them. Lingering resentment shows the extent to which the village's political problems have invaded the original social relations of the community. While residents of *nishi nichōme* do know very well who their fellow cooperative-group members are, where they live, and where they hail from, and also might know what their hobbies are and what their children are doing today, they generally do not know how they market their rice—it is simply not a topic for discussion among farmers of different marketing associations.

Rice Farming and Business Intertwined

Although rice is a political hot potato in Ogata-mura, most settlers of the national project continue to concentrate on its production today—only a few have become fed up enough with the issue to quit growing the crop altogether. Therefore, the village tends to function according to a uniform rhythm—quiet and tranquil in winter, busy and bustling in spring, watchful and diligent in summer, and then busy and bustling once more in the autumn. During planting and harvest time, most residents are too distracted with their work to engage in side activities. Those who are not too busy are the black sheep, in a word, and they sometimes feel obligated to explain why they are at leisure to attend English class on a sunny day. But Ogata-mura's rice agriculture is very efficient and relatively clean, and each farm is of a size that grants much satisfaction to its owner when he gazes across the sea of flooded paddies reflecting the color of the sky in the spring, when he walks among the fields in the summer and listens to the sound of the plants rustling in the wind, and when he counts the truckloads of harvested grains in the autumn. The main problem today is that the farmers' wallets do not grow nearly as thick from their hard work as they did before.

Different farmers in the village also grow their rice in different ways. Most are trying hard not to rely much on chemicals, and some try harder than others, or even completely avoid them—at least where some of their fields are concerned. But rice marketing is at least as variegated in Ogata-mura as rice growing. Today there are a number of different rice marketing methods and institutions. Most farmers are still using the methods and companies they have been using for the past twenty or thirty years, but some selectively market their rice, changing their strategy almost annually. At the beginning, there was a sharp line between those who used the Country Elevator and those who did not, and a settler's position in relation to that line clearly revealed whether he had obeyed the government. Now this line is not as clear, for some who were always loyal to the government and who always used the Country Elevator now sell only some of their rice to it, or perhaps none at all. Some who sell to it say they do so only because they feel sorry for it (*kawaisō dakara*). One thing is fairly clear, though—those who were turned away by it in the past are not selling to it today. Rice marketing strategies in the village, therefore, still reflect many of the original social relationships of Ogata-mura. Dōyūkai and Nōyū membership, for example, are clearly connected to the settlers' arrangement into cooperative farming groups when they first took up residence in the community.

At one time, profitability differed widely between rice marketing strategies. This was also related to cooperative group membership, and it is still echoed somewhat in the differences between settler homes—even today, now that profit margins for one rice farmer are just about as small as those for another, regardless of their business practices (although farm size matters). As the village economy began to change, and as regulations became less and less able to constrain the settlers, those who moved quickly and took the right kinds of risks when the time was right, and who managed their money carefully, got an early lead on their obedient neighbors—a lead that has yet to vanish. The situation has resulted in much lingering resentment among some settlers and their families, which acts as a barrier to overall village unity today. But despite all of this, residents of the village can, overall, enjoy cordial relations with one another—as long as they do not get into political discussions with certain people. Friendships relating to cooperative group membership, place of origin (also connected to the former), street arrangements, and hobbies and other interests are not always affected by politics and ideas about rice production. These relationships can coexist. But rice production and marketing philosophies are also quite rigid in Ogata-mura. Perhaps the settlement scheme resulted in creating a village with more stubbornness than would normally exist in any other community. Perhaps, also, allowing rice to become the main crop of the village at the beginning was a mistake on the part of the planners, for it is odd that the crop—massive production of which is not vital to Japan today—should be so deeply ingrained (pun intended) in the village's political sphere. Rice is everything in Ogata-mura, which is why some settlers decided to get away from it. The entire political landscape rests ultimately on rice issues.

Notes

1. There are a number of settler households that rent farmland out to other producers. In effect, therefore, the number of large farms is actually greater than the official figures show.
2. There are, however, cases of younger sons of farmers setting up their own households in the village. One day while I was walking the streets doing some map survey work, I met a child I recognized from the kindergarten. Her father was outside, washing the car. He turned out to be the second son of a settler—his older brother had become his parents' successor. This young father had joined the village firefighting brigade, where he was employed full-time. He had a new, fairly small house on the west side of the village among the homes of other public employees, and no farmland, but at least he could be close to his parents and brother. As the son of a village farmer, his new household was entitled to a lifetime supply of excellent rice from his brother's fields, and his children had their cousins to play with. Furthermore, he could be close to the main ancestral graves and *butsudan*—the Buddhist family altar dedicated to the ancestors located in his natal household and maintained by his older brother and brother's wife—and the ancestral tablets (*ihai*) as well.
3. An interesting special case: one settler granted one half of his fields to his son and the other half to his daughter. But since the son had already established his own household and the daughter had married into another, this did not constitute the creation of a new branch household.
4. Planting rice one year, then wheat the following spring, and then soybeans in the fall, followed by rice again the third year is said to be rather effective.
5. There is no longer any business relationship between the village agricultural cooperative and the Country Elevator.
6. Some producers reported in 2001 that a farmer who sold his rice to one of them could receive three to five million yen more than a farmer who sold only to the Country Elevator.
7. Both are clearly doing good business and seem to be in advantageous positions to adapt quickly should the current agricultural situation—rice prices, for example—change for the worse.
8. Although the national government has recently done away with the legal distinctions between public and private corporations, the former are generally considered to be doing better business than the latter, and they may therefore have an easier time gaining customers' trust from the beginning.
9. Follow-up spot checks in the neighborhood have indicated very little change in rice production or marketing strategies since 2002—probably under 5 percent.
10. This member of Tony Farm is actually the younger brother of the original settler, who for an unknown reason backed out of the settlement program at the last minute over

forty years ago. The younger brother elected to settle in Ogata-mura in his place, but he was actually a member of the third wave, so his fellow group members had a two-year head start on him.

11. Since the block was one of the first in the village to be settled, the farmers named their streets in this manner.

12. The owner of the larger house was the head of the Board of Education for a number of years, and therefore received a salary in addition to his farm income. This may help explain the great difference between his house and the one next door.

13. This lends some support to the decision to separate group members in later settlement waves.

14. This finding was supported by a simple test involving the assignment of index values for the different house types (represented by Figures 4.7 through 4.11) and comparing these numerically with rice marketing strategies (Wood 2004: 271–279).

15. Richard Moore, personal comment, November 2002.

5

POLITICS AND THE NEW SOCIAL ORDER

Votes in Ogata-mura are the same as bundles of rice. . .
—Sadayoshi Miyazaki, former head of the Ogata-mura JA

Politics in Ogata-mura is serious business. One result of the small size of the community is that candidates—especially those who run for council seats—can essentially count their fellow villagers' votes and tell with surprising accuracy how people from whom they expected to receive support actually voted. In this situation, the secret ballot loses some of its meaning. Although candidates can sometimes garner a few votes based on old ties—having the same place of origin, belonging to the same cooperative farming group, or simply living on the same street—how people actually cast their ballots depends far more on one major factor: whether a candidate has remained loyal to the Country Elevator. A secondary factor, which has grown out of this situation, is whether a candidate has been complying in recent years with the crop reduction/diversion programs. True, compliance in this is completely voluntary—no law requiring farmers to limit their rice production exists today—but whether a household has been following the rules or not says a great deal about their past rice marketing activities and their philosophy on the future of village agriculture.

This division between farmers of Ogata-mura does not appear only at election times; it pervades every facet of their social lives, and it tends to be strongest between men, whether they are settlers themselves or the sons of settlers. In March of 2002 I asked the parents of elementary school children in the village whether rice marketing was a factor in their relations with one another through questionnaires—distributed on my behalf by the school.[1] Just over one-third of the parents answered "sometimes, depending on the case," while 64 percent answered "no." Thirty-two percent of women responded in the positive, compared

---

Endnotes for this chapter begin on page 188.

to 53 percent of men. There also appears to be some correlation between positive responses to the above question and whether villagers use the Country Elevator to market their rice. Breaking the parents down into four categories based on their answers to the questions "Do you use the Country Elevator?" and "Do you have trouble getting along with other PTA members who use or do not use the Country Elevator?" I found that there is a lower tendency to have problems with others among those who do not use the Country Elevator (see Table 5.1). Perhaps this only means that those who do not use the Country Elevator simply do not care what others think, but the fact that over one-third of all young parents felt that associating with others who market their rice differently was still difficult at times indicates the depth of the problem.

Table 5.1: PTA members' relations with reference to rice marketing strategies.

	Some trouble	No trouble
Use Country Elevator	20%	21%
Do not use Country Elevator	16%	43%

The Interplay of Opposing "Parties"

Since the start of the rice quarrels in Ogata-mura, the noncompliant farmers have increasingly become identified as one political party. Until August of 2000, they were the *yatō*, or opposition (minority) party. They tended to vote as a block against Mayor Miyata in each election up until 1996, but were always fewer and less powerful than his supporters. The dominant party (*yotō*) in the village (also until August of 2000), while always larger and stronger than the opposition group, has been somewhat less cohesive and a little harder to define. For example, not all residents who supported the former mayor, Miyata, and other candidates loyal to the national government—and who continued to use the Country Elevator—agreed with all of his initiatives. They may have believed in the merit of using the Country Elevator, or have trusted the dominant Liberal Democratic Party (LDP; Miyata was a member), but still have been skeptical of his large-scale events and the liberal use of village revenues for other tourism or image-building projects. I have run across more than one loyalist farmer in the village who believes that Shinichirō Sakamoto should be mayor, and I have heard him contrasted with Wakui of the Akita Komachi Corporation a number of times. "Sakamoto-san is a real farmer. Wakui-san is just a businessman," said one very bitter first-wave settler in late 2001. This man expressed strong regrets over having relocated to Ogata-mura in the first place when reflecting on the results of the previous year's election.

This situation constantly simmers beneath the surface of the village society, but when an election year comes along everything gets dragged out into the open, and the "parties" are once again defined in terms of the current big issues. In 1992 Tōru Wakui, president of Akita Komachi Corporation, ran against Mayor Miyata for the first time. He was soundly defeated, by 507 votes (1,300 to 793), but this did not lessen his resolve to run again four years later. The 1996 election centered around two matters—rice and big spending. Many Ogata-mura residents—both those who used the Country Elevator and those who did not—were opposed to the mayor's allocation of village monies for events such as the solar races and projects such as the *bunkajin* neighborhood. Most noncompliant farmers wanted the village government to get out of the image-building business and back into a focus on improving the community's agricultural base. They said things like, "They should sell rice at the new hotel . . . after all, this is a farming village." Furthermore, many wanted the government to do more to help village households that were slipping into financial insolvency. Even though a number of compliant farmers felt this way, as had been the case in the past, few were willing to vote against Mayor Miyata in favor of a noncompliant candidate—especially Wakui, a leader among rice overproducers. Clearly, the tide was starting to turn against the mayor, but Miyata scored his sixth straight win, once again defeating Wakui. This time, however, he prevailed by only 188 votes (1,238 to 1,050). Indeed, this election revealed a major political shift. The fact that enough compliant farmers—perhaps many who had always been somewhere more centrist—decided to cast their votes against Miyata shows how much his support was weakening over the big-spending issue.

As noted above, not all supporters of Mayor Miyata were completely happy with his policy of placing high priority on village image improvement, and especially at high cost. On the other hand, to make matters more confusing, not all village settlers who were politically opposed to Miyata were against his pet projects. Even though Wakui had made the spending issue central to his campaign to oust Miyata in 1996, Takeru Isono was still very happy about the solar events in the following year. He said:

> I'm all for it—really. We do that here, and then the technology and the solar car spreads out from Japan throughout the entire world, and then the planet's environment will really become clean, and our own grandchildren . . . they can live in a better world. That's why I completely support it.

Like many, Takeru was already questioning the *bunkajin* project and the Nanohana Festival because their value to the village and to the farmers was unclear, but unlike many he showed no concern at all about financial cost. Of course, the reclamation museum had yet to be built, and the full extent of the village's debt was still unknown to the public. But Takeru is probably not representative of his (rice) overproducing, free-marketing, anti-Miyata peers. His love for the village is undying, and at least at that time was disconnected from the political arena. This is not the case for the more pragmatic Nobuhiro Machida. When asked about the solar races in 1997, he said:

> Well, I think Ogata-mura's image has improved quite a bit, but there's no economic benefit at all for the residents. The village's image has gotten better, but it's absolutely the opposite situation, you know. They sell bonds and it creates a big burden for the villagers. So, as far as doing all that goes, if you want to know if that's a plus for the individual villagers, there's no plus at all. But, I'd say that it does raise the village's external image. That's fine, you know, to do that in various ways. So, from the old *yami-gome* and other problems, that dark image has turned around and become a good image for Ogata-mura. But, on the other hand, the villagers' problems have multiplied, to put it bluntly.

Not surprisingly, his wife Takako was of the same sentiment, and both were also opposed to the *bunkajin* project and the Nanohana Festival. But Nobuhiro was never emotional in his condemnation of the mayor's PR efforts—he faithfully adhered to the Japanese ideal concept of *shikata-ga-nai* ("oh, well—it can't be helped") fatalism in his take on the issue. This is not the case for Isao Satake, who was as emotional in his criticism of the amount of money spent on the solar events as Takeru Isono was in his support of the races at the same time. In 1997 Isao said:

> Simply as "events" they're alright, but they don't do anything for the village. There's no economic benefit, either. Also, villagers can't really participate much. The Nanohana Festival, too—they do that just at the busiest time of the year for us. That's why villagers don't think too much of these things—the Nanohana Festival and the solar events and such. Who are they doing it for? The mayor probably thinks they're doing it for the young people—for the future of Ogata-mura.

Isao's wife, Hiroko, was less strongly opposed to the events in 1997, but she wished the races had not been moved out to the special track, with its starting line at the southern edge of the village land. She said:

> The first year, the solar car race started over behind the community center. From there, they drove around the village on the public streets. The villagers and the race participants could at least rub shoulders and communicate a bit then, but now there's that new course way out there. There's no more of that [closeness] any more.

Isao was strongly opposed to the *bunkajin* project, but Hiroko, being more interested than her husband in general social activities within the village and in having more interactions with nonfarmers, felt that the *bunkajin* project might benefit her and her peers somehow, and so she was not too eager to pass judgment on it.

The tension over these issues in the small community in the latter half of the 1990s even permeated the village schools. In September of 1996, on the Monday after votes had been cast and the results announced, I was working as the assistant English teacher in the middle school. During the morning meeting, it was declared by the assistant principal that no mention of the election results was to be made in front of the students for fear that doing so might increase tensions between them—not so much because of the narrow margin by which the incumbent mayor had won, but because several compliant settlers (and strong Miyata supporters) had surprisingly lost their positions on the village council to members of the opposition party—one of them to the son of a settler and Dōyūkai founder who had a son of his own in the school. Former students generally deny that there was any trouble between them based on their families' respective actions or political beliefs during the 1970s or 1980s, but by 1996 the gap between anti-Miyata and pro-Miyata farmers had grown very wide due to the big-spending issue, and many of the former were becoming quite upset over it. The impact of this on the students was made clear to me when the questionnaires I administered to them in 1997 revealed some very strong anti-Miyata comments. In response to the question, "What do you dislike most about this village?", one girl wrote, "I hate the way the mayor spends so much money on useless projects and events that have nothing to do with agriculture. It's stupid." Another girl penned a similar remark. The general consensus among the teachers was that the children had merely absorbed these ideas from their parents—certainly correct. The most interesting aspect of this episode was not so much the comments themselves but the reaction of the teacher responsible for the class from which they came. He was visibly nervous, and was so concerned about sparking a political backlash that he implored me to keep the comments private. I assured him that I would do so at least until the mayor changed. The results of the 1996 election did send shock waves through the village, but this was nothing compared to what happened four years later.

The Election of 2000

Shortly after Miyata won for the fourth time in 1988, a settler named Sadayoshi Miyazaki, a major figure in village politics who was content to remain mostly in the background until he became head of the agricultural cooperative in 2001, began thinking seriously about how to change the political situation. Miyazaki already had strong ties to the leaders of the Dōyūkai and Nōyū, and also to Tōru

Wakui of the Akita Komachi Corporation. In fact, he was largely responsible for Wakui's two political campaigns against the incumbent Mayor Miyata. In the months leading up to the election of 2000, Miyazaki decided that it might not be very good for the CEO of the second-largest rice-marketing corporation in the village to be mayor. One reason for this was because of the obvious potential for conflicts of interest. There was also concern that the corporation might stumble if its leader was too busy trying to run the village. Furthermore, there was the likelihood that if a person as closely tied to the political quarrels of the past as Wakui—especially someone so strongly aligned with one specific side—were to become mayor, the gap between the two opposing political camps would be widened. Given this situation, "Where," wondered Miyazaki, "are we going to find a candidate who might both defeat the mayor and help unite the two sides?" Suddenly, then, everything changed. Miyata surprised the public by announcing in March of 2000 that he would not seek reelection.[2]

Miyazaki moved quickly. He collaborated with Wakui and the presidents of the Dōyūkai and Nōyū in building a strategy to take advantage of the situation and finally prop up an opposition candidate who could win. They decided that a woman would be the best choice. A female candidate, they reasoned, would have a good shot at garnering support from women in general, and would also be more likely to attract the attention of compliant farmers who wanted a break from old quarrels, in addition to winning the votes of noncompliant farmers. They decided to ask Kita Kurose, whose husband—fifth-wave settler Tadashi Kurose—had led the resistant farmers during the 1980s. Mrs. Kurose, born in Beijing during the Japanese occupation of China, had already been a strong leader among women in the village for some time. She had also held leadership roles in her home prefecture of Shiga before migrating to Ogata-mura with her husband. Kurose eventually agreed to enter the race, but suggested that it would be easier for her to manage the job should she prevail if the members of the village council were not all male. Miyazaki and his associates were then faced with two tasks—making certain that Kurose would be the next mayor of the village, and finding and supporting a woman candidate for the village council. How they succeeded in their second task is an interesting story, and it illustrates very clearly the ways in which the original social arrangements of Ogata-mura (based on places of origin and cooperative farming groups) and later ties (stemming from political differences regarding agriculture, farm life, marketing, and the identity of Ogata-mura) conflict with each other when the time comes to cast votes.

Wakui became the official primary sponsor of Kurose's campaign, and he and the others began their search. They eventually found their candidate among a group of women who had started a biodegradable, "all-natural" soap and household detergent manufacturing association in 1989—a group that had originally banded together to help defeat Mayor Miyata's proposed golf course. They had

Figure 5.1: A party at the community center (*kōminkan*) attended by members of the English conversation class in 1997. Yukiko Kusakabe sits at the far right. Five of the other women were also married to farmers. The other two were married to men who worked for the prefectural junior college, but they no longer live in the village today.

always had a hard time obtaining any real recognition or financial support from Miyata's administration, and of course they were all from opposition households, which probably explains the lack of interest in their environmental endeavors on the part of the village government. Therefore, each was considered a good potential candidate for a seat on the village council by Miyazaki and the other noncompliant leaders. Unfortunately, all of the women had excuses for not getting too involved in community politics—all but one, that is.

Yukiko Kusakabe (see Figure 5.1) is not only the wife of a fifth-wave settler, but also the eldest daughter of Takeru Isono of Essa Farm, a third-wave settler from Niigata (see Figure 2.5).

When Takeru finished his training period in late 1969 and was joined by his family in the village, Yukiko was already in junior high school, so she finished her compulsory education in Ogata-mura. Therefore, she is one of the few children of settlers who can remember very well how life was before coming to the village, and so shares with them a lingering nostalgic attachment to the former homeland. One day in early spring of 1974—during the fifth-wave settlers' training period—Takeru was asked if anyone from his household could lend a hand in the annual task of preparing polytunnel greenhouses to hold rice seedlings by Rokunosuke Fukui, the second-wave settler whose migration to Ogata-mura had inspired Takeru to move there in the first place. Fukui had asked Takeru for help because both were from Niigata, and so they met up from time to time when the members of the Niigata Prefecture association assembled. Takeru sent his eldest daughter, Yukiko, to help Fukui that day. At the same time, Fukui also asked a young settler from the fifth wave to help him. Hiroshi Kusakabe had come to Ogata-mura from Tochigi Prefecture, but the fact that his father was originally from Niigata made an instant link between the young unmarried settler and Fukui and other members of the Niigata association. Hiroshi's father, who later joined his son in Ogata-mura, had been born into a Niigata farming family but was too far down in the pecking order to inherit any property, so he went to Manchuria during the occupation. Upon the surrender of the Japanese forces, he was taken to Siberia to labor. During his exile he contracted pneumonia, which probably saved his life because a nurse in the hospital there took pity on him and arranged to have him sent home. Upon returning to his homeland, he found an opportunity to buy some property in Tochigi, so he resettled there only to find that he had purchased fields high in the mountains—not an uncommon story. Fortunately, his quest for a good farm ended with his eldest son's acceptance to the Hachirōgata settlement program. It was thought that Yukiko Isono and Hiroshi Kusakabe might make a nice match, so eventually an official meeting (*omiai*) was arranged and the two were wed. Connections to the homeland run deep.

In the summer of 2000, Rokunosuke Fukui collaborated with Miyazaki in trying to get Yukiko Kusakabe to enter the race. They called her father, Takeru Isono, to Fukui's house and ran the idea past him. Once they had him on their side, they went to Yukiko herself. They also asked President Kawabuchi of Nōyū to speak to her personally and assure her of the company's support (her husband is a founding member). Shocked, she tried to say no, but the activist in her was unable to refuse, and she came to see the situation as a prime opportunity to help make changes for the better in her adopted community. She agreed to enter the race, and Wakui had his candidate to run alongside Mrs. Kurose.[3] Yukiko received most of her initial backing and support from the members of her soap-making group—two of the three necessary campaign positions were filled by them—and also from other Nōyū families.

Yukiko Kusakabe was the first female candidate for a position on the village council, which made the 2000 election all the more interesting, but there were also two other young candidates who had been brought to the village by their parents. One of them was Hiroto Takahashi, the son of a second-wave settler who has always been loyal to Mayor Miyata and the Country Elevator, and who also once served as CEO of the company.[4] Takahashi—not belonging to any of the smaller, definable marketing associations—received his support, as well as the initial nomination, from other young users of the Country Elevator in his neighborhood. The other young candidate, who had already agreed to enter the race that year, was Yutaka Nitahara, the son of a first-wave settler and member of the Dōyūkai—the membership of which had originally selected him as their candidate for the election. Nitahara was certain to receive votes from all households in the Dōyūkai, as well as others from noncompliant first-wave settler households and from many former schoolmates in the village, which made him a virtual shoo-in for a seat on the council. Yukiko Kusakabe's success, however, was far from certain. Although about ninety votes from Nōyū households were essentially guaranteed, she still needed to garner at least another forty in order to win a seat. She looked to some members of her neighborhood and the other households belonging to her husband's former cooperative farming group, but these could not all be counted on because differences over rice marketing supersede older alliances. A good possible source for extra votes was, in fact, the Dōyūkai since her father is a founding member. This meant that some Dōyūkai voters might have had to decide whether to support her or their own candidate, Yutaka Nitahara. The situation was further complicated by the fact that Yukiko's brother and Nitahara were both serving as officials of the Dōyūkai at the time of the election, meaning that they worked closely together nearly every day. The ambiguous vote-splitting matter caused some tension between Yukiko and her brother, and was giving the Dōyūkai president a real headache. The situation was solved, however, one night on a bus. Mr. Sugisawa, the Dōyūkai president, happened to be returning to the village from a wedding reception in Akita City when the Niigata association head, Rokunosuke Fukui—also a passenger on the bus and a guest at the wedding—moved into the seat next to him. "How's it going with that vote-allocation matter?" Fukui asked the president. "Oh," replied the tired business leader, "it's driving me crazy. I don't know what to do about this." "I have an idea," ventured Fukui. "Why don't you just suggest to all Dōyūkai households that the older couples—the founders—cast their votes for Takeru Isono's daughter and that the younger couples back Yutaka Nitahara? That way, Mr. Nitahara's son will still be assured of victory and Mr. Isono's daughter will get the support she needs, too." The suggestion worked, and Sugisawa's headache disappeared.[5] However, there was also the issue of Essa Farm—Takeru Isono's old cooperative farming group. Of the six households in Essa Farm, two others are also Dōyūkai founding members (Figure 5.2). Isono had long been close to these two settlers, so votes from their households were secured. He and his wife, therefore, made a point of visiting the other three and asking for support for their daughter even though she had married out years before.

The Nakada family across the street marketed their rice on their own, so gaining their votes seemed possible, and although Mr. Itō down the street still used the Country Elevator at least to a degree, the fact that he also sold some rice to Wakui's company meant that there was a chance of Kusakabe's getting at least a vote or two from his household. The one household that could not be counted

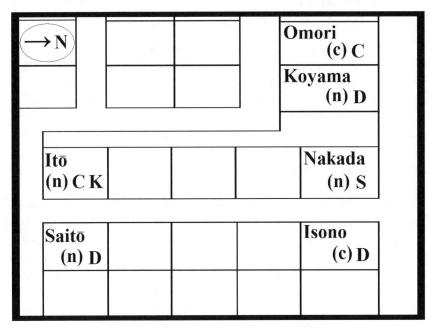

Figure 5.2: Households of Essa Farm (Rice marketing: C = Country Elevator, D = Doyukai, S = self or independent, K = Akita Komachi Corporation; House type: n = new, c = composite or integrated).

on, despite both the Niigata and cooperative group connections, was the Omori household. Mr. Omori, formerly the principal of the village kindergarten, not only has been loyal to the Country Elevator and Mayor Miyata since the beginning, but also is an alumnus of Tokyo Agricultural University, as is the much younger Hiroto Takahashi—a compliant candidate for the village council. These factors negated any possibility of netting his support for his fellow group member's daughter (even though he had taught Takeru to ski years earlier). Connections to the homeland do run deep, but they cannot compete with contemporary political concerns.

In the end, all three young candidates won places in the village government— Yukiko Kusakabe became the first female council member with 188 votes (only 130 had been needed), and Kita Kurose the first female mayor. Despite the fact that all went well for both Yutaka Nitahara and Yukiko Kusakabe, some tensions over the affair lingered between the latter and her brother, for when I told her that I would like to discuss the election with her brother, she asked me not to mention the matter to him at all—even eighteen months after the announcement of the results. Company ties, economic ties, and political ties form a tangled web to top off the comparatively simple familial and cooperative group relations that comprised the original social structure of the village.

Developments following the Election of 2000

The 2000 election resulted in a number of firsts. For the first time, a noncompliant farmer became mayor, a woman became mayor, a woman was elected to the village council, and the opposition party finally succeeded in balancing out the composition of the council itself—although still outnumbered, noncompliant members amounted to six while another eight still remained loyal to the Country Elevator. In the past, the mayor always hand-picked the assistant mayor (*joyaku*), but after Kurose's election it was decided that an official from the Akita Prefecture government would assume the position in order to increase the village's ties with the regional administration and to attempt to ease bad feelings among the formerly dominant compliant faction.[6] The new assistant mayor soon began initiating changes that may have had exactly that result. For example, from April of 2002 the village government—entrenched far too deeply and far too long in factional politics—made efforts to further separate itself from agricultural matters and concentrate instead on community and social needs. Local agricultural policy, support, and guidance since that point have fallen much more under the auspices of the Ogata-mura JA (the agricultural cooperative), headed by Sadayoshi Miyazaki at the time. It was hoped that this would help increase the feeling among the losers of the 2000 election—the compliant farmers—that the village government was everyone's government. This was not, it should be stressed again, the way opposition farmers had felt over the past twenty years. Not long after her election, while having lunch with Yukiko Kusakabe and me at the hotel, Mayor Kurose remarked with a frown that under her predecessor's administration noncompliant residents who tried to get support from the village on any kind of initiative nearly always received the same response: "No." Yukiko agreed; her soap-making group was not the only such association that had failed to obtain any official help or recognition. Mayor Kurose, on the other hand, made many efforts to support more grassroots movements in the village while in office. All the same, however, members of the compliant faction remained bitter after the sea change of 2000. One older woman remarked:

> Oh, the new mayor? I'm not impressed. When I saw her I thought she was just another "regular mother" (*futsū no okāsan*). I don't see what good she can do. You know, it seems like we should have done what the new mayor and all the others did, too—we should have gone out and sold illegal rice and all that. We lost in the end, anyway.

The actual workings of the government and the handling of the major issues can be easily seen by checking the pages of the quarterly newsletter that the council office publishes. One of the major issues following the 2000 election was how to help village families that were deeply in debt to the local agricultural cooperative—somewhere between sixty and eighty households. It was generally agreed that the worst cases were people who followed crop reduction programs, neglected to increase the size of their farms, and remained loyal to the Country Elevator. However, the situation is not really so simple: some farmers have over-extended themselves by counting on high rice prices while taking out loans for investing in venture businesses, for buying rental property in residential centers like Akita City, or simply for rebuilding their own houses. Many others have successfully done these things, but some have made bad judgments concerning timing, amounts, and types of investment.

Changes Made to the Projects of the Miyata Administration

After assuming office, Mayor Kurose set about altering the projects of the Miyata administration that she was able to change. The hotel required no major adjustments, for it was already showing promise as a business venture, and proving itself useful to villagers. The biggest change was the expansion of products sold in the shop near the front counter. The land reclamation museum, a major point of contention for Kurose and her supporters, proved to be essentially untouchable—little could be done besides shaving a bit off of its operating budget. (Some changes came later, however, as noted in chapter 3). The projects that the new mayor and council were able to alter soon were the solar and electric vehicle races, the *bunkajin* project, and the Nanohana Festival.

Mayor Kurose took action on the solar sports early. Under Mayor Miyata, the village office had been quite proud of having the only solar division—a small bureau within the village administration—in the country. No other municipal office had such a special unit, with a head and full-time staff. However, as a public venture it had long been seen as frivolous by the opposition camp. Mayor Kurose was quick to disband the solar division. However, the electric and solar vehicle races could not simply be canceled—some kind of organization was needed to handle them. Therefore, the village office helped establish an NGO, Clean Energy Alliance, charged with managing the events. The NGO came to be headed by Tsutomu Tani, who was the final *joyaku* under Mayor Miyata. Miyata serves as an honorary member of the NGO, and Hisahiro Yamamoto, the hair stylist who brought the solar race idea to the village in the first place, has also been deeply involved. Clean Energy Alliance is located inside the central village area, occupying some office space inside the villagers' center (*son-min sentā*), where funerals are usually held today. This office space was donated to the NGO by the village, but it is not very involved in the organization's operations now. Whereas the solar and electric races were staffed by village employees who were required to work the events when Miyata was mayor, today they are staffed by whomever Clean

Energy Alliance can mobilize as volunteers. So far this seems to have worked well enough. The main problem for the events is that the money all but dried up, for not only has the village backed out of supporting them, but Akita Prefecture has done so as well. Funding for the races has thus been low since 2000, and this is reflected in a lack of special financial help for foreign teams. Consequently, they rarely enter the events today—especially the car races. The scale of the events has also shrunk. In their heyday the solar car races attracted over about eighty teams and the bicycle races in excess of one hundred. Today these numbers are much lower—down by roughly half. On the surface, this might seem bad for the events, but being run by people who really want to see them succeed, and being staffed by people who truly want to be involved, is probably better. Furthermore, they are no longer a direct drag on the village's resources, and so are basically removed from the political environment. The only sticking point is the maintenance of the race track—this still costs the village quite a lot each year, but this would have to be done anyway lest the administration be accused of wasting a major resource. Many, though, wish that the track had never been built. Also, the majority of the opposition-party village residents do not actually view the solar events and other races as having changed fundamentally.

As for the *bunkajin* project, Mayor Kurose had long been opposed to this by the time she took office. Some new delegates on the village council wanted to end it completely due to the expense. Kurose initially expressed similar feelings, but she also had to be sure that the people who had been accepted under the program would be taken care of and could still feel comfortable in the community. In the end, the village did not scrap the project, but it stopped using the problematic *bunkajin* label and instead began referring to the special settlers by their official title (which had actually existed all along)—Ogata-mura Transmitters of Information (Ogata-mura Jōhō Hasshin-sha)—and also stopped offering monthly payments for new applicants. Despite this, though, some appeared in the mid-2000s and several were accepted, including the younger brother of a former principal of the village junior high school, whom I knew in 1995–1996 when I taught English there. This new member of the community has proven to be quite sociable and resides in the village most of the time. He maintains a website featuring information about the village and interviews with settlers, and at the time of this writing is involved in compiling a comprehensive history of the community. In 2008 there were nine houses in the special neighborhood. Relations between the residents were still rather thin, but there was hope for greater activity and personal interaction because of the decision to admit more people. To be sure, the situation with the program is far better now than I predicted it would be in 1999. Changes to the Nanohana Festival have been fairly minor. It still occurs each year in May, but the scale has been cut. Particularly expensive attractions, such as professional models flown in by helicopter and high-priced musical acts, are no more. Also, the village's *nanohana* fields have decreased in size due to the building of an assisted-living facility for elderly people (*rōjin hōmu*).

Education, rebuilding the village schools, completing the assisted-living facility, supporting local agricultural improvements, protecting the Country Elevator Corporation from insolvency, cleaning up the water in the Hachirōgata reservoir, improving the quality of the drinking water, and general environmental concerns were among the major issues being addressed in the first few years of Mayor Kurose's tenure. Where an assembly member stands politically has always determined how he or she votes on these issues—for example, a noncompliant member will be less likely to push for funneling money into the Country Elevator and more likely to focus on improving the water or rebuilding the schools (something that began in 2010). Different residents have different ideas about which would be more important in the long run.

Ogata-mura Decides to Go It Alone

One of the biggest issues that came up during Mayor Kurose's first term in office was the question of whether to merge with the neighboring city of Oga, covering the entire peninsula of the same name, just to the west of the village. The great municipality merger of the Heisei era (*Heisei no dai gappei*), which began in the year 2000, sought to reduce the number of cities, towns, and villages across the nation even more than had been accomplished during the successive postwar amalgamations of the Shōwa era. As mentioned in chapter 1, the number of municipalities in the nation was drastically reduced during the first decade of this century—to only about 1,900 as of March 2006, fewer than 200 of which were villages (in 1945 there were over 8,500 villages). Under the merger plan, cities, towns, and villages of the nation have been encouraged by their respective prefectural governments to open merger discussion councils (*gappei kyōgikai*), comprised of local elected officials and representative residents. The recommendations of these councils are to be taken into consideration in official deliberations over mergers. By late 2002 early discussions between Oga, Ogata-mura, and the small town of Wakami-machi, which was sandwiched between the two, were underway. It seemed clear from the start that Wakami would become a part of Oga. Meetings were held, but it would have gone against Mayor Kurose's style to decide either way without knowing how village residents actually felt, so in November of 2003 a referendum on the issue was held in Ogata-mura. In the end, 62 percent voted against merging, so the village broke off discussions with its neighbors and declared that it would remain independent. Today it is one of only three villages in Akita Prefecture, all of which owe over one million yen per capita.

Preserving the village's name and identity was a big reason for most residents who voted against merging to do so. If Ogata-mura had joined with Oga, its name might have vanished completely. At the very least "Ogata" would have become a mere label for the area, subservient to the city name of Oga (although they appear similar in roman letters, there is no relation between the names of the village and the city). Also, many residents were unwilling to let their village become a subdivision or distant residential area of Oga. There was also the question of the merit of merging with a city like Oga that has a lot of territory to manage with few resources other than fishing and tourism, which are not exactly booming (see Matanle et al. 2011: ch. 9). When it comes down to it, Ogata-mura has it all over its more populous neighbor in terms of arable land and per capita income. Even tourism is at least as lucrative in Ogata-mura, despite the excellent scenery that the peninsula affords, because the village is compact and has a high degree of coordination between its constituent elements. However, even many who voted against the merger realized that it may have to occur in some form in the future, especially considering the shrinking rice market and falling rice subsidies and prices. The mayor, who was personally opposed to merging with Oga, conceded this as well. In fact, most village residents do recognize that the village would probably be able to receive special consideration in its debt repayments and get greater tax grants if it were to merge with another municipality. Villagers who voted against the merger either hoped to simply avoid it as long as possible while the young village's still shallow sense of identity deepened, or were holding out for a more attractive option to present itself—such as joining Akita City. Given current trends, it is not too big a stretch to speculate on an eventual division of the entire prefecture into north, central, and southern sections. Becoming part of a greater northern county would probably please—and benefit—villagers more than joining Oga could have done.

The Election of 2004

In the summer of 2004, Ogata-mura residents went back to the polls to decide whether Mayor Kurose would be granted a second term in office. Tōru Wakui again served as her official sponsor. In order to run against the incumbent mayor, Hiroto Takahashi, the son and successor of a second-wave settler who once served as CEO of the Country Elevator, vacated his seat on the village council, which he had won in 2000. Being a member of the second generation—brought to the village as a child by his parents—Takahashi was not personally involved in the original political divide that opened up between settlers over compliance with or defiance of national rice policy. However, he was no stranger to the village political scene when he announced his candidacy. In addition to having served on the village assembly for four years, he had also sat on various committees, including that of the land reclamation museum, the Farm Improvement Committee, and the village Young Farmers' International Exchange Council. Takahashi had also long been a major figure among his generation of settlers' successors (*kōkeisha*). Having spent two years in the United States in a young farmers' exchange program after graduating from Tokyo Agricultural University in 1983, his English is also quite good. In addition, in 1990 he spent several months in an agricultural study program in Brazil, from where his (ethnically Japanese) wife hails. By all accounts, Takahashi was a qualified and formidable candidate.

On the one hand, the 2004 election was largely a battle between the same two sides that had fought it out over the mayor's chair in all of the previous elections. Mayor Kurose was backed by Wakui and Miyazaki, and the pro-free-market (opposition) settlers that had backed her before, and Takahashi received his support from the remnants of the political machine that Seiki Miyata had built, wounded by its defeat in 2000 yet still very much alive and kicking. The head of the village council at the time, a compliant settler, had also held that position during the last term of Mayor Miyata, and he emerged as a main supporter of Takahashi, as did Tsutomu Tani, who had been the last assistant mayor under Miyata and who later took over the NGO that supports the solar and electric vehicle races in the village. Yet on the other hand the election of 2004 deviated substantially from anything that had come before, for despite the similarity to prior elections in the official backing of each candidate, the platforms and composure of their broadest support bases were actually quite different. Takahashi's platform was titled "Open the Possibilities of Ogata-mura." The word *open* was written with the same Chinese pictograph that is used for the verb *reclaim*, as in land reclamation, an obvious allusion to the origins of the village itself and the hopes and dreams that the original settlers brought with them. It was an attempt at a restart of the village in the hands of the second generation, and a reevaluation of the village's identity. To opposition farmers, it represented yet another attempt to highjack the village's history and redefine Ogata-mura primarily according to the terms of the overthrown former administration—or "Miyata Light." The platform basically comprised a blend of reconsideration of the accomplishments of the Miyata administration (which Mayor Kurose and her supporters had downgraded as much as they could) and new plans for social, educational, and financial investments, with a distinctively youth-oriented angle. But the most prominent aspect of Takahashi's manifesto was a call to reconsider merging with another municipality, if not Oga. It was a progressive challenge that he could publicly make, and one that helped differentiate his platform from that of the incumbent mayor, because she herself had turned down the merger the year before (based, of course, on the wishes of the majority). Takahashi's most noticeable backers were in fact seniors of the formerly dominant compliant faction, but he had received his original support for a seat on the assembly from other young farmers of the second generation in the election of 2000, and it is clear that he garnered many votes from farmers of his generation in that election and in 2004 as well.

In contrast to the Takahashi campaign, Mayor Kurose's platform concentrated on her various accomplishments. For example, it was noted that she had increased public support for several village associations for the elderly, that she had extended the operational hours of the village nursery school, which now closed at 6 p.m. (at the request of many young farming mothers), that she had whittled down the scale of the Nanohana Festival begun by Mayor Miyata as she was asked to do by many village farmers who disliked having the community's streets clogged by the cars of incoming tourists just at the peak of planting time, and also that she had increased the number of days when rice is served for lunch in the public schools at the expense of bread days. In addition, her success at trimming the municipality's budget by streamlining the staff and absolving the village from running the solar and electric vehicle races was noted. After Kurose took office, it became generally known that the village was more deeply in debt than had been suspected, and she was rather successful at setting Ogata-mura on course for fiscal improvement. In 2004 it was made clear that the village was in fact 169 million yen above the red line, and that its tax base amounted to 874 million yen, up 21.6 percent from the previous year. But, at the time Ogata-mura still owed 3.5 billion yen to the national government and on stocks and bonds issued in the past. Mayor Kurose had been chipping away at this figure since taking office in 2000.

However, the most prominent claim of the mayor's platform for her 2004 campaign was that she had succeeded in making the governing of the village into a much more participatory and transparent process, freely sharing her time with residents of any political persuasion and allowing them to cast their votes for or against propositions such as merging with other municipalities—something that her predecessor never did. Indeed, Mayor Kurose always kept her office door open for visitors and remained very accessible. As for her support, the mayor's most active and vocal backers in 2004 were clearly women. Most of her campaign materials were prepared and disseminated by a group that called itself "The Association of Women Hand-in-Hand" (Te o Tsunagu Josei no Kai)—which could also be read as "The Association of United Women." In the end, Kurose was returned to the mayor's office on August 29 for another four years by a fairly narrow margin of 130 votes—she received a total of 1,251 votes to Takahashi's 1,121. Following the election, Takahashi remained very much involved in village affairs, although in an unofficial sense. He sat in on all meetings of the village assembly, he networked tirelessly, and he continued sending out regular newsletters, offering his ideas about current topics, to village households. The election of 2004 proved three things: (1) that many villagers were pleased with Mayor Kurose's work; (2) that a significant number of other villagers were ready to hand over the political reigns to the second generation; and (3) that the old factional divisions, although somewhat blurred, were still far from gone. Indeed, as the structural effects of the earlier social arrangements of the village gradually fade, relations and political positions become more complex.

A Fracture Forms in the Opposition Party

Unfortunately for Mayor Kurose and the faction of disobedient (opposition) farmers who helped get her elected, a deep fissure began to develop between the mayor and her strongest supporter, Tōru Wakui of the Akita Komachi Corporation, not long after her initial election. In 2002, Wakui and seven other village farmers banded together to form a new corporation, Organic Farm Ogata. They then drew up a plan under which the new company would purchase from the Akita Prefecture government a large parcel of land on the southern side of the reclaimed land area (within the polder dam) that was originally part of an experimental farm, and use the land to grow soy beans—and not rice—organically. This land had been left unused after the settlement program was cut short in the mid-1970s. Wakui and his colleagues knew that a proposal to use the land for growing rice would have stood no chance of acceptance. With their organic soybean plan, they applied for *nintei* accreditation for the company, and also of course for each man since they owned the company jointly. This was granted by the village. After receiving the status, Organic Farm Ogata, with Wakui acting as sole representative, presented its plan to the national government and requested a Super L loan from the AFC (the Agriculture, Forestry, and Fisheries Finance Corporation) for 1.26 billion yen, which was also granted. The money was used to purchase a 148 hectare area of the aforementioned land from the prefecture—a transaction that was completed in April of 2003. All would have gone well had the eight men actually produced organic soybeans as promised. However, Organic Farm Ogata was found to have diverted the land to wet rice fields and to have already begun rice production (*kakōmai*) in early 2005.

Many people both inside and outside of the village were incensed. Of course, Ogata-mura farmers who had always obeyed the government (and who never agreed with or admired Wakui in the first place) were especially angry, since the entire village is basically held responsible for such problems by public officials. Even many opposition party members, who had always sided with Wakui politically, were very unhappy. More than a few of these settlers accused Wakui of planning to plant rice from the beginning, charging that the fields were already being prepared for the grains. "Sure," they said, "everyone knew they were getting ready to plant rice on those fields from the start. It was obvious." Even those of Wakui's political faction who served on the village council at the time were very displeased, as was the mayor herself. Most perturbed, though, were the officials of the national and the Akita Prefecture governments, who wanted to see rice production decrease and not increase, and the fact that the prefecture had allowed the land to be used in such a way did not help matters. With the Tokyo politicians and bureaucrats breathing fire down the backs of their Akita counterparts, the Akita Prefecture assembly members took no time in deciding that the village needed to rescind the *nintei* accreditation of Organic Farm Ogata. This, of course, put the mayor in a difficult position, for Wakui was her strongest supporter and was directly responsible for her being elected mayor in the first place. Although the village council at this time was filled mostly by settlers of the opposition party who had always been on Wakui's side politically, it was overwhelmingly against him on this matter—by the autumn of 2005 the council had produced a strictly worded resolution condemning Organic Farm Ogata for its behavior, and calling on the village to take away the company's *nintei* status. This was soon done. Consequently, Organic Farm Ogata faced the daunting task of returning the borrowed money, for the original long-term payback plan had become null and void since the special status had been lost. However, because legal provisions for handling such a situation did not exist, there was no agreement on exactly when the money had to be repaid.

Finally, as if the entire situation was not bad enough, it got worse when Organic Farm Ogata filed a lawsuit against the village in early 2006, arguing that the municipal office had treated it too harshly by taking away its status and subjecting it to possible bankruptcy because of the ensuing need to return the borrowed money early. As a new crop of rice seedlings were poking their tops above the water line in Organic Farm Ogata's 148 hectares of paddies the following spring, the plaintiffs and the defendants were still awaiting the start of the trial, and the power base of the opposition faction remained damaged. Yet many of Mayor Kurose's supporters stuck with her, feeling certain that she would be able to win again in 2008 even without Wakui's support. They charged Wakui and Miyazaki of having supported Mayor Kurose's election in the first place with the hope of manipulating her—using her like a marionette. At any rate, most villagers merely scoffed at the idea of Organic Farm Ogata suing the village, sure that the company had no legal ground on which to stand. Furthermore, there was speculation that Wakui had filed the lawsuit simply to delay having to pay the government back for the loan—perhaps to buy time to prepare money. In late 2007 the trial began at the district court in Akita City, and Wakui got his chance to plead his case. The hearings dragged on into the first half of 2008, as the village was gearing up to decide who would serve as mayor for the next four years. In the end, the Akita district court ruled against Wakui and his seven associates on August 28—the very same month as the village's elections—citing their early shift from soybeans to *kakōmai*, and continued production of rice, as evidence that they had intended to do this from the beginning (Akita Sakigake Shinpō 2008b). Wakui expressed agreement with the ruling, calling it "expected," and indicated that he would not subject the village to greater publicity or suffering over the matter by appealing the verdict. Both Wakui and the village administration gave vague remarks to the press about the possibility of reaching some kind of agreement on how to handle the situation from that point, and the problem quietly faded away.

Tensions between the Village Government and the Agricultural Cooperative

Just when the tension between Organic Farm Ogata and the village government was at its peak, Ogata-mura residents were surprised when the head of the agricultural cooperative, Sadayoshi Miyazaki, suddenly announced in June of 2006 that the JA (Figure 5.3) had conceived a plan to open a convenience store in the village and that the store would sell fresh vegetables grown by villagers. First of all, Ogata-mura is quite unusual in that it is one of the few municipalities in the country with no convenience store. This was one reason for wanting to open such a franchise. But the main cause of the JA's hastiness was the impending "Wakasugi" National Athletic Meet, due to be held in Akita Prefecture in September and October of 2007. The JA wanted to have a convenience store completed by then since the boat races were scheduled to be held in Ogata-mura—on the remaining water of the Hachirōgata reservoir.

In response to Miyazaki's surprise announcement, the grandmothers who had for years been selling their products in the village's direct marketing center

Figure 5.3: The Ogata-mura JA.

immediately cried foul. Along with many others, they argued that a new convenience store would be in competition with the direct marketing center, and that this would be bad for everyone. Furthermore, many of the JA's roughly one thousand members feared that their cooperative would suffer economically by embarking on such a venture, especially since it had been in bad fiscal shape when Miyazaki took over its management shortly after the election of 2000.[7] Considering this history in addition to the falling rice prices, a significant number of village residents were unwilling to welcome the appearance of a JA convenience store in 2006.

While public opposition to the plan was apparent from the start, this was not the only problem. The JA wanted to acquire a large plot of village-owned property on the highway running north–south along the western edge of the settlement for building its proposed store. Currently the home of the village's Tourism and Product Support Promotion Corporation (Ogata-mura Kankō Bussan Shinkō Kōsha), a public entity owned by the village itself, this corner lot sits across the street from the JA's gasoline station and next door to the land reclamation museum and its connected direct marketing center. The four-way intersection sports one of the few sets of traffic lights in the village, so vehicles passing through often have to stop there anyway, making the spot one of the best possible locations in the village for a convenience store. Also, the Akita Komachi Corporation is located only several hundred meters to the north along the same highway. The problem for the JA was that the village proved unwilling to rent or sell the land to the JA for its proposed retail enterprise. A meeting of the village assembly confirmed this.

It seems that the leadership of the Ogata JA miscalculated the feelings of the villagers in making its plan. Whereas some opposition to the convenience store idea had been expected, it was thought that allowing locals to sell vegetables in the proposed store would help placate villagers and garner enough support to allow the plan to pass. Instead, however, things went the other way. A struggle was already emerging by the end of 2006, and this caught the attention of the local media. A series of articles appearing in the pages of the *Akita Sakigake* newspaper brought the story to the residents of the prefecture as it unfolded over the first half of 2007. It was decided in January of that year that the JA would distribute questionnaires to about three thousand concerned people and check the results before moving forward—an unusual move considering the number of individuals involved. Adult members of the JA (mostly resident farmers of Ogata-mura), high-school-aged and older dependents of settlers, and people working in the village but living elsewhere were all to receive questionnaire forms. In the end, the nine hundred or so JA members who responded were split almost evenly over the plan. Young people who were not members of the JA were largely supportive, while those who were not residents of the village were overwhelmingly so. After the results were announced, however, unhappy JA members pointed to a problem regarding the wording of the questions. Instead of asking respondents how they felt about the *JA* opening a convenience store, the questionnaire simply asked how the respondents felt about having a convenience store in the village. Of course, most residents would like to have a convenience store—they just did not want the JA to fund it. Therefore, opponents argued that the numerical support for the JA's plan would have been lower if the most important question on the form had been more specific.

In an attempt to stop the JA, opposing residents banded together and held a meeting at the village hotel in early March of 2007. The mayor, ten of the twelve village council members, and about three hundred other people attended. At least one opponent of the JA's plan publicly voiced concern about connections between Tōru Wakui of the Akita Komachi Corporation and the problem-laden Organic Farm Ogata, and Miyazaki, head of the JA. In addition, the fact that Wakui had held a high-level executive position in the JA since Miyazaki took over the headship had long worried much of the JA's membership. Collusion between the two men was suspected by many, especially since the Organic Farm Ogata fiasco had brought new shame upon the village. At the meeting, a public advocate from Fukushima Prefecture with much experience on the topic lectured on the economic dangers of opening a convenience store without careful planning. He stressed that there were quite a few public bodies, corporations, and individuals currently facing bankruptcy due to their opening a convenience store, and supposed that it would be difficult for the Ogata-mura JA to improve its financial situation through such an undertaking.

By the end of 2007 the JA had given up on opening a new store, in accordance with the wishes of the majority of its members. But the sudden appearance of tension between the JA and the village government raised more than a few eyebrows in the village. Members of the pro-Miyata compliant faction began to pick up on the formation of cracks in Mayor Kurose's original support base, and ideas about who might occupy the mayor's chair following the election of 2008 were kicked around as early as late 2006. Finally, it became completely clear that Mayor Kurose would not be able to count on the support of Wakui and Miyazaki—two heavyweights in village farming—in 2008. Miyazaki remained sympathetic to Wakui, whom he recognizes as the father of entrepreneurialism in the village, all the way. In late 2006 he showed no interest in supporting Mayor Kurose again, speculating instead that the son of a settler would make the best mayor. However, he would never have thrown his weight behind Hiroto Takahashi. "Votes in Ogata-mura," he said one day while in his office, "are the same as bundles of rice, and a woman just isn't prepared to handle the business of rice." This was an analogy between a single vote (*hyō*) and a sixty kilogram bundle (a *tawara*, also pronounced *hyō*) of dried unpolished rice grains—because any vote cast in the village is tied tightly to rice, and both have the same phonetic sound although they are written with different Chinese pictographs. In early 2008, Miyazaki's position on the village's political situation—and on the reelection of Mayor Kurose—remained unchanged. The failed convenience-store plan aside, the mayor's giving in to outside pressure and rescinding Organic Farm Ogata's *nintei* status had made him too unhappy. "She should have just maintained our unity instead of doing what the prefecture asked," he said, lamenting that the issue had become so big. "There was no real need to do what she did." In other words, Miyazaki blamed the mayor for making a concession to outsiders on the surface, or in the formal arena, and allowing the conflict between the village and outsiders to invade and disrupt the in-group, where no conflict should exist, according to the model proposed by Ishida (1984: 17). However, one could just as easily blame Wakui for putting the mayor in a bad position, and for bringing new negative publicity to the village, for anybody could have guessed that the media would pounce on the story like a cat on a mouse, and that the prefectural government would be angered by Organic Farm Ogata's use of the purchased land for rice production. Wakui could be charged with creating discord among in-group members and allowing it to be seen by the outside world. And, in fact, many did charge him with this. That the village had already been through a nasty period of infighting and illegal activities made it all the worse. Of course, it is true that the mayor could have turned a blind eye to Wakui's actions, but this would have only delayed the inevitable. The news would have reached the press, or the local authorities, sooner or later—and probably sooner. Speculation aside, feelings changed, and the former opposition party cracked; "I went ahead and helped her get reelected that time, but . . .", said Miyazaki in early 2008, foreshadowing the outcome of the next mayoral poll.

The Election of 2008

On August 24, 2008, Ogata-mura residents cast ballots to determine whether Mayor Kurose would serve another four-year term or give up her position. This time, she had to deal with two opponents—it was the first three-way race for the office of mayor since 1988, when Seiki Miyata easily trounced his two adversaries for his fourth straight win. Hiroto Takahashi had announced his candidacy in April, as expected. The incumbent mayor formally entered the race about two months later, this time without the help of the two men who had been central in putting her in office in the first place—Tōru Wakui of the Akita Komachi Corporation, and Sadayoshi Miyazaki of the Ogata-mura JA. In 2006 Miyazaki had hinted that a young farmer he knew might run in the 2008 election, and this is exactly what happened. Hajime Kobayashi declared his own candidacy in July. The son of a first-wave settler related to Tarō Omori of Essa Farm, Kobayashi had served as an administrator of the JA under Miyazaki for a few years before becoming president of Mizuho. There were at least some similarities between Takahashi and Kobayashi—both were the sons and heirs of settlers, and they were not too far apart in age (the former was forty-eight years old and the latter forty-one, at the time of the election). But the similarities ended there. As had been the case in 2004, Takahashi was backed by former Miyata supporters and steadfast users of the Country Elevator Corporation, and also by various other young men of the second generation. Kobayashi entered the race with Wakui, members of the Dōyūkai, and the JA (led by Miyazaki) behind him—a significant part of the old opposition party. Although Kurose did not have the support of these men and their organizations, she still had her strong grassroots movement, centering on the core of women who had been with her all along.

Each candidate's political machine turned out flyers and other printed materials as polling day drew nearer. Takahashi stuck to his central pledges: raise the income of the farmers and improve the village's economic base through shoring up and protecting its agriculture, partly through the production of *kakōmai*. Mayor Kurose's platform was similar to that of the 2004 election—focusing on her achievements in establishing and maintaining transparency in the village government, on cutting back spending wherever possible, and on improving social programs. Kobayashi's platform stressed his youth, attempting to convince the electorate of the need for a younger, fresher mayor less involved with the old rice quarrels of the past. Kobayashi also pushed his proposition of opening up a village satellite store in Tokyo in order to sell its special products there. Although Kobayashi's political machine had significant financial backing from Wakui, the Akita Komachi Corporation head kept a low profile during the campaign. Takahashi's supporters published a small, *manga*-style booklet about his life, from the time he immigrated to the village with his parents as a small boy to the aftermath of the 2004 election, which he lost. In it, episodes in his early life, highlighting his determination to succeed at *kendō* (Japanese swordsmanship), are cast as influences on his qualities as a leader and his desire to be one. It is clearly noted that he spent time studying agriculture in the United States, and that he was strongly affected by the black market rice episodes and political divisions that formed within his adopted home village in his youth. The booklet also made it crystal clear that Takahashi, if elected, would respect the results of the 2003 referendum on merging with another municipality, in which villagers voted against such an arrangement, even though he had been for it at the time (a major difference in strategy as compared to his campaign four years earlier). In addition, the booklet capitalized on Takahashi's loss in the 2004 election, graphically depicting his disappointment, and how he quickly got back on his feet again with the help of his friends who had supported his campaign. One interesting aspect of this particular election was the absence of harsh, negative campaigning on the part of all of the candidates. Both Takahashi and Kobayashi accused Kurose of lacking vision and clear direction, and Takahashi charged her with creating a "closed community" environment (which was true in a sense, due to her austerity measures), but this was the extent of their attacks. Kurose also refrained from negative campaigning. Overall, it was a very congenial race, and not a particularly thrilling one. In truth, there was little that either of the mayor's opponents could hurl at her, and vice versa.

In the end, Takahashi's perseverance paid off. He soundly defeated both of his opponents, garnering 954 votes to the incumbent's 804 and to Kobayashi's 539.[8] Promising to fulfill his campaign promises to increase farm income and strengthen the village's finances, and also to help the community overcome the divisions stemming from the rice quarrels, Takahashi took office on September 5, the day after Kurose had walked out of the village administration building as mayor for the last time. And so, once again the village had elected a mayor loyal to the Country Elevator Corporation. Kurose's supporters grumbled and groaned, worried about a return to the "old ways"—which, Takahashi pledged, would not happen. After all, Takahashi is different from his earlier predecessor, Miyata. For one thing, he is a member of the second generation—born outside the village but very much attached to it (having no other place to call "home"). He is also not affiliated with any national political party, as was Miyata (the LDP). And, even though Takahashi's family has been firmly rooted in the pro-government (loyalist) camp, much time has passed since the *aogari* and black-market days, and in the early autumn of 2008 there was hope that he would focus on contemporary matters and not let the thorny issues of the past cloud his judgment; he had given his fellow villagers reason enough to believe this through his actions since 2004.

However, one of Takahashi's earliest acts as mayor gave members of the old non-compliant faction cause for concern. Scarcely two months after taking office, Seiki Miyata was appointed CEO of Rural Ogata, the company that manages the village's hotel. This means that Miyata is effectively in charge today of Sun Rural Ogata, regardless of who actually holds the position of general manager. In addition, the village came up with funds to make numerous improvements and small additions to the hotel after the 2008 election. More than cause for concern, actually, the combination of the appointment and these expenditures greatly disturbed many of the former mayor's adversaries.[9] In other ways, though, Takahashi has turned away from Miyata-era policies. For example, capitalizing on its "lone wolf" status—reinforced by the 2003 decision not to merge with another community—the village produced a new guidebook in November of 2010. Of course, as mayor, Takahashi is featured prominently. The guidebook brings the issue of identity to the forefront, with a cover reading "As the color changes day by day, our identity matures." The guide also stresses the importance of the village's "agricultural identity." Furthermore, adding emphasis to Takahashi's pledge to not merely return to the "old ways," the guide unveils a new development scheme—one to completely replace the Miyata administration's Rurec Plan. Dubbed the "Third Ogata-mura Active Plan," this scheme consists of three primary endeavors: (1) village improvement reflecting the identities of its residents; (2) cultivation of industries that make good use of the village's greenery and its vast amount of land; and (3) the establishment of a new system responsive to all villagers' concerns. If Takahashi wins a second term in the summer of 2012, then this plan might be deemed a success.

The Changing Political Landscape

Ogata-mura's peaceful appearance belies an astringent political environment. Observant residents of Akita Prefecture who have been around for a while accept that overproducers of rice who made a big fuss years ago and loyalist farmers who have remained obedient to the government are perpetually pitted against one another inside the village. But this is not the whole story; even the matter of who opposes whom—and vice versa—is often very murky, as are the reasons. Groups of people who are united on one issue might be divided on another. Even old rice alliances may be tested—or perhaps obliterated—by the shifting political tides as they ebb and flow with the currents of business and politics. But when the time comes to vote for a mayor or for representatives on the village council, loyalties are usually quite clear—every four years the lines in the sand are drawn again and tested, as the villagers vie over their conflicting ideas about money, rice, and the meaning of Ogata-mura.

Nevertheless, this may be starting to change. More than any other factor, Kita Kurose lost the 2008 election because the old opposition party cracked down the middle during her tenure as mayor. Rather than attempt heroic measures to save Wakui, her main supporter, she did what she had to do as the highest elected official in the village, and she did this knowing what might happen. In addition, she held her ground against Miyazaki, as well, when he attempted an unpopular move. These men's actions only added fuel to the allegations that they had put Kurose in office in order to manipulate her, but she still lost the 2008 race. This may signify the beginnings of a true change in the village's politics: a shift from a situation in which all the issues are defined by the settlers and their past actions to one in which the second generation—and perhaps soon the third—comes to define the issues, structure the agendas, and set the pace. After all, it is they who will have to steer the village in the coming years. This is clearly starting to happen; although Yukiko Kusakabe retired from politics in 2004 after serving only one term, Yutaka Nitahara went on to eventually become head of the Dōyūkai, and Hajime Kobayashi replaced Sadayoshi Miyazaki as president of the Ogata-mura JA in 2010.

Notes

1. These were the same questionnaires mentioned in chapter 3 (return rate: 111 out of 155).
2. Perhaps Miyata was concerned about the very real possibility of losing. At the time, he was said to be considering getting into regional politics beyond the village level, but he did not do this. Instead, he retired from politics gracefully, having never lost a mayoral election. He received an Order of the Rising Sun medal from the national government for his political service in 2010. (For the 2000 village mayoral election, Miyata's supporters backed a settler who had always been a very strong advocate of his policies.).
3. I visited the Kurose home in 1997 in order to ask Mr. Kurose about his motives for fighting the government over rice marketing—the meeting having been arranged by Yukiko Kusakabe, whom I had already come to know due to her interest in learning English.
4. See Wood (2005: 47) for a photo of Hiroto Takahashi's father serving as a guide in the village museum.
5. See also Bestor 1989: 99-101 on vote-splitting within households.
6. This situation eventually changed; the mayor began appointing assistant mayors, as had been done in the past.
7. In February of 2002 Miyazaki estimated that the JA might only last another ten years before having to merge with another. This has not happened, however.
8. Kobayashi had clearly pulled votes away from Kurose. Some had wanted him to wait until 2012 before running for mayor for fear of this happening. After the 2008 election he reportedly promised his backers that he would run again in 2012.
9. Commencing construction on a new school complex—situated to the north of the original buildings (see Figure I.2)—in 2010 (rather than simply refurbishing the existing buildings) also upset many.

6

What Can We Learn from Ogata-mura?

This village is the best place in Japan. It's the best in the world!

–Takeru Isono

Somebody who knew nothing about farming planned this place with a pen, and this is the result.

–Isao Satake

Ogata-mura today is largely a product of its planning and settlement. At the same time, subsequent agricultural and regional policies have also had a great impact on the village. This chapter represents an attempt to bring evidence of these from previous chapters together in a coherent whole, and also to answer the question of how the village might be able to fulfill its intended role as a modern model for the future of Japan's agriculture—a problem that also involves government policy and international trade. As for the issues of planning and settlement, policy, and structure and individual agency, there are two main ways in which these need to be understood: in terms of how the village society as a whole has grown and changed over time (the "big picture" view), and in terms of how individual people have adjusted to the village (the "small picture" view).

Plans, Policies, and Politics—The Big Picture

Ogata-mura's course of development has been affected to a great degree by the way it was designed and by the circumstances of its establishment. It began as a highly controlled, centrally planned, rice production project based on concepts of efficiency and mechanization, and on ideals of homogeneity and harmony—a thoroughly modern village to pave the path to a new national agriculture for the

---

Endnotes for this chapter begin on page 219.

twenty-first century (cf. Nishida and Kase 2000). Cooperative farming groups (with private property ownership) were established early, and these allowed settlers to acquire the necessary machines to begin their work. They also encouraged relatively tight social ties to form between the settlers. The initial socioeconomic arrangement served its purpose for the first few years, but the collective labor arrangements fell apart early. The decollectivization that occurred in the village, centering on the dissolution of the farming groups, also contributed to a weakening of the old social order. Both collective farming-group solidarity and relations according to street of residence lost their importance with time, although they linger today in some cases. Instead of these, relations between members of the same block, or *jūku*, have taken prominence, as have individual relations between members of different households with similar interests or with other ties.

In addition, just as the settlement project was nearing completion, concern about not being self-sufficient in rice suddenly flipped over and went the opposite direction. The national government reversed course and began forcing the farmers of the country to cut back on its production. This may have been acceptable to many smaller-scale farmers, who were already relying heavily on regular, wage-based employment. They, after all, could do a bit less work and get payments for that (although not all of them were happy with the situation). But for larger-scale growers with no or little outside earnings, the sudden turnaround presented a more serious problem. As it if was not bad enough to be robbed of the satisfaction of running their own farms as they pleased, many had to endure staring at empty fields and also diminishing returns—not fun for career farmers. A tiny minority in Japan's agricultural sector, these are the farmers who supported the defiant settlers of Ogata-mura, who had not only come to the village expecting to grow large quantities of rice but also given up any land they had held or had been set to inherit in their home areas.

Ogata-mura is not completely unique as a small, planned farming community—there are many other examples. Heterogeneity has been desired, but it has generally not lasted, as is the case with Ogata-mura. Nevertheless, the village is not an abject failure—it has problems, but it still exists and it has cohesiveness. Not all who live in it love it, but many truly do. They take pride in the fact that they built the community themselves, or that their fathers and mothers—or grandparents—did. Change in homogeneous, planned farming communities, or in tightly controlled, socialistic farming villages, has often come from the inside—with individuals taking great risks to produce or market their goods themselves outside of government channels. This has happened in Ogata-mura. Also, such actions have at times been responsible for lengthening the lifespan of centralized economies, smoothing out the distribution process and making up for inherent shortcomings (Grossman 1977). However, this has not happened in Ogata-mura.

In the village, the actions of recalcitrant settlers, if anything, served to break the state-mandated system down and weaken it.

Mayor Miyata and others feared this from the beginning. He warned his disobedient neighbors many years ago, accusing them of "spitting into the heavens," and saying that that their spit would "fall back on them" (Sanger 1991, quoted in Moore 1993: 286), meaning that they would later have only themselves to blame for destroying the system that had been protecting Japanese farmers for so many years. Indeed, the actions of the disobedient settlers also attracted the attention of foreign diplomats in Japan who were eager to use the case to argue for the relaxing of the country's rice marketing scheme (Sanger 1991). Their behavior was met with fierce resistance, both from the state itself and from many of their fellow settlers, and some of their relatives were even threatened by government agents. Two settlers had their fields taken away from them by the government in 1999, and because they had continued to farm those fields after that year, Tokyo later slapped them with massive fines for "damages." Eventually, though, the majority of the noncompliant villagers were forgiven, in a sense, as the government gradually relaxed its policies, and then granted them the freedom to grow and market as they pleased in the 1990s. Then, they were almost completely exonerated, in the same sense, when the minister of agriculture publicly took Akita Prefecture to task for imposing penalties on them and on other overproducing farmers in late 2009. In the end, the modern farming model and experimental community that the government built and struggled to maintain became a model for something quite different from what it had originally intended, partly due to its heavy-handedness.

Ogata-mura can be studied as a transition economy. It began with a high degree of central control, with cooperative work groups and communal machine ownership, with strict regulations on rice production amounts, with rice prices that were set in Tokyo and not at all by a market, and with no private marketing channels for rice, either. Settlers had migrated to the village knowing most of these things, and at the beginning they were able to quietly change some of the arrangements that they felt were unsuitable. Cooperative labor, for example, was generally disliked. Some compared it to "eating cold rice" (*hiya-meshi*)—an expression conjuring up images of extreme poverty. On the other hand, cooperative equipment ownership made sense. The settlers altered these conditions selectively, and the Jigyōdan acquiesced. The decollectivization process in Ogata-mura was therefore quick, simple, and painless. Following this, other trends typically seen in transition economies, such as the appearance of private (illegal) marketing channels, the loosening of production limits, and relatively open markets, came along. These have been hotly contested issues. Although many settlers have merely shrugged their shoulders over the changes in government policy, some (Shinichirō Sakamoto, for example) have complained passionately. But these changes were at least partly caused by the creation of private marketing channels and rice markets—direct results of the actions of particular settlers.

As has been noted by many researchers (Dana 2002, 2005, Pomfret 1996, Pryor 1992), illicit markets and parallel economies are common in transition economies, the development of an entrepreneurial environment tends to occur unevenly, and the very term *entrepreneur* is often considered synonymous with activity of dubious quality. Indeed, the original entrepreneurs of Ogata-mura were, and sometimes still are, viewed negatively by neighbors. In Ogata-mura, many settlers chose to overproduce rice and then had to forge their own marketing arrangements and make their own distribution channels when they were turned away by the Country Elevator. Yamano (2003) has argued that members of the third settler wave were less likely overall to do this, but this is probably due at least partly to the fact that Mayor Miyata was a member of that settlement wave. I have not tried hard to quantify and sort such factors in the settlers' choices on that matter—that would be a topic for a different study—but there are indications that settlers of the fourth and especially the fifth waves were more likely to defy the government for several reasons, such as the poor water drainage of their fields, their higher land costs relative to those of the earlier migrants to Ogata-mura, and probably also the fact they did not have to toil quite as hard as their predecessors did at the beginning.[1] In general, though, cooperative group membership and place of origin (related factors in most cases) have clearly affected the choice to obey or to defy the government.

In its transitions, the society of Ogata-mura was affected strongly by the political conflicts that arose within it—a theme that has not been very well explored in ethnographic studies of Japanese farming villages up to now. As mentioned above, certain settlers became pitted against one another because of vastly different beliefs about the meaning of farming and the relationship between the producer and the state. These conflicts were exacerbated by the high-priced image-building campaign of Mayor Miyata—his appropriation of the village's modern identity. Two classic, opposing theories on the relationship between conflict and social cohesion espoused by Coser (1956) and Dahrendorf (1959) are very relevant here. Dahrendorf's assertion that endemic social conflict weakens overall community solidarity has been demonstrated in the preceding chapters, although irresolvable, class-based strife in the Marxist sense has not appeared. But Coser's charge that conflict creates new, sometimes shifting, kinds of social cohesion is also clear. In the Japanese cultural context, the distinction between in-group and out-group is very important.

Ishida (1984) has demonstrated that conflict between such groups can be resolved as long as neither side loses too much face. In Ogata-mura, two relatively tight in-groups appeared over the issue of compliance or noncompliance with government regulations on rice production, and the matter of production lingered as a moral issue even after the question of legality had faded away. The opposition group, or party, became accustomed to losing face over many years as it failed again and again to stop the paternalistic Miyata administration from spending large quantities of money on big projects and events. The only one it was ever able to stop was the golf course plan in the late 1980s, but that was actually due to the high degree of unity between political camps over that particular issue, and besides, opposition to the golf course did not arise out of financial concerns so much as environmental ones—loyalist and law-breaking settlers alike were worried about the ill effects of chemical run-off and the damage that might be done to their crops (even though it was supposed to be a "chemical-free" enterprise). In the year 2000 the dominant loyalist party lost much face when the wife of the opposition leader was elected mayor. And in addition, within that group (or existing on the fringes of it) the faction loosely centering on Shinichirō Sakamoto lost the most, for by that time many of them were experiencing serious financial problems, and the new administration was not especially concerned about their plight—at least not in comparison to the administration it had replaced. In the middle part of the first decade of this century the new dominant party cracked down the middle over the Organic Farm Ogata and JA convenience store fiascos, and then the old core of the party lost face when Mayor Kurose was defeated by a candidate closely tied to the Miyata administration and supported largely by the remains of his political machine, reborn with a younger look.

Quite a bit more time may be necessary for the two main sides in the long-standing argument over rice, money, and power to fully make up, if Ishida's model is correct. The problem was the main point of an article about Kita Kurose that appeared in an English-language newspaper just after her initial inauguration. In addition, the split between her and her two main supporters, Tōru Wakui and Sadayoshi Miyazaki, also conforms to Ishida's model in that the two men were unhappy with the mayor for allowing what Miyazaki, at least, saw as an in-group issue to spill out into the open. However, in the eyes of many villagers the two men had caused the situation. Either way, conflicts between settlers over rice politics and public spending are tightly connected to settlement plans and conditions, subsequent agricultural policies, and the transition of Ogata-mura's rice economy from a centrally controlled one without private markets to one based almost entirely on such markets and channels. Ogata-mura's story up to this point centers on these issues.

Plans, Policies, and Politics—The Small Picture

The three individual settlers focused on in the preceding chapters—Takeru Isono (from Niigata), Nobuhiro Machida (from Toyama), and Isao Satake (from Akita)—have adjusted to Ogata-mura in different ways, as have their wives. For two of them the village has become a new "home"—a *furusato*—and for one it has not. Takeru Isono is now one of the most successful settlers in Ogata-mura, in a number of different ways. For one, thanks to his quick thinking in the 1970s he was able to set a good pace for himself and his two fellow Essa Farm members by collectively buying new machines. Also, he held out on radically altering his house for many years. Of course, he did enlarge it, but even in the late 1990s the original peaked roof was easily seen from the street. Instead of investing heavily in a new house or in property outside the village, as many did, Takeru invested in his own farm and in the Dōyūkai. This paid off, for he now possesses over thirty hectares, making him one of the largest landowners in the village. His son, Katsuo, has also turned out to be a very able farmer, and has been very active in running the Dōyūkai. In addition, Katsuo's son, Kenji (see Figure 2.5), returned to the village after graduating from a school in Sendai around 2004 in order to become his father's successor and take over the farm when his turn comes; and not only this—he brought with him a wife who gave birth to a daughter shortly thereafter, and then a son later. This means that the Isono household in Ogata-mura now spans four generations, and even five if one considers that the great-great-grandparents (Takeru's mother and father) spent their last years there and have been entombed in the cemetery park. In fact, it was the marriage of his grandson and impending birth of a great-grandchild that finally prompted Takeru to raze his village house in 2006 and build a new one (Figure 6.1). In addition to

Figure 6.1: Takeru Isono's new house stands amidst snow in February of 2008 (of course, he was away skiing on this day).

the stability of Takeru's own household, his two daughters—Yukiko Kusakabe and her younger sister—are both married to village settlers and have grown-up children (and successors) of their own.

Takeru's love for and confidence in Ogata-mura have remained unshakable. He has never had any serious problem with the symbolic aspect of Ogata-mura's identity as a modern village. As noted in the previous chapter, even when his close neighbor and political enemy—Seiki Miyata—was mayor in the mid-1990s, Takeru was overwhelmingly supportive of the solar racing events. But ten years later, when a mayor he had supported was in office, he disparaged these projects and events over their cost and condemned the former mayor for leaving him and his fellow villagers saddled with debts because of them. By then, he had become convinced that the solar races were not helping to make the village "greener" and that everything else was just expensive fluff. Moreover, he was especially unhappy about the building of the land reclamation museum, which he said should not have been constructed at all. Takeru had internalized the argument of the anti-museum activist villagers who had called for remodeling and enlarging the community center (*kōminkan*—see Figure I.5) in the middle of the settlement—which had always served as an ad hoc museum of sorts—and making part of it into a proper reclamation memorial and museum. "They should have just done that," he said, "because it would have been cheaper and it would have brought more people into the center of the village." One reason for Takeru's change of heart was the community-wide realization, after the beginning of Mayor Kurose's first term in 2000, that the village was far more in debt than anyone had thought. And, despite the fact that his about-face came hand-in-hand with a cornucopia of new concerns about the future of agriculture (including falling rice prices) and even of the village's economic base as well, his change in attitude reflected only a strengthening of love for Ogata-mura and not the opposite. His statement serving as an epigraph to this chapter comes from the mid-1990s, but he was saying the same thing ten years later. For Takeru, Ogata-mura is the place of opportunity, risk, and success. Even today he longs sometimes for his old place in Niigata, but the land his father once owned and which he himself worked is gone, only very distant relatives now remain, and the community there has changed too much for him to call it "home." In fact, Takeru does not hesitate to call Ogata-mura his *furusato* today, and acknowledges that his former one exists only in his heart, in the form of memories of a place long gone.

In contrast to Takeru, Nobuhiro and Takako Machida have not changed their opinions of the village's big events over time, even though Nobuhiro did his own about-face regarding compliance with national agricultural policy. Practical, financial concerns have always taken precedence over symbolic ones for Nobuhiro, and Takako is of basically the same mindset, so it is no surprise that neither of them has ever been particularly excited about the *bunkajin* project or any other

Figure 6.2: The Machida and Tanaka families pose for a shot in the town of Hachirōgata in 1997. From top left: Nobuhiro Machida, Hiroaki, Takako Machida holding her grandson Yūsuke, Kōki Tanaka's mother, Kōki Tanaka (Asako's husband), and a friend of Kōki's. From bottom left: Kōki's father, Asako Tanaka, and a friend of Asako's (also the daughter of an Ogata-mura settler). Kōki's friend at the top right and Asako's friend at the bottom right later married.

enterprise undertaken by the Miyata administration. On the other hand, Nobuhiro is not especially passionate about his dissatisfaction with them, either. That the former mayor left the village's taxpayers to foot the bill for the projects and events is to him a simple fact, and that the costs must be met is also clear. He shrugs his shoulders and softly laughs about it today, and then mentions that merging with another municipality one day might help the village better manage the debt.

Although Nobuhiro was at one time very unhappy with the government's agricultural policies and its attitude toward him and his fellow Ogata-mura settlers, he has now settled rather well into Ogata-mura, and it is slowly becoming a *furusato* for him. This is also the case for his wife. In the late 1990s, she especially expressed a continuing strong sentiment for her natal home in Toyama, mainly because her parents were still living there. But even at that time, Nobuhiro's feelings of attachment to Toyama were growing thin. One strong reason for the couple's ability to accept Ogata-mura as a new *furusato* was the marriage of their daughter, Asako, into a family by the name of Tanaka in the neighboring town of Hachirōgata in March of 1996. Moreover, by the following year a grandson, Yūsuke, had been born, giving Nobuhiro a potential heir for his farm and business. This was still an important issue for him at the time, although he was not losing any sleep over it

Figure 6.3: The Machida house today.

because he also had a son of his own. Asako's brother, Hiroaki, was born around the time Nobuhiro helped found the SKK (Seiji Keizai Kenkyūkai) in the early 1980s, but in the late 1990s he was still a college student and showed no interest in farming (Figure 6.2 shows the Machida and Tanaka families).

After graduating, however, Hiroaki returned to Ogata-mura and started helping his father with the farm work and the business, in preparation for taking over in the future. In 1997 Nobuhiro declared that he was planning to sell his farm and business to Hiroaki should he decide to follow in his footsteps. After all, Nobuhiro bought his Ogata-mura land himself—he did not inherit it. He said, "I'm thinking of doing it American style and just selling everything to him if he wants to farm. I'm not talking about just passing on ancestrally inherited farmland. I'll make my son buy my rice fields. If he says he wants to farm, that's what I'm thinking of." But when reminded of this statement ten years later, Nobuhiro simply laughed, and said, "Well, I guess that's up to him!" Actually having Hiroaki around to help, ready to take over, has made Nobuhiro too happy to stubbornly stick to such an idea. Besides, rice prices have dropped since he spoke those words. Today, Nobuhiro, Takako, and Hiroaki live together in their large and spacious Ogata-mura house (Figure 6.3), which was built in the late 1980s while Asako was in high school, and while the rice Nobuhiro was spiriting out of the village was fetching very high prices through covert sales.

Not only is Hiroaki now his father's heir and successor, but he is also running a new rice marketing firm, Inaho Beikoku, which purchases unpolished rice (*genmai*) and scrap grains (*kuzumai*) that cannot fetch a high price on the food market. The former may be polished and sold to consumers, or sold as is, and the latter can be sold in bulk to companies that will process it into other products. Thanks to the passage of time and to the many good things that have come with it, Nobuhiro and Takako are now very well settled in Ogata-mura. The village is becoming their *furusato* more and more every day.

Isao Satake has had a much harder time adjusting to Ogata-mura. Like Takeru Isono and Nobuhiro Machida, he defied the government and the local administration, and faced certain hardships for that. But unlike the others, Isao applied to the settlement program because he wanted a fulfilling farming lifestyle. Isao wanted to live near his fields and to live for farming, rather than to farm for a living, in a manner of speaking. His wife, Hiroko, also shared this dream. Unfortunately for them, however, that dream could not be realized in Ogata-mura. In this case, and as Isao's statement at the beginning of this chapter illustrates, the negative effects of planning are perhaps most visible. Isao has not been able to enjoy the satisfaction of viewing his fields from his own house—a point noted by Shirai (1976) and Rutherford (1984)—and he also was not able to grow rice as he pleased from the very beginning (at least not without pressure). For many others these were not such serious problems, but for Isao they have been. In complete rejection of Ogata-mura as a legitimate modern version of a traditional farming village, he said,

If you go to Hokkaido, there's still a lot of farming village scenery there. Among the fields there are houses. They're spread out. Here, there's no scenery like that. You see, your typical tourist comes here thinking he'll see a farming village that really looks like a farming village, but this place isn't like that at all. There are no houses—no people—in the fields, right? This is an industrial farming village. Even though it was made from nothing, they could have made it more like a traditional farming village.

In addition, Hiroko was disappointed at one point to find that she could not even enjoy raising animals outside her home when she tried keeping some chickens:

I raised them from eggs into chicks. I was so happy when they hatched! There must have been about ten or twelve chicks that hatched. There were both hens and roosters, too, and the roosters cried. Then, a neighbor complained that they were too noisy, so I gave up on raising chickens. I thought, "We're farmers and we can't even raise chickens!"

In 1997 Ogata-mura was not a *furusato* for either Isao or Hiroko. Although both of them appeared to want to feel more attached to the village, neither were able to reconcile Ogata-mura's identity as a modern model with its identity as a farming village, and they were still strongly connected to their hometowns. At the time, this was even more the case for Hiroko than for Isao. Since her parents were still living in their house in the place where she grew up, only about ten kilometers away, she did not even have to waver about the question of her *furusato*—it was back home, where her parents were. Isao, on the other hand, appeared to be somewhat in limbo between the home he grew up in and Ogata-mura. His parents were both still living at the time, but his elder brother and brother's wife were poised to take over their household and farmland (tiny compared to Isao's Ogata-mura property). As the fourth born of five sons, there never was anything for Isao to inherit there, anyway. "I don't want to be buried back there . . . but I don't think I really want to be buried here in this village, either," he said in 2006. He did replace the original block-house with a large and comfortable one in the late 1980s (Figure 6.4), which made the village more satisfactory for him and his wife, but that was not enough to make it a *furusato*. As for the big events of the Miyata administration, Isao and Hiroko have always been fairly negatively disposed to them, although Hiroko not as strongly as her husband. But in 2006 both were quite unhappy about the amount of money that had been spent on the major projects— especially on the museum. Isao, on the other hand, has always been steadfast in his opposition to anything not directly related to agriculture.

Figure 6.4: The Satake home in the autumn of 2006.

Sadly, in January of 2004, Hiroko was diagnosed with spinocerebellar degeneration (SCD)—a disease of unknown cause that results in shrinkage of the cerebellum. Effects include a progressive loss of coordination as the cerebellum becomes unable to do its job effectively. As the upper part of the brain is unaffected, however, there is no loss of cognitive function. By late 2006 Hiroko was having trouble walking and speaking, but was still able to move around fairly well alone, at least at home or outside in the village. She could not write or drive a car, but she was riding an adult tricycle to and from the JA store, Agri-Plaza, and doing her shopping largely on her own. Her overall attitude was good, and Isao was working hard to take care of her. In the winter of 2005–2006 the two of them traveled to Hawaii where they met a nephew of Isao's and the eldest daughter of their next-door neighbor in the village, who was married and living in Honolulu. In contrast to Japan, they found it relatively easy for Hiroko to move around in a wheelchair—the U.S.A. (or at least Honolulu) being more accommodating of people with physical disabilities.

This unfortunate development has had a great effect on Hiroko's feelings about the village as a *furusato*. As her condition worsened, she realized that it would not have been as easy to get around in a larger town or city, and she also learned about who she could truly rely on. People around her, and especially her close neighbors, have done much to help her, and she began to appreciate being a part of the community more than ever before. Isao and Hiroko used to talk about retiring in Hawaii one day, but considering Hiroko's current condition, and also knowing that it can only be expected to worsen, that dream seems very impractical now—if not impossible. Although Hiroko was able to go out shopping alone sometimes during 2007, she was having more trouble getting around inside the house by early 2008, and using a walker. The couple began to rely on the services of a home helper, who visits frequently. With no children and no heir, however, Isao and Hiroko's future in Ogata-mura is unclear, and Hiroko's disease makes that situation worse, even if it has (ironically) helped her to feel more attached to the community itself. Still today, Ogata-mura has not exactly become a *furusato* for the couple, and certainly not for Isao. For him, it is more of a workplace, which leaves him in the position of having no home to return to for rest.

These three settlers and their families have adjusted to Ogata-mura in different ways and at different speeds, despite the fact that all chose to defy the government and overproduce rice initially. Their approaches may be related to their backgrounds. Takeru Isono grew up in a family that did not depend on regular wage labor to supplement its farm income, and later he found a way to generate good profits and enlarge his farm without having to run a business on his own by joining the Dōyūkai with fellow cooperative group members. Running a private business out of his own home or a small office has never appealed to him. His successes in Ogata-mura have made him happy enough to love the village and to feel very settled, even though there are things that bother him. Nobuhiro Machida had the experience of working for the JA in his hometown for wages as a farmer, so he came to Ogata-mura with a good understanding of bureaucratic matters, agricultural policy, and the frustration of farming around a regular work schedule. He turned out to have a strong business and entrepreneurial sense and so he was made the CEO of Nōyū, but being answerable to himself and his family only was much better for him, so he struck out on his own instead. Farming and business can go hand-in-hand for Nobuhiro, and Ogata-mura has given him the chance to make this happen. He therefore loves the village in his own way, but not unconditionally, and he does not take it at face value. For him, the entire community is somewhat of a business enterprise, and this has affected his acceptance of the village as a new *furusato*. For Isao Satake, that Ogata-mura is a kind of industrial farming enterprise is exactly the problem. He longs for a "pure" farm life that he cannot have in the village. He has tried to get as close as he can to it, by avoiding tedious business issues (at the expense of higher profits), but Ogata-mura will probably never be for him what he wishes it could be, which has very strongly affected his own adjustment to the village. The impacts of plans, policies, and politics on these three settlers are parallel to the impacts on the entire community.

A Model Farming Village?

When Gordon wrote in 1965 (p.82) that the Hachirōgata settlement project would probably not "be more than an interesting, even enviable, example of 'model farming,'" he meant that the model would probably never translate into reality—would never really mean anything—for the vast majority of Japanese rice farmers. Was he correct? Can Ogata-mura fulfill its mission and serve as a model for the future of Japanese agriculture? This requires a reconsideration of national policy vis-à-vis the village, and its place in the grand scheme of things.

We can begin by briefly reviewing a two-part special program on the changing rice agriculture of Japan that aired on NHK's main TV channel in late 2007. The program hits straight at the core of the greatest concern for most Ogata-mura farmers (and most Japanese rice farmers) today—the rice price and the security of the domestic market. It opens with the explanation that Japan's food self-sufficiency ratio is currently about 39 percent (compared to over 100 percent for Australia, the U.S.A., Canada, and France, among others), and that this number may drop to 12 percent should all foreign rice and other foodstuffs be allowed to freely enter the country, and then asks the troubling question, "Who is targeting our food [supply]?" Part one of the program focuses on rice as a business commodity. Companies in Japan that buy large quantities of rice for prepared meals delivered to corporations or facilities are shown to be very happy to switch to cheap, imported rice in order to protect their shrinking profit margins, amidst an overall national drop in rice consumption. World Trade Organization agreements made in 1995 require Japan to import 10 percent of its rice, which makes this kind of choice possible for businesses. Then, the program takes the viewer to California, where high-quality rice brands such as Hitome-bore, Akita Komachi, and even Niigata's beloved trademark, Koshi-hikari, are being produced in vast amounts at a fraction of what it costs to grow them in Japan. It is also stated that, contrary to popular claims, these grains are virtually indistinguishable from their Japan-grown counterparts with regard to flavor. An experienced international trader, "Michael," who is of Chinese ethnicity, attests to this as he tastes samples while visiting with various growers, a representative of the U.S.A. Rice Federation, and the CEO of a major rice marketing firm, all of whom want very badly to get a larger share of the Japanese market. Michael then visits a high-end department store in Shanghai, where bags of domestic (Chinese) and imported (Japanese) versions of Akita Komachi and Koshi-hikari line the shelves. A three-kilogram bag of Chinese Koshi-hikari is priced at 45.8 yuan (about 730 yen), while a two-kilogram bag of the same brand imported from Japan carries a price of 198 yuan (about 3,200 yen). One can easily imagine what might happen to Japan's rice market if this rice were allowed into the country in large quantities.

Next we see Michael in Niigata, the heartland of Koshi-hikari production in Japan. He makes a deal with a young entrepreneurial farmer named Sasaki who agrees to export ten thousand kilograms of his rice to Taiwan, where it is to be marketed as a very high-end product. Sasaki says, "Of course, I'd like for Japanese people to eat what I produce. That's how it should be. I mean, it's quite something to ship rice from here to Tokyo, but to send it overseas . . . well, that's a completely different matter. But if that's what it takes to survive, then that's what I'll do." Sasaki accompanies Michael to Taipei, where they visit an expensive sushi restaurant which has recently switched to Sasaki's rice. However, each patron must pay about thirty thousand yen (about U.S. $330) to eat lunch there—a prohibitive cost for most people. Later, Sasaki is surprised to find Koshi-hikari produced in places such as the U.S.A., Thailand, China, and Taiwan on the shelves of a supermarket—something not seen in Japan. "It's scary," he says. "If this happens in Japan . . ." Later, Michael and Sasaki visit a Taiwanese rice wholesaler. They hope that the company might agree to handle some of Sasaki's high-grade Koshi-hikari. Instead, however, Sasaki is surprised not only to be refused, but also to be shown a warehouse stocked with tons of Taiwanese rice that the company hopes to export to Japan. "We're very interested in the Japanese market," a representative explains. Again, the farmer is visibly frightened. In concluding part one, NHK visits with three Japanese experts on the issue in order to seek an answer to the question of who should produce Japan's rice. First, Nobuhiro Suzuki, a University of Tokyo professor of agricultural economics and former employee of the MAFF, argues for protecting self-sufficiency in rice production at all costs, largely out of concern for national security. University of Tokyo agricultural economist Masayoshi Honma argues for the opposite, explaining that rather than worry about self-sufficiency in rice and taking heroic measures to maintain it, Japan should make many friends through trade, import rice, and concentrate on exporting its advanced technology to balance its imports. Finally, economist/critic Katsuto Uchihashi, who often appears on NHK and other network programs, makes a case for protecting national self-sufficiency, arguing that there is no telling how long Japanese corporations (and perhaps the government) will be able to purchase foodstuffs from overseas at the rates asked.

Part two of the program focuses on rice production in Japan, concentrating on current initiatives and problems, and presents some cases to illustrate its points. It shows that there are many hurdles and dangers associated with starting up and maintaining hamlet-level farming (*shūraku einō*) initiatives. A number of small-scale farmers in Iwate and in Akita are seen struggling to find ways to improve their fields and make their joint projects more economical, but these efforts are stymied by disagreements about water drainage and field location, and also about equipment use—some of the problems that proved impossible to overcome in Ogata-mura at the beginning. In one Akita town, Akita Komachi rice is being produced by twenty-four different households in fields filling narrow mountain valleys. It is noted that about 40 percent of all rice grown in Japan is produced in such areas, the farming of which defies most attempts to make it more efficient. A sixty-nine year old farmer who owns slightly over one-half of a hectare is introduced. Although he can only barely survive on such a tiny parcel of farmland, he is determined to keep growing rice to the end, largely because the fields were farmed by his father and grandfather before him. An employee of the town comes and explains that it is going to become more and more difficult for him to receive any government support if he does not make headway on consolidating his fields and operations with others and increasing the overall efficiency.

The program then looks at another area of the same town where more progress has been made in consolidating fields and increasing farm efficiency. A number of producers are worried about the falling rice prices, and they have another problem: they set up a hamlet-level farming operation but purchased three large-scale combines at a total cost of ten million yen before completing their land and agriculture improvement plans and securing government assistance. How to acquire the support they need, and how to pay for the machines, vexes them. Again, the show turns to expert analysts. First, Masayoshi Honma of the University of Tokyo argues that Japanese rice agriculture must change with the times—that it must react sensibly to market forces. This necessarily includes the departure of some producers from farming and a growth in average farm size, and of course greater efficiency. This view is basically in line with recent government policy, and is the type of pragmatic/realist philosophy that upsets Shinichirō Sakamoto and other like-minded farmers. Next, economist/critic Katsuto Uchihashi makes a case for defending farmers and their operations from unbridled market forces, claiming that "natural" farming, the rural environment, and village culture will suffer in the push for greater efficiency. Furthermore, he argues that food quality, and also concern for quality on the part of consumers, may be compromised. Having consulted these experts, the program points out that, in light of current trends, it will be harder and harder for Japanese rice farmers to secure heirs if they do not work towards increasing their efficiency and raising their profits—a point argued by Nobuhiro Machida of Ogata-mura (in reference to Shinichirō Sakamoto's farming philosophy and practice).

At last, the program turns its eye to Ogata-mura, beginning with a sweeping bird's eye view of the flat, geometrically rational landscape. First, Shinichirō Sakamoto is introduced. He is seen harvesting grain on his fifteen hectares of paddy land, and it is mentioned that he had a farm income of twelve million yen in 1993, when the government bought virtually all rice from the country's producers and guaranteed them relatively high returns. However, this pales in comparison to the figure of thirty to fifty million yen annually for the more competitive rice farmers of Ogata-mura during the village's "golden era" (early 1980s to mid-1990s). Then, it is made clear graphically by the program that the price of Akita Komachi has dropped steadily since the market was partially opened to foreign rice in 1995, and that it now hovers at around 11,650 yen per sixty kilogram bag (*tawara*), which is only 650 yen more than what it costs Sakamoto to produce a this amount. It is also made clear that Sakamoto has fallen deeply into debt—to the tune of seventy million yen—due to this development, and that his household has survived on a sliver of farm income and his pension. Sakamoto shows a letter from the Ogata-mura JA asking him to begin returning the money he owes, and he is then seen entering the JA building. An employee speaks with him about his debts, but since he has well exceeded the official limit, they will not loan him more, and they ask for payback. "I won't be able to plant a crop next year," laments Sakamoto.

Next, Tōru Wakui is introduced, as the enterprising owner of fifty-three hectares. It is mentioned that top-grade rice handled by his company, Akita Komachi Corporation, fetches a price of about fifteen thousand yen per sixty kilogram bag— well above that of rice sold to the Country Elevator. We see Wakui outside. He is explaining that successful farming does not depend on area as much as it depends on thought, making a joke that the *nō* in *nōgyō* (agriculture) could be rewritten with a different *nō*—that meaning "brain." In contrast to the financially ailing Sakamoto, Wakui appears confident and optimistic. However, the program reveals that even Wakui's business has been declining in terms of the overall number of contracts and purchases—dropping from a peak of three hundred thousand in the recent past to about fifty thousand today, due in Wakui's own estimate to the drop in per capita rice consumption and the (still rather small) influx of cheaper rice across the country's borders. Next, a young employee of Wakui's corporation in a business suit is seen attempting to appeal to a retailer in Tokyo, asking it to put the corporation's Akita Komachi on its shelves. "Everyone is growing delicious rice these days," says the representative of the retailer, as he snubs the plea and turns the young man away. Finally, the scene shifts to the ballroom of Sun Rural Ogata, the village hotel, on the afternoon of September 11, 2007, the day on which it was announced that JA branches across the country were planning to pay farmers less for each sixty kilogram bag of rice than they had the previous year. Numerous Ogata-mura farmers have gathered to listen to Wakui speak. Among them, greeting and chatting with his fellow settlers, a suited Sadayoshi Miyazaki, head of the Ogata-mura JA and longtime cohort of Wakui, can be seen. The farmers are there because Wakui has promised to continue paying them fifteen thousand yen per bag for a three-year period as he had originally vowed. "As long as I'm still living . . . I'm going to keep my promise," he declares from behind the podium with a confident smile. However, most farmers appear unimpressed. "The price will only drop from this point," says one with a cynical grin. "We have to expect that. We have to steel ourselves for that. If even this 'model village' can't survive in the current environment, Japan's rice agriculture will surely go under." The farmer's grin vanishes quickly at the end of his statement.

The NHK reporter, standing in an Ogata-mura field, explains that Sakamoto and Wakui both entered the village in the fourth settler wave in 1969, and adds that both are facing hard times despite their vastly different approaches to agriculture. (It seems that Wakui and Sakamoto are destined to be compared to one another forever.) Once more, the program turns to the academic experts—the first one being Nobuhiro Suzuki of the University of Tokyo, who is of the opinion that not even Ogata-mura will be able to adequately compete against cheap imports should the current shield be lifted. He says,

> Large-scale farmers like those of Ogata-mura, who rely 100 percent on rice, will be unable to compete with cheap imports if the borders are opened. Some feel that Japanese farmers may be able to compete against rice imported from the USA or Australia, but it's completely unthinkable. From an economic perspective, just considering the sheer numbers, there's no way.

Next, Masayoshi Honma appears again, arguing that the time has come for Japan to seriously reevaluate its stance on rice production and the position of rice in the national diet:

> Rice should be treated as just another crop, like any vegetable, and not as the main crop and staple food—self-sufficiency in which must be

maintained at all costs. Then, people can concentrate on how to appeal to consumers and sell it to them. It's time to stop clinging to the 'if we grow it, it will sell' mentality regarding rice.

Finally, Katsuto Uchihashi returns to once again champion the position for protecting the Japanese rice grower and the staple crop. "No country has been able to survive without a viable domestic agricultural sector," he says, and continues:

> How long can a country depend on others for its own survival? Any country that can't maintain a degree of self-sufficiency is suffering, as the poorest people [in any country] suffer. It's a [justified] public expense to support the farmers, and basically all countries around the world are trying to protect their farms. The countries of Europe, for example, are striving to maintain their agricultural sectors. Protecting farming and making it attractive to the next generation in order to secure successors—this has a certain social value. It's not just about feeding the population. Gradually, this is being recognized, and the country needs to keep at it and do even better.

That Ogata-mura would feature so prominently in a nationwide NHK program says much about its position in Japan's rice-growing environment. Here, the village is being upheld as a model for Japanese rice agriculture in at least one way—a model for big, efficient farms and a system that stands the best chance of working if the state ultimately fails to protect the domestic market in the future. As was explained in chapter 1, Tokyo has been trying for many years to make Japan's farms more efficient. Earlier efforts included encouraging a rise in mechanical tool use and reorganizing and improving fields. But the total number of farms did not shrink much, which means that individual operations did not become more efficient once they reached a certain threshold. Instead, households held on to small plots and began relying more and more on outside income. Farmers aged and in many cases became unable to secure heirs, which resulted in a large number of elderly, small-scale producers. The JA organizations that support (and depend on) them have tried hard to protect them from imports. Recently, this has been most visible in the JA's unified opposition to the Trans Pacific Partnership (TPP), which is intended to erase nearly all tariffs on imports (including the roughly 770 percent levy placed on rice) and which the U.S. government currently wants Japan to join (see Nakano 2011, Suzuki and Kinoshita 2011, Takarajimasha 2012). Consequently, both the farmers and JA (Nōkyō) have been vilified by many bureaucrats, econometricians, and analysts (but generally not by politicians, who need their votes—see Tabuchi 2010).

Inspired no doubt by the NHK show, a large article (Ueba 2007) on Japan's rice agriculture appearing in the pages of the *Daily Yomiuri* newspaper in the same year criticizes small-scale farmers and JAs for being too conservative and accuses individual farmers of being unwilling to sell their fields to larger-scale producers—not because of sentimentality or legitimate financial worries but because of greed. They are charged with holding out for more lucrative deals—a shot at selling to a corporation that wants to develop the land, for example. Part-time, small-scale producers, it is argued, will choose these kinds of options over attempting to streamline their operations. But blaming such growers for the problems with the nation's agriculture is nothing new—it is exactly what Jussaume (1991) argued against over twenty years ago, concluding, "The effective and stubborn resistance that farmers maintain towards changes in agricultural policies is based in considerable measure on their recognition that there are no other means by which they could maintain the standard of living they have achieved and perceive to be desirable" (see also Fukutake 1967, 1980). Unlike certain Ogata-mura settlers, most Japanese farmers—and their JAs—have been concerned with maintaining the status quo more than anything else for good reason.

Even Ogata-mura farmers are worried about the current situation. After all, they are dependent on a very tenuous support system—one that is subject not only to (highly controlled) domestic market fluctuations but also to external forces via the WTO. They are very much aware of this. How long their government can hold out against the pressures it faces, nobody knows. Also, as the NHK program shows, there are a variety of opinions on the role of agriculture in the national economy and the value of the agrarian sector, and of agrarian life. Of course, lest we become too despondent, it is important to remember that Japan is not alone in its efforts to protect its national agriculture from foreign pressures and domestic political currents. Even the United States, champion of the principles of free trade, goes to great lengths to do exactly that, and the party in power at any given time is never immune to the farm lobby. Total crop subsidies paid to U.S. farmers by the United States Department of Agriculture exceeded sixteen billion dollars in 2009, concentrated primarily in the heartland (Rucker 2011). Although all U.S. farmers were supposed to gradually become independent of government subsidies over a seven year period from the passing of the 1996 "Freedom to Farm" act, a new support bill was passed in 2002, and a 286 billion dollar bill was passed by the House of Representatives in July of 2007 (Hanson 2007). And, at the request of Brazil and Canada, the WTO launched an investigation into the United States' farm support policies in December of that year (Daily Yomiuri 2007). Indeed, farmers in the United States also often keep some of their land out of production each year in order to qualify for federal subsidies (Allen and Dillman 1994: 51).

The idea that Japan's rice farming sector should be allowed to die by reason of economic rationality, and that this can be offset by boosting industrial output and exports, seems suspicious at best. As the disaster that struck Tōhoku on March

11, 2011 has shown, other nations can be counted on to help in many ways in a time of crisis, but this is different from expecting them to provide a country of tens of millions of people with its staple food for an extended period—even if it is economically beneficial to the producer nations. The kinds of problems that can disrupt production and trade are too difficult to predict, and each country, after all, is concerned first and foremost with itself. In addition, there would be questions about food quality and safety. Perhaps one day the nations of Earth will be united enough to work together in such a way, but not now. In addition, the nuclear plant disaster in Fukushima Prefecture that was caused by the earthquake and tsunami of March 11, 2011, has also proven that a country cannot always count on smooth production and export to support its economy. Energy shortages impede production, and international worries about radioactive fallout do the same to exports, not to mention investments. Furthermore, mass production requires energy and there is always a cost (and a risk) to energy production (Kirby 2011: 188–192). Just the same, it is hard to perpetually justify the exaltation of rice as a special-status crop. And certainly, Japanese agriculture—particularly rice agriculture—needs to adapt more to changing times. Honma is correct when he speaks of a national farming crisis (Tabuchi 2010). For one thing, agriculture would benefit from being weaned off the handout-based, carrot-and-stick support system currently in place; it is fraught with problems, such as the fact that it tends to encourage farmers to evict tenants from their fields in order to let those fields lie fallow and receive the lump sum payments (Miyazaki and Uetake 2010).[2] If this is to be done, Ogata-mura can probably serve as a model in at least three ways: as a good example of effective entrepreneurialism, as a model for large, rationalized farms, and as an ecofriendly agricultural village. But first, we must finish addressing the question of where Ogata-mura currently fits into the overall picture, and what the nation's policymakers actually desire.

It does seem clear that the national government still wants Ogata-mura to serve as a kind of modern model. For one thing, Tokyo has tried to encourage greater feelings of entrepreneurialism among the farmers of the nation. In November of 2007 the Economy, Trade, and Industry Ministry (METI) and the MAFF jointly announced a plan "to support farmers who are willing to use information technology systems and collaborate with other industries and universities" (Yomiuri Shimbun 2007d). Increased support is to be given to: (1) farmers who "use IT for production, inventory, and sales management;" (2) farmers who "develop food and medical products that use the waste produced by standard production methods by using new technology developed by universities and other organizations;" and (3) "nonprofit organizations that run natural food restaurants using locally produced organic vegetables." Japan's political environment changed in August of 2009 when the Democratic Party (DPJ) finally defeated the Liberal Democratic Party (LDP) in a general election—something it had been trying vainly to do since its founding in 1998. With the inauguration of a new cabinet, all ministers—including the prime minister—were replaced by DPJ politicians, and their agendas were notably different from those of their LDP counterparts.

To be sure, since that time there has been far more talk and speculation than action where the nation's agriculture is concerned, but the strongest indication of what is to come right now is probably the DPJ's new plan to abolish the policy of penalizing "sales-oriented farmers" (*hanbai nōka*) who do not cooperate with production quotas by withholding subsidies from them, which has been going on for quite some time now. This plan (Nōgyō Kobetsu Shotoku Hoshō Seido) will essentially absolve the prefectural governments from having to keep their farmers in line and punish them. What the government wants instead now is for each municipality to work together with its producers and thereby maintain certain production levels as a unit—a more community-based approach. This process officially began in Ogata-mura in February of 2010. According to the plan, when a farmer fails to break even on a certain crop, he can receive money from the government to make up the difference. Also, across-the-board subsidies will be available to all participating market-oriented farmers. Each can receive fifteen thousand yen for each ten ares that he plants with certain designated crops, for example. This means that if an Ogata-mura farmer grows five hectares of *kakōyōmai* (rice designated for processing), for example, he stands to get 750,000 yen, or about U.S. $9,600, just for doing so. As of March, 2010, there were indications in Ogata-mura that many overproducing farmers were seriously considering participating because of the low rice prices. The village office indicated—boldly—that as many as 90 percent of its producers might sign up. Many scoffed at this figure, but after all, on 10 June of that year Mayor Takahashi was happy to announce in a village assembly meeting that of the 523 farming households, 442 (or 84.5 percent) were participating in the new program (Akita Sakigake Shinpō 2010). What made this so impressive was the fact that 183 settlers who had never cooperated with crop reduction programs had suddenly decided to do so. These are among the more entrepreneurial farmers of the village, and their change of strategy reflects a utilitarian economic decision in line with the thinking of Nobuhiro Machida, from Toyama, and not a sudden change of heart brought about by feelings of indebtedness to the government. It reflects the shared worry among all Ogata-mura rice farmers about plummeting rice prices and uncertain state protection.

Just before this the village had once again found itself at the center of national agricultural policy issues. The new minister of agriculture under the DPJ, Hirotaka Akamatsu, visited Ogata-mura in November of 2009 and spoke with Akita Komachi's Tōru Wakui, the JA head Sadayoshi Miyazaki, and others, and heard first-hand from them about the penalties that had been imposed on them by Akita Prefecture for many years up to that point (in line with LDP policy). Symbolically this was very important because no major government official had ever paid any serious attention to the noncompliant Ogata-mura settlers. Shortly thereafter Akamatsu publicly announced that since Akita's action was illegal (actually, would soon become so) under the new plan, Akita would be excluded from the national scheme if it did not cease the practice immediately, meaning that none of the 561.8 billion yen set aside for subsidies would be granted to any of the prefecture's farmers at all. This put both Ogata-mura and Akita on the front pages of many national newspapers, and caused no small degree of chaos inside the prefectural government headquarters in Akita City. After a number of emergency meetings, the prefecture decided to abolish its penalty system, but then had to set a new interim support program for farmers of the area who had observed government rules from the start. Some of them referred derisively to Ogata-mura as *baka-matsu-mura*—a play on words combining *baka* (crazy or stupid) with *matsu* (instead of "Akamatsu") to express their displeasure with the minister and the village at the same time. Meanwhile, overproducing Ogata-mura farmers like Tōru Wakui, Takeru Isono, Nobuhiro Machida, and Isao Satake could be happy about not being singled out anymore, yet those who were always compliant wondered why in recent years the actions of their disobedient neighbors had come to be condoned by the state, echoing the complaints of many following the village election of 2000.

Entrepreneurialism

Ogata-mura might serve as a model of entrepreneurialism. Farmers in Ogata-mura who made the right decisions at the right time have found ways to build agricultural enterprises that their heirs might want to inherit, or that others would probably want to purchase or at least invest in. On the other hand, the Tamagawa Dam settlers who entered the village in 1978 were unable to make these kinds of decisions due the restrictions placed on them by the prefecture government—no doubt one major reason for their relative lack of success. Tōru Wakui certainly has accomplished something. He built his massive corporation from nothing, with the help of some associates, and owns more farmland than some entire hamlets. But he has also angered many people in his village—and not only the supporters of the former mayor, Miyata. Economic motivations might not always mesh well with social relationships, if good social relations are desired. The members of the Dōyūkai and Nōyū might serve as models for healthy entrepreneurialism. They have done something that some larger-scale farmers across the country may be able to do if they can manage to work well enough together, and they probably would not have to make moral sacrifices. Nobuhiro Machida might also be a good model. He actually switched from "bad" to "good" by becoming an accredited farmer and observing production guidelines in order to receive subsidies. Nevertheless, it is interesting to note that none of these Ogata-mura settlers would have been candidates for "model farmer" status twenty years ago—not by any means. The government's about-face on this issue has contributed in a major way to the current confusion across the nation about what exactly *is* a good model for Japanese agriculture, which makes answering the question of whether Ogata-mura can be one all the more difficult.

However, a very interesting new venture in the village is now turning heads across the nation—one which does not closely relate to rice politics as they have played out locally up to now. In May of 2009 a group of about thirty "Shibuya Gals" (young women of Tokyo who tend to cluster around the Shibuya area and who sport a distinctive style of clothing, makeup, and hair) descended upon Ogata-mura and got to work hand-planting rice seedlings in several flooded paddies. This was due to the efforts of Shiho Fujita, a "Gal" and businesswoman, who had arranged to rent the fields and produce rice to be sold in Tokyo. She had also organized the rice-planting tour that brought the flock of Gals to the village for a good muddy slog—another business venture. The planting event attracted the attention of not only the local media (Akita Sakigake Shinpō 2009) but also the national press (Yomiuri Shinbun 2009). In her enterprise, Fujita negotiated with Hajime Kobayashi (a candidate for mayor in 2008) and arranged to have Mizuho (the child company of the Dōyūkai, which Kobayashi headed at the time) market her rice. The first crop was harvested in autumn of 2009 and today bags of this "Shibuya-mai" are being sold through Mizuho's website (around 2,500 yen for five kilograms). They are illustrated with an image of ripe, dry rice plants with the buildings of Shibuya behind them, and a large silhouette of the famous Akita dog Hachikō, whose statue is a well known landmark of Shibuya, in the center. The plastic inside the dog's image is clear, which allows the rice grains to be seen by potential buyers. Fujita has stated that she wants to help change the image of agriculture, and Kobayashi, of course, was also hopeful. Many Ogata-mura farmers are also interested. Perhaps this kind of venture will help achieve this, and Ogata-mura is an ideal place to try. We might recall here the words of Nobuhiro Machida (quoted in chapter 4 and above)—even though he may have changed his mind about selling his farm to his son, the attitude that a settler's son is not required to take over is important. For healthy entrepreneurialism, an enthusiastic attitude is more crucial than a sense of duty. Moreover, as explained in chapter 4, Nobuhiro sees the situation as not so much one of finding a suitable person to take over his farm as one of having the responsibility of building a farming operation that is worthy of being passed down to an heir. This is the attitude that has been fostered in Ogata-mura through the joint effects of settler selection, settlement, policy, and the village's economic and social transitions—a facet of the "third monkey" way of thinking (to quote Tadashi Kurose—see chapter 3). Although the attitude is not shared by all, it could be a worthy export for the village. Unfortunately, Tokyo does not appear to have caught on to this very well.

Larger, More Efficient Farms

More than twenty-five years ago, echoing Gordon's (1965) concerns, Rutherford (1984: 94–95) commented:

> Hachirōgata is perhaps a laudable showpiece but has been achieved at considerable cost. Its experiment in large-scale, co-operative farming on a highly mechanized basis seems to have not met with much success. It certainly has not provided a full solution to a serious rural problem in Japan, the inadequacy of farm sizes. Few traditional areas could afford to create new farms, as large as one finds here. Whether they would be more successful in overcoming the problem of smallness of farms by co-operation among neighbours is still in doubt, though if it meant co-operation among longstanding neighbours, perhaps social tensions would not be as great as they have been reported to be in Hachirōgata.

Probably, Rutherford was unaware of the true nature of the social tensions between Ogata-mura settlers, and it is doubtful that more harmonious cooperation could be forged between longstanding neighbors, as problems with the establishment of *shūraku einō* cooperative farming initiatives across the country show. But *shūraku einō* notwithstanding, if Tokyo truly wants more efficient, larger farms, then Ogata-mura might serve as a model. As time passes it seems certain that the farms of the village—and of the entire country—will continue to shrink in number while growing in size, and that overall efficiency will go up even more. As this happens in Ogata-mura, Tokyo might be pleased because then the village would be able to serve as an even better model of consolidation and economy. But now the village government is still grappling with the problem of how to bail out its endangered residents, limit suffering, and preserve the community, which might work against the village serving as a model for consolidation (Shinichirō Sakamoto is still farming in Ogata-mura as of 2012, as are nearly all settlers who were in dire straits in 2007). Yet consolidation is occurring just the same. Takeru Isono and Tōru Wakui, among others, were able to expand their farms by purchasing fields from their neighbors who either scaled back or quit farming. Just how far this trend will progress in Ogata-mura from this point is unclear, but nearly all agree that it will continue for some time, and that ultimately the number of farming households in the village will probably drop to about one-half of the original number of settlers—perhaps going down to about three hundred if not lower. As already mentioned, production costs in Ogata-mura per unit of land are below the national average, and these costs are actually lower for the larger-scale Ogata-mura farmers, such as Tōru Wakui, Takeru Isono, and Nobuhiro Machida.

Noted, farm expansion and consolidation cannot work across all of Japan as it works in Ogata-mura. First, even if a farmer with several hectares and a full-time job takes out a loan and buys five more hectares (provided that they are available) he probably cannot afford to quit his job, because he will only have barely enough land to survive. But he cannot take care of so much land while working full-time, either. And, even if he tries this, he will need to make sure that even more available land exists nearby, for he will need to expand again as soon as possible. Not many Japanese farmers will actually be able to do this in the coming decades. For most, going into debt in order to buy more farmland when rice prices are so low simply does not make sense (although growing other crops is an option). If Ogata-mura is to be a model in this way, farm expansion and consolidation across the nation will have to follow a fairly rough path, and the difference between large landowners and small landowners will certainly grow, with small producers gradually disappearing altogether. Increased regulation (and more incentives) would be needed to encourage smaller-scale farmers to sell land to larger-scale producers (see also Hayami 1991: 103). Perhaps the "traditional" farming village environment can still be preserved to a degree amidst such change (although it will also have to evolve). The words of Nobuhiro Suzuki of the University of Tokyo are worth noting again—some form of government protection and support will most likely be needed in the future, for even a fifty- or one hundred-hectare farm in Ogata-mura would have a hard time if Japan's borders were fully opened to foreign rice (hence, fear of the TPP—Tabuchi 2010).

Ecofriendly Agriculture

It is perhaps the ultimate in irony that by destroying a delicate ecosystem the government created a remarkably ecosensitive farming society. This might be the most important way in which Ogata-mura could serve as a good model for the agriculture of the entire nation in the current century. One reason for the increased amount of time available to Japanese farmers of Meiji through Shōwa times (1868–1989) for doing *dekasegi* labor away from home was the growing use of chemical fertilizers across the country. This, plus the fact that their holdings were tiny, helped encourage the development of a massive part-time national farming industry (Jussaume 1991), which was shored up by state policy (Moore 1990; Mulgan 2005b). But Ogata-mura is full of farmers with relatively large land holdings and free winters, who are generally more concerned with improving the efficiency, output, and reputations of their farms than taking on other work, and tend to enjoy hobbies in their downtime.[3] Ecological concerns stem from this and the ever present problems with the water quality of the remainder of the Hachirōgata reservoir. As mentioned in chapter 2, the children of the village's junior high school sample the water of the former lake, analyze the water, and report on the changes in pollution levels annually—sharing their data with the village council.

Short articles on the changes in the Hachirōgata water often appear in the pages of Akita's leading newspaper. Also, the village government's plan to build a golf course inside the polder dam in the late 1980s brought the settlers together in near-unanimous opposition—the first time they were able to unite on any political issue since 1975, and the last time such a large number of them were able to agree on anything relating to rice production until 2010, when nearly 85 percent chose to participate in the DPJ's new rice-farming support system. The wives' group that has produced and sold natural soap made with recycled oils in the village for the last twenty years sprang from that movement, and Yukiko Kusakabe, who became the first female member of the village council in 2000, is a founding member of that group.[4] Instead of a golf course, the village sports a bird sanctuary along the main highway leading to it from the south—a spot that was featured in a popular nature show on NHK's main TV channel in early 2010, and again in March of 2012.

Ogata-mura also has the solar and electric vehicle races. It is true that these are not as popular now as they were in their heyday, when the village managed them through its solar division, but they still exist and so does the track. The NGO in charge of the events—Clean Energy Alliance—is not a financial drag on the village, and the name sounds good, but it does not have the kind of funding that the former Solar Division had. Perhaps greater pan-village support could be generated for the zero-emission vehicle events, and if they could be better tied into Ogata-mura's overall energy/lifestyle/agriculture package, then the NGO could truly live up to its name. The village might, in fact, be moving closer to this now. In April of 2010 a new clean energy business enterprise—a joint venture between the village, Akita University, TDK Corporation, and several smaller businesses—was launched. Termed "Local Smart Grid," and based at Road Station Ogata (the rest stop on the highway comprised of the special products center and the land reclamation museum), this project combines wind and solar power with fuel cell batteries in an attempt to create a clean and dependable energy network for the village, the technology for which is of course intended for eventual use elsewhere in addition to Ogata-mura (TDK Corporation 2011). Three large, five-kilowatt solar arrays (Figure 6.5), a 700-watt fuel cell battery, and a windmill capable of putting out up to twelve kilowatts (Figure 6.6) are now helping to provide the museum with electricity and to power LED streetlights in the area. Concrete results here have not yet been generally noticed by the public, but the project has received support from the national government and at least it looks promising. In addition, in March of 2012 the village announced a plan to form a new wind power corporation and build two windmills, capable of generating 1,990 kilowatts of power, and start selling the electricity by 2015, and it announced at the same time that a wind power enterprise founded by Hisahiro Yamamoto (originator of the solar vehicle races) had agreed to invest in the proposed company (Akita Sakigage

Figure 6.5: Solar arrays behind the land reclamation museum.

Shinpō 2012). The proposed project is related to a new feed-in tariff scheme (Edahiro 2011), and it mirrors the current aspirations of numerous other high-tech companies (Kyodo News 2011b). How this plan actually plays out remains to be seen, but it would be a major step in the right direction—albeit a gigantic one—if Ogata-mura could eventually reach a point at which it no longer needed to rely on the national power grid. At least it might one day be able to generate enough power by itself to operate its three large pumping stations, which must run around the clock to keep the lagoon from reclaiming the village. There is plenty of space in Ogata-mura for windmills and solar arrays.

The low use of chemical fertilizers in Ogata-mura is tied to the kinds of concerns illustrated by the golf course episode and clean energy ventures. According to a comprehensive 2001 village study, the amount of nitrogen, phosphoric acid, and potassium elements put into its lands in 2000 were all well below the national averages for these substances (Table 6.1). Overall, the village's farmers tend to use many organic nutrients, and appear to employ even fewer fertilizers than other Japanese farmers. For example, the national average amount of nitrogen from naturally produced, nonfecal supplements used by farmers in the year 2000 was 3.2 kilograms per one thousand square meters (ten ares), while the amount used in Ogata-mura was only about 1 kilogram over the same area. Comparing figures for the village with those for the entire nation regarding the use of pesticides, antibacterial agents, and herbicides also indicates a much

Figure 6.6: The windmill towers over the museum parking lot.

lower reliance on such substances in the village than in other parts of the country (Table 6.2). Although the figures for Ogata-mura generated by this study are now more than ten years old, conversations with village officials and with farmers indicate that they have remained at these levels or dropped since then—they have not risen.

Table 6.1: Average amounts (in kilograms) of nitrogen, phosphoric acid, and potassium elements used in Ogata-mura soils, compared with national averages, for the year 2000.

	Nitrogen	Phosphoric acid	Potassium elements
Ogata-mura	4.9	2.7	1.3
Japan	7.8	10.7	8.6

Source: Ogata-mura village data (Ogata-mura 2001).

Table 6.2: Average amounts (in kilograms) of pesticides, antibacterial agents, and herbicides used in Ogata-mura soils, compared with national averages, for the year 2000.

	Pesticides	Antibacterial agents	Herbicides
Ogata-mura	0.6	0.2	0.5
Japan	1.5	1.9	1.8

Source: Ogata-mura village data (Ogata-mura 2001).

There are also two particularly interesting clean agriculture ventures in the village today. O-LISA (Ogata Low Input Sustainable Agriculture) was founded in 1991 by a consortium of settlers who wanted to research and utilize environmentally friendly farming methods, such as the use of ducks and organic farming that does not involve plowing (*fukōki saibai*—mentioned in chapter 4). These farmers have managed to involve researchers from Akita Prefectural University and Tōhoku University and a variety of other interested people from other parts of Akita—and even outside Akita—in their group. In 2007, in celebration of their 15 year anniversary, they published a book containing many short chapters written by members of their association detailing a wide variety of low-input agricultural methods and discussing a range of ecological issues (Atarashii Suiden Nōhō Henshūiinkai 2007). The other group—Ogata-mura Yūki Nōgyō Suishin Kyōgikai (here, OYNSK), dedicated specifically to advancing organic farming methods—was founded in 2008 by 126 settlers. This large group concentrates heavily on promoting the use of non-chemical fertilizers, and currently has about 750 hectares of rice paddy land devoted to organic farming practices. The association made headlines in March of 2012 by winning a MAFF Minister's Award in an annual environment-protection methods contest—the first time any group or individual in Akita had ever won the award (Morimoto 2012). There are also indications that pan-village unity is being promoted by these two groups (as a side-effect): Although O-LISA largely centers on settlers who have been loyal to the Country Elevator, some non-loyalist village farmers were invited to contribute articles to its 2007 volume, and OYNSK appears to contain a blend of settlers. In addition to these impressive ventures, there are quite a few village farming households that have earned a special designation from the Akita Prefecture government for success in lowering the amount of synthetic chemicals they use. Furthermore, that seepage or blowing of chemicals from one man's fields to another's is often a cause of friction in the village, as mentioned in chapter 4, is testament to the seriousness of ecological issues surrounding farming in Ogata-mura.

All of this suggests that the Hachirōgata land area may serve as a good model for Japanese agriculture in the ecological sense—even if other farmers cannot possess such large fields, they can at least try to limit their reliance on chemical fertilizers, too. Small-scale farmers can also release ducks in their paddies, as Nobuhiro Machida has been doing for some years now. They (like some fish) eat bugs and produce natural fertilizer. Despite the recent shrinkage in the market for high-end, naturally grown (and costly) rice, all of the major rice marketing firms of the village—and the majority of the smaller ones—continue to concentrate on these products (and to produce their own organic fertilizers). This has recently paid off in a big way. In the wake of the massive March 11, 2011, earthquake off the coast of Miyagi Prefecture and the resulting multiple tsunami that ravaged the Pacific coast—severely damaging a nuclear power plant in Fukushima Prefecture—orders poured in from across the country for Ogata-mura's ready to cook, chemical-free, *musenmai* rice. Nōyū, Toru Wakui's Akita Komachi Corporation, and the village Country Elevator all sold record amounts during the three weeks following the quake (Akita Sakigake Shinpō 2011). Individuals and corporations that have taken the right risks and made the right strategic decisions—and not only during the transition economy period of the village's history—have profited, and tapping into the ecological farming movement continues to pay off.

The strong ecological aspect of Ogata-mura's farming system not only feeds into the business side of life there. It also fits in well with the village's position as a model village for the current century (and possibly beyond). While clean water and "pure" farming are part of the image of the quaint, isolated, *furusato* or *satoyama* (locally-managed forest areas) of Japan so well promoted by travel companies and others in their campaigns (e.g. Ivy 1995; Williams 2010), the real villages and small towns of Japan do not exactly conform to this pattern, as contemporary anthropological studies have shown (e.g. Guo et al. 2005; Ivy 1995; Schnell 1999; Thompson and Traphagan 2006; Traphagan and Knight 2003). But Ogata-mura is supposed to be a modern version of the "traditional" village, and its built-in ecological concern—even if partly inspired by a desire for financial profits—may in fact prove to be its biggest saving grace. There can be no doubt that safe (and affordable) food will be one of the most important issues facing Japan in the coming decades, considering its currently low rate of self-sufficiency and the pressure to import more food, in addition to the growing realization that the country is not necessarily as ecologically clean and safe as it has often been made out to be (Kirby 2011)—a point that has been driven home in a most brutal way by the disaster of March 11, 2011. Ogata-mura may be able to lead the way to a new style of agriculture that is larger, more efficient, and clean, but still fulfilling to the farmer—and not only fulfilling, but fun. Kirby (2011: 187–192) shows how foreign pressure has influenced Japan's attitudes toward sustainability in recent years. Perhaps Ogata-mura can be a catalyst for a similar movement in agriculture.

Ogata-mura would be easy to criticize. One could take an extreme position and assert that the land it occupies should never have been created in the first place. Some of its residents do in fact feel this way. They may be right. One day the consensus may in fact be that it was not worth the financial cost to make or maintain, or the loss of the Hachirōgata ecosystem. Protein culled from the lake might in the end prove to have been more valuable to the public than the carbohydrates and vegetables grown on the land. Ogata-mura may be vilified as yet another example of failed "high modernism" (see Scott 1998). But this would be the easy route, and it would ignore the fact that the village still exists, and functions. It would also waste the opportunity to learn something from Ogata-mura. What, then, can be learned? As a social experiment, its community model might not be the best one to follow. Although there are many residents who are content with the linear streets and clean, orderly living areas, the satisfaction of residing close to one's fields is noticeably missing. For the majority of settlers, a hamlet-based arrangement allowing them to live near their farmland would probably be better.[5] Also, given the general difficulty of maintaining egalitarian systems around the world, it might also have been better to allow each settler to choose how much farmland he would buy from the start. Those who were more serious about staying would have bought more and then also bought the fields of neighbors who eventually left (and assistance could have been provided for that), and then larger, more efficient farms would have appeared earlier. Entrepreneurialism and efficient, clean farming could have been better encouraged to rise in tandem with one another. If the national government had done the above things and also at least exempted the settlers from its rice reduction and cash handout policies Ogata-mura could stand up even better today as a modern farming village and a model for the future of Japan's agriculture. If the last six decades of government agricultural policy is any indication of the next six, however, Ogata-mura is going to have to find a way to do this without reliance on Tokyo and with greater internal unity. This is the challenge facing the village today.

Notes

1. This is a difficult topic to discuss with most village farmers without first establishing a rapport and a good degree of trust—it basically involves posing the question, "Did you break the law, and if so, why?"
2. Here, "tenants" refers to farmers who cultivate fields owned by another and who generally pay "rent" in the form of a share of the earnings from each crop sold, and not as "tenants" in the prewar sense.

3. This last point, of course, relates to the facts that: (1) they were actively discouraged from doing *dekasegi* work (or even leaving the village) in the winters from the beginning, and (2) good side-work was always scarce in the Hachirōgata area.
4. Incidentally, Yukiko Kusakabe has now converted her home into an inn (*minshuku*) that she operates under the umbrella of a prefecture-led green tourism program—a movement that seeks to bring residents of urban areas to rural areas for agriculture-related touristic activities.
5. Interestingly, some of these points may soon be tested. On November 18 and 19, 2011, a group of 23 civil servants and other representatives from the city of Tagajō in Miyagi Prefecture visited Ogata-mura to evaluate its potential to serve as a model for rebuilding their city, 34 percent of which had been inundated by the tsunami that hit it on March 11 of that year (Ogata-mura 2011b:3).

AFTERWORD

Studying Ogata-mura over the past seventeen years has been like trying to solve a jigsaw puzzle with a piece count that perpetually grows: each time you think you're almost finished, you find more pieces to deal with. For example, on March 31, 2012, a 156-page booklet about the village based primarily on interviews with Seiki Miyata, mayor from 1978-2000, was published by Tokyo-based Kōjinsha, but by the time I obtained a copy it was too late for me to incorporate its contents into this book. Miyata is listed as primary author and the three university professors who conducted the interviews (and also some on-site fieldwork in Ogata-mura) are listed as co-authors. The booklet, very rich in detail, sheds light on major issues in the village's development from the earliest years to the election of 2008 and its immediate aftermath. In addition, although the publication comes across as a fairly one-sided celebration of Miyata's political career, the fact that its academic co-authors did their homework is clear; they spoke at length with Miyata's detractors and adversaries in advance, which guided the questions they posed to Miyata and gave some balance to the booklet. Unfortunately, however, the three researchers who guided the project and actually wrote up the booklet have ignored the entire body of geography-oriented work on Ogata-mura and Hachirōgata, as well as all of the English language material, which limits the scope and also the universal applicability of the finished product.

Another case of suddenly appearing puzzle pieces: the day after I sent the corrected final manuscript of this book to Berghahn a short article written by a former student of mine at Ogata-mura's junior high school—the heir of a settler—appeared in the *Akita Sakigake* newspaper. Kenji Tanaka was in the seventh grade when I arrived at the school in 1995 and was in the ninth grade when I left, and I remember him quite well because he was one of several students who helped me host an in-school lunchtime English broadcast program on Wednesdays. As of this writing, Tanaka is posted in Bangkok as an employee of Hokuto Bank, the second-largest financial institution in Akita. In his April 2012 report from

Bangkok he noted the popularity of Akita Komachi rice among consumers there who can afford to pay the price—approximately five times that of locally-grown rice. Tanaka, of course, was pleased to find rice from home selling in stores in Thailand, but the situation with the price recalls the examples in the NHK special mentioned in chapter 6. It is unclear whether high-end overseas markets can actually help sustain Japan's rice industry in the long run.

Yet another example of proliferating puzzle pieces: the day after the above essay appeared in the paper, the *Sakigake* prominently featured on its front page two articles bearing a strong relation to this book. One of these was about Ogata-mura serving as a model for post-tsunami reconstruction on the Pacific coast, and the other was about rice growers in California boosting production of short-grain varieties in anticipation of Japan's joining the Trans-Pacific Partnership (TPP) and dropping its protectionist rice tariffs (also reported in other papers, including *The Japan Times*). The former article focused mainly on visits to Ogata-mura by representatives of tsunami-stricken areas who were interested in learning from it as they considered rezoning their own communities for better safety. Mayor Takahashi's explanation in the article about the convenience and efficiency of neatly separating farming space from living space, while understandable, should not be taken at face value in light of some of the findings of this book.

The second article is more serious. The TPP is probably the single largest agricultural issue facing Japan at the moment. At best, its very existence seems to be preventing the MAFF from doing any kind of creative thinking about farm reform. At worst, it has pitted the country's agricultural sector (which strongly opposes the TPP, and is therefore widely considered to be conservative and selfish) against its business world (which is seen as progressive and heroic): paranoid reactionaries thwarting the valiant efforts of enlightened captains of industry— Henny Penny versus Andrew Carnegie. This has been a very unfortunate sideeffect of the United States' placing pressure on Japan to join the TPP talks. Amidst ongoing (but informal) discussions it has repeatedly pressed Japan to honor its "international obligations" with its friends, meaning that allied nations should not do such antisocial things as place trade barriers between one another. However, each nation's regulation of its own economy is ultimately its own responsibility and right. Despite Japan's relative economic strength, its agricultural sector is weak, partly due to the fact that its arable land amounts to only about 12 percent of its total area (compared to about 20 percent for the U.S.A.), and also to the political issues outlined in this book. The simple fact that an item can be produced in country A cheaper than in country B neither necessitates nor justifies the latter's ceasing production of that item and instead buying it only from the former. Of course, some people would profit from such an arrangement, and some would suffer. But who would benefit, and who would pay the price? Clothing can be made in China cheaper than in the U.S.A., but U.S. senators were incensed upon discovering that the uniforms for the 2012 U.S. Olympic team had been fully manufactured in China, and this was purely a symbolic issue and not about actual job losses at all.

Relatedly, anthropologist Steven Gudeman (2008) convincingly argues that calculative reason—basically, profit-oriented "bottom-line" economic thinking—is nurtured and proliferated by competitive trade, as it grows and expands. This is a process that threatens to undermine the "base" of a community, which Gudeman defines as its "shared materials and services" (28). Importantly, Gudeman's complex concept of "base" allows for great a variety of constituent components across cultures, and it also acknowledges that the base is tightly interconnected with individual and group identity. Considering the historical importance of rice in Japan and its deep connection to group identity, coupled with the direct economic and social value of rice farming to most regions of the country—its prominent position in Japan's base—it is no wonder that JA has been so strongly opposed to the TPP. Becoming reliant on imported rice would cause significant damage to that base, upsetting the balance between anonymous market commerce and mutual trade relations that Gudeman so carefully outlines (see esp. pp. 13–15). Likewise, although the automobile was not invented in the U.S.A., it has long held a central position—both material and symbolic—in the nation's base. Concern about the security of the United States' still-struggling auto industry in mid-2012 prompted Ford and other American auto-makers to press the Obama administration to prevent Japan from joining the TPP, ostensibly due to worries about job loss, but the symbolic factor cannot be ignored. As an example of the symbolic side of international motor vehicle trade, I recall a Harley-Davidson TV add I saw years ago in Texas in which a gleaming "hog" was introduced with a deep-voiced narrator's bold assertion: "This ain't no rice-burner!" In other words, American motor vehicles are tough and burn gasoline, while Japanese motor vehicles are wimpy and burn rice. Yes, rice—even Harley Davidson dealers would acknowledge the symbolic connection between rice and Japan, yet the US Rice Producers Association and certain members of Congress would have Japan sacrifice its domestic rice industry and imperil many of its agrarian regions for their own benefit. This, I believe, is something that allied nations should not do to one another.

I contend that the TPP is exactly what Japan does not need now because its domestic rice-producing industry would not be able to survive, and the damage to the country's regions would be devastating, if its massive rice tariffs were removed within the next ten years, which would have to be done if Japan were to join the partnership. Japanese proponents of joining the TPP have suggested that the U.S.A. might grant some form of allowance on these tariffs, but given the rhetoric coming from across the Pacific, and considering the precedents set by the WTO, this is highly unlikely.They are simply hoping to get something for nothing. Masayoshi Honma of The University of Tokyo (see chapter 6) has suggested that the TPP might be just the shock that Japan's agricultural sector needs for its rejuvenation (Tabuchi 2010), but this is also wishful thinking—promising to drop all trade tariffs within ten years at this point would be far too much of a shock. Without steady leadership and reliable support—both notably lacking—there is no hope. An anthropologist might be expected to take this this position, and would expect in turn to be criticized for doing so by economists, but not all of the latter are convinced of the absolute merits of fully open trade.

With the best interests of the U.S.A. firmly in mind, economist Ian Fletcher makes a very strong case against the kind of reasoning that produces simple "open=good/closed=bad" economic formulas in his 2010 book, *Free Trade Doesn't Work*. Directly relevant to the TPP issue, Fletcher argues in the 2011 edition that free trade "gives up some of the best tools humanity has to shape what *kind* of economic globalization we get: tariffs and non-tariff trade barriers" (20, emphasis in original). By glossing over the fact that any community's economy is deeply embedded in the social relations that comprise that community—that economy is always social—Fletcher commits a typical economist's error, but his argument is nonetheless clear and powerful, and the fact that it does not rely on cultural evidence probably makes it resonate all the more strongly with those interested in such macro-economic issues. Fletcher's book should be read by anyone who believes in the universal goodness of free-trade, including Ogata-mura'sTōruWakui (CEO of the Akita Komachi Corporation), who appears to have become confused about his status as a relatively small-scale industrial farmer dependent on state support. Wakui can be seen arguing for joining TPP on YouTube, but he is mistaken. To compare Wakui and Shinichirō Sakamoto one final time, the latter's attitude toward TPP is closer to the mark—at the very least, Japan must fix its internal agricultural problems before it even begins to think about dropping its tariffs on incoming rice. In a special program on Ogata-mura produced by an Akita TV studio that aired in February of 2011, Katsuya Okada can be seen campaigning in Ogata-mura in mid-2010, when he was Minister for Foreign Affairs. Holding an envelope addressed to Okada in one hand, Sakamoto works his way into the line of people waiting to greet Okada, but a secret agent spots the envelope at the last moment and quickly takes Sakamoto aside while inquiring about its contents. With one arm wrapped paternalistically around Sakamoto's lower back, the young agent communicates with colleagues using a small device attached to his lapel as Sakamoto opens the letter that was in the envelope. Of course, it is a plea to Okada to refuse the U.S.A.'s overtures on TPP."It doesn't matter now—he's gone, anyway," says Sakamoto just before he is led further away by three agents.

Politically, in addition to the "us and them" situation that has arisen between farming and business interests in Japan over the TPP, there have been some curious effects of the pressures placed on it by the U.S.A. over joining. First, the

Liberal Democratic Party (LDP) switched from a supportive position to a mildly anti-TPP platform, and the now-dominant Democratic Party of Japan (DPJ) came out strongly in favor of joining. However, the LDP's switch was clearly inspired by public opinion and its historical ties with JA and the farm sector, and now the DPJ leadership appears to be hoping that the issue will quietly fade away—little is being said by its members about TPP at this time, and no serious steps toward joining have been taken. Considering this and the opposition to Japan's involvement on the part of the U.S. auto industry, the issue may soon become a non-issue after all. Even if this happens, though, it is sure to surface again in the future.

As for the future, in concluding the final chapter of this book I declared that Ogata-mura needed to face it with greater unity. One promising enterprise recently featured on Akita's local TV news, appears to be helping on this front. The Ogata-mura Komeko Project capitalizes on the MAFF's current *kakōyōmai* subsidy scheme to produce a variety of products from flour processed from village-grown rice (or, *komeko*). It also hinges on direct support from the MAFF, which covered one-half of the 11.6 trillion yen tab for starting up the project out of a special fund established for rejuvenating first-sector production areas. This fund is tied to a MAFF scheme creatively labeled "Sixth Sector Industrialization," the figure of six being reached by adding one (representing the primary sector), two (for the secondary sector), and three (for the tertiary sector),and symbolizing the project's aim to encourage the creation of self-contained, complete systems that successfully link production areas and functions of these three sectors of the national economy.

The remainder of the start-up costs of the Ogata-mura Komeko Project was paid by the project's constituent elements, which include the Country Elevator and the Akita Komachi Corporation. Both produce flour from rice grown in the village, and the latter also processes some of that into pasta and other noodles, such as *udon*. It also includes the Osaka-based Gyōza Keikaku Corporation, which recently opened a factory in the village that produces *gyōza* (Chinese dumplings) and frozen bread dough from the Country Elevator's rice flour, and additionally Delica Food Research Corporation, which is in charge of research, development, and marketing. The Ogata-mura JA and the village itself are deeply involved as well, serving to coordinate the overall effort. As with the village's infant solar/wind power enterprise, it is too early to pass judgment on this project, but this unprecedented cooperation between Ogata-mura business and political entities is attracting attention and looks very encouraging. The inaugural ceremony for the project, held at Sun Rural Ogata in November of 2011, even featured an address by the DPJ's Hirotaka Akamatsu, who made headlines in Akita in late 2009/early 2010 when he was head of the MAFF(see chapter 6).

Increased unity, new business opportunities, and positive media attention: things did appear to be looking up for Ogata-mura as of the middle of 2012.

However, another mayoral election loomed, and these usually have social effects akin to pouring gasoline on burning embers. Mayor Takahashi declared his candidacy in March of 2012—six months prior to the end of his first term, and just as the village announced a new plan to invite some 250 retirees with special technical skills to move to the community (with their spouses) from Tokyo and other major centers and live in housing to be built near the Ogata-mura campus of Akita Prefectural University, which used to be the prefectural agricultural junior college. Under the plan, the incomers were expected to use their specialized knowledge in productive ways, and thereby contribute to the village's economic base and possibly to its new high-tech enterprises. In return, they were to receive unspecified tax exemptions. Secondarily, the proposed micro-community of retirees was to serve as a model "healthy elderly community" (*genki na kōreishakai*) for the entire country—not a completely unimportant issue to the society of Ogata-mura because it is now beginning to show signs of aging and possible successor shortages in the future due to a growing number of unmarried heirs and a declining average number of children per household.

However, the parallels between this scheme and the problematic *bunkajin* project that had first appeared about two decades earlier were obvious from the start. Many village residents immediately bristled at the prospect of their tax revenues being used to build such housing units. Moreover, the mayor's political opponents were especially worried that having so many non-farming households in the village would result in a loss of political power on their part in two possible ways; there was concern that non-agricultural issues would come to take precedence over agricultural ones because the newcomers would not be particularly concerned about the latter, and it was thought that the political loyalties of newcomers might lie with the mayor who had invited them. Of course, those worrying about these things were the same villagers who had been strongly opposed to Mayor Miyata's non-agricultural image-building and revitalization endeavors in the 1990s, so to them this new development represented a continuation of the "old ways." During the weeks that followed the announcement political opposition to the mayor coalesced somewhat around this issue, which was not a very preferable situation for him or his administration, so when pressed on the matter in the June 14 assembly meeting, Mayor Takahashi carefully explained that the village actually had no concrete plan to embark on such an endeavor and that it had never even seriously considered it. He also added that the March announcement had been made prematurely, but that he would be not be opposed to exploring related plans in the future.

In early August Mayor Takahashi was still standing unchallenged, with Election Day set for Sunday the twenty-sixth. However, a certain member of the village assembly was widely expected to announce his candidacy at any moment. Seiichi Kimura, the son of a first-wave settler from inside Akita Prefecture, had been employed by the village before resigning to run for the assembly in 2008, and since winning a seat in that election he served as the primary political representative of the anti-Miyata pro-free marketing faction that had lost the mayor's office in the same election. It was Kimura, in fact, who grilled the mayor in the June 14 assembly meeting over the village's March announcement that it would consider bringing a large number of retirees to settle, and also for spending roughly 120 million yen on building wedding ceremony facilities for the hotel, Sun Rural Ogata, which Seiki Miyata had taken control of soon after Takahashi's election. In other words, the political tussles centering on big spending that marked the final decade of Miyata's rule had once again become the norm in Ogata-mura. In fact, the faction that lost the 2008 election had become so galvanized over all of this by 2012 that former assembly member Yukiko Kusakabe—daughter of Takeru Isono—decided to emerge from her 2004 political retirement and attempt to reclaim a seat for herself, alongside one other woman of the same political orientation. And, to make for an even more interesting election, it was said that Tōru Wakui would put up a female candidate of his own. Furthermore, Nōyū and the Country Elevator were both expected to field strong candidates as well. Kusakabe decided to enter the election knowing that it would be tough, but since she had by that time become head of the village Women's Association (*fujinkai*) she had a large pool of potential supporters behind her. There was no telling how the 2012 election might pan out at the time this afterword was completed in early August, but it was clear that the outcome would at least give a good indication of the balance between the weight of current political issues and that of cooperative ventures such as the Ogata-mura Komeko Project and others mentioned in chapter 6, and also largely determine how the village as a whole would stand up to the challenges of the next four years.

Fortunately, the publication schedule of this book allowed me just enough time to add this final comment to the end of its afterword—on the day after the village's 2012 election. It is the last puzzle piece to be included in the book's pages. After all, the only two people widely seen as potential challengers to Mayor Takahashi in 2012—Hajime Kobayashi (who ran unsuccessfully in 2008) and Seiichi Kimura (mentioned above)—declined to run against him. The fact that it would be virtually impossible for someone to head the JA while serving as mayor was apparently a major reason behind Kobayashi's decision not to run, and Kimura would have had to vacate his seat on the assembly to do so (as Takahashi had done in 2004), and would have therefore found himself completely out of village politics for at least four years if he had lost. Considering, especially, that three men of great influence in the Country Elevator Corporation (including a former president and the current president) were running for election to the assembly, it seemed safer for Kimura to defend his place in that body than to take a great risk running against the relatively well-entrenched mayor.

On August 21 at 5pm it became clear that Takahashi would serve a second term because nobody had filed papers for candidacy—the first time in the village's brief history that this had happened. When interviewed by the press, Takahashi mentioned the fading of the compliant/noncompliant division as a major factor. The local media also focused on the effects of the mayor's "green" initiatives and the promising Komeko Project. Hints of problems to come were also included in the comments of reporters and the mayor himself: (1) the TPP threatens to undermine the livelihoods of Ogata-mura's farmers, (2) the village society is on the threshold of having to grapple with a growing proportion of elderly people and a shrinking proportion of youths, and (3) relating to the previous point, the village may be able to play a role in helping to create a healthy and happy society of elders. In other words, the mayor has probably not given up on finding a way to pursue the aforementioned plan to bring retirees from urban centers to live in the village at some point. It would mesh with his assertion that the village needs to diversify and see itself as more than "just" a farming village. The parallels here with the policies of the Miyata administration are clear; the main question is how well Mayor Takahashi can sell his vision to the rest of his fellow villagers, and especially to members of the old anti-Miyata faction (party), over the next four years.

The fact that villagers still see many political issues (including big spending) along lines drawn years ago resulted in 15 people vying for 12 assembly seats. In the end, the assembly election results yielded a rather strong verdict on Mayor Takahashi's performance during his first term, helping to make up for the fact that there was no race for his office—and therefore no vote tally—to use for gauging his real popularity. To summarize, all three Country Elevator candidates easily won assembly seats, and the Nōyū president (see chapters 4 and 5) claimed a seat for himself as well. Although Yukiko Kusakabe did her best, the 110 votes she received (out of 2,236) were not enough to return her to the assembly; one candidate barely won a seat with 118, so she actually lost by a very narrow margin. A woman close to Kusakabe (politically and socially) did successfully defend her seat, and a woman who once headed the JA's Women's Association (separate from the village's *fujinkai*) won a seat. This candidate may have received behind-the-scenes support from Sadayoshi Miyazaki and Tōru Wakui, but this remains unclear. A surprise bigger than the triumph of all three Country Elevator candidates was the defeat of a notable Dōyūkai member who had originally entered the assembly in the election upset of 1996 (see chapter 5). Moreover, an even bigger surprise was the defeat of Seiichi Kimura, who had won a seat in 2008 and who had served as the most vocal opponent of Mayor Takahashi since then. In fact, Kimura garnered the smallest number of votes among all candidates (96).

Added to the fact that each of the new Country Elevator candidates received over 150 votes, Kimura's loss indicates that a large number of villagers are basically pleased with Mayor Takahashi's performance. He will probably have an even easier time implementing his plans during his second term, since the assembly is likely to be somewhat more supportive. On the other hand, the lines between the village's two main political factions are not quite as clear today as they were even in 2008—the DPJ's current rice farming support system (Nōgyō Kobetsu Shotoku Hoshō Seido, see chapter 6) having done more to erase those lines than the passage of time—so there is no guarantee that fellow Country Elevator users will always be cooperative, or that former noncompliant faction members will always be unsupportive. After all, Takahashi's clean energy projects are generally quite popular, and the Komeko Project links many people and organizations. One thing, at least, is certain: the farmers of Ogata-mura realize now more than ever before that they are bound by a common fate. Disagreements over financial issues and large projects may continue for years, but the volatile political schisms of the past do finally appear to be fading. In other words, the village's political situation described in chapter 5 has indeed begun to change. Whether or not this process continues smoothly will depend largely on how the mayor chooses to navigate the village's political waters over the next four years, and for the verdict on this we will have to wait until the next election in 2016. The publication of this book, however, cannot wait.

August 27, 2012
Akita University

BIBLIOGRAPHY

Akita Keizaihōkadaigaku Keizaigakubu Keizaikenkyūjo, ed. 2002. *Akita de Chiiki o Kangaeru.* Akita: Akita Bunka Shuppan.

Akita-ken Nōgyō Shikenjō. 1970. *Hachirōgata Chūō Kantaku-chi Dojō Setsumei-sho (Dai-ichiki Dojō Chōsa).* Akita: Akita-ken Nōgyō Shikenjō.

Akita-ken Kōsaku Hōkichi Taisaku Kyōgikai. 2009. "Kōsaku Hōkichi Saisei Riyō no Torikumi Hōshin ni Tsuite." *MAFF Home Page* (http://www.maff.go.jp/j/nousin/tikei/houkiti/h_zenkoku_kaigi/pdf/01.pdf, retrieved Mar. 30, 2012).

Akita Sakigake Shinpō. 2006. "Mura no Dokujisei o Jūshi—Nōsei no Henkaku ni Kikikan mo." *Akita Sakigake Shimbun* (29 April): 1.

——. 2007a. "Chihō no Shakkin Kakusa 500-bai." *Akita Sakigake Shimbun* (8 April): 1.

——. 2007b. "Kōfuzei ni Tokubetsu Waku Teian." *Akita Sakigake Shimbun* (19 November): 1.

——. 2007c. "Shusshinchi-betsu no Kingaku Tōitsu: Kankon Sōsai no Mōshiawase." *Akita Sakigake Shimbun* (2 April): 22.

——. 2008a. "Tokureisai ga Tanomi no Tsuna." *Akita Sakigake Shimbun* (17 March, evening edition): 1.

——. 2008b. "Genkoku no Seikyū Zenmen Kikyaku." *Akita Sakigake Shimbun* (30 August): 24.

——. 2009. "Nō-gyaru Doronko Osawagi: 'Shibuya-mai' 30-nin Taue." *Akita Sakigake Shimbun* (24 May): 30.

——. 2010. "Shi-chō-son Gikai." *Akita Sakigake Shimbun* (11 June): 25.

——. 2011. "Musenmai no Chūmon Tsuzuku." *Akita Sakigake Shimbun* (1 April): 20.

——. 2012. "Ogata-mura, Fūryoku Hatsuden Jigyō ni Sannyū e 15 Nendo Made ni Baiden Kaishi." *Akita Sakigake Shimbun* (http://www.sakigake.jp/p/akita/politics.jsp?kc=20120308c, retrieved Mar. 9, 2012).

Albrecht, Don E., and Steve H. Murdock. 1990. *The Sociology of U.S. Agriculture: An Ecological Approach.* Ames: Iowa State University Press.

Allen, George C. 1981. *A Short Economic History of Modern Japan.* London: Macmillan.

Allen, John C., and Don A. Dillman. 1994. *Against All Odds: Rural Community in the Information Age.* Boulder: Westview.

Anbai, Kō. 1991. *Tōjō wa Umi no Mura.* Tokyo: Gendaishokan.

Aoki, Shirō. 1985. "Seikatsu Kaizen Fukyū no Konnichiteki Yakuwari." In *Chiiki Nōgyō Shinkō to Murazukuri,* ed. Akira Kasegawa. Tokyo: Bunmei Shobō, pp. 1–19.

Asahi Shimbun-sha. 2001. *Asahi Gakushū Nenkan 2001 (Tōkei).* Tokyo: Asahi Shimbun-sha.

Atarashii Suiden Nōhō Henshūiinkai. ed. 2007. *Atarashii Suiden Nōhō e no Charenji: Ogata-mura ni Okeru Sangaku Kyōdō no Seika*. Tokyo: Atarashii Suiden Nōhō Henshūiinkai.

Bailey, Jackson H. 1991. *Ordinary People, Extraordinary Lives: Political and Economic Change in a Tōhoku Village*. Honolulu: University of Hawaii Press.

Beardsley, Richard K., John W. Hall, and Robert E. Ward. 1959. *Village Japan*. Chicago: University of Chicago Press.

Bestor, Theodore C. 1989. *Neighborhood Tokyo*. Stanford, CA: Stanford University Press.

Brown, L. Keith. 2006. "Tōhoku: A Place." In *Wearing Cultural Styles in Japan: Concepts of Tradition and Modernity in Practice*, ed. Christopher S. Thompson and John W. Traphagan. New York: SUNY Press, pp. 197–206.

Bunkachō Bunkazai Hogobu. 1971. *Hachirōgata no Gyorōshūzoku—Mukei no Minzokushiryō Kiroku, Dai 15 Shū*. Tokyo: Bunkachō.

Cancian, Frank. 1992. *The Decline of Community in Zinacantan: Economy, Public Life, and Social Stratification, 1960–1987*. Stanford, CA: Stanford University Press.

Chiba, Jihei. 1972. *Ogata-mura—Aru Dai Kantaku no Kiroku*. Tokyo: Kōdansha.

Connors, Theodore T. 1963. *The Reclamation of Kojima Bay, Japan*. Unpublished M.A. thesis, Department of Geography, University of California at Los Angeles.

Coser, Lewis A. 1956. *The Functions of Social Conflict*. Glencoe: Free Press.

Dahrendorf, Ralf. 1959. *Class and Class Conflict in Industrial Society*. Stanford: Stanford University Press.

Daily Yomiuri. 2007. "WTO Launches Probe into U.S. Farm Support." *Daily Yomiuri* (19 December): 9.

Dana, Leo Paul. 2002. *When Economies Change Paths*. Singapore: World Scientific.

——. 2005. *When Economies Change Hands: A Survey of Entrepreneurship in the Emerging Markets of Europe from the Balkans to the Baltic States*. New York: International Business Press.

Dennō, Jun'ichi. 1999. "Akita-ken Ogata-mura ni Okeru Tochi Riyō to Nōgyō Keiei no Henka." *Shūdai Chiri* 46: 33–38.

Dore, Ronald. 1959. *Land Reform in Japan*. London: Oxford University Press.

——. 1978. *Shinohata: A Portrait of a Japanese Village*. New York: Pantheon.

Edahiro, Junko. 2011. "Japan Begins Feed-in Tariff Scheme to Accelerate Renewable Energy Promotion." *Japan for Sustainability Newsletter* (http://www.japanfs.org/en/mailmagazine/newsletter/pages/031395.html, retrieved Apr. 20, 2012).

Embree, John F. 1939. *Suye-mura: A Japanese Village*. Chicago: University of Chicago Press.

Feige, Edgar L., and Katarina Ott, eds. 1999. *Underground Economies in Transition: Unrecorded Activity, Tax, Corruption and Organized Crime*. Aldershot: Ashgate.

Fitzpatrick, Sheila. 1994. *Stalin's Peasants*. New York: Oxford.

Fukutake, Tadashi. 1967. *Asian Rural Society: China, India, Japan*. Tokyo: University of Tokyo Press.

——. 1980. *Rural Society in Japan*. Tokyo: University of Tokyo Press.

Gavron, Daniel. 2000. *The Kibbutz: Awakening from Utopia*. Lanham, MD: Rowman & Littlefield.

Ghirardo, Diane. 1989. *Building New Communities: New Deal America and Fascist Italy*. Princeton: Princeton University Press.

Gill, Tom. 2001. *Men of Uncertainty: The Social Organization of Day Laborers in Contemporary Japan*. New York: SUNY Press.

Gordon, Douglas H. 1965. *The Reclamation of Hachirogata*. Unpublished M.A. thesis, Department of Geography, University of Hawaii.

Government of Japan (Ministry of Land, Infrastructure, and Transport). 2003. "Zenkoku Sōgō Kaihatsu Keikaku." *Ministry Home Page* (http://www.mlit.go.jp/kokudokeikaku/zs5/hikaku.html, retrieved Mar. 17, 2008).

———. (Sōmu-shō). 2008. "Nihon no Chōki Tōkei Keiretsu." *Ministry Home Page* (http://stat.go.jp/data/chouki/index.htm, retrieved Apr. 12, 2012).

———. (Sōmu-shō). 2010. "Gappei Information." *Sōmu-shō Home Page* (http://www.soumu.go.jp/gapei/, retrieved Feb. 26, 2010).

———. (Sōmu-shō). 2011. "Nihon no Tōkei 2011—Kanren suru Tōkeihyō." *Sōmu-shō Home Page* (http://www.stat.go.jp/data/nihon/g1507.htm, retrieved Mar. 30, 2012).

Graburn, Nelson H.H. 1995. "Tourism, Modernity and Nostalgia." In *The Future of Anthropology: Its Relevance to the Contemporary World*, ed. Akbar S. Ahmed and Chris Shore. London: Athlone, pp. 157–178.

Grossman, Gregory. 1977. "The Second Economy of the USSR." *Problems of Communism* 26(5): 25–40.

Gudeman, Stephen. 2008. *Economy's Tension: The Dialectics of Community and Market.* New York: Berghahn.

Guo, Nanyan, Seiichi Hasegawa, Henry Johnson, Hidemichi Kawanishi, Kanako Kitahara, and Anthony Rausch, eds. 2005. *Tsugaru: Regional Identity on Japan's Northern Periphery.* Dunedin: University of Otago Press.

Hachirōgata Kantaku Jimusho. 1969. *Hachirōgata Kantaku Jigyōshi.* Tokyo: Nihon Doboku Gakkai.

Hachirōgata Shinnōson Kensetsu Jigyōdan. 1976. *Hachirōgata Shinnōson Kensetsu Jigyōdan-shi.* Akita: Hachirōgata Shinnōson Kensetsu Jigyōdan.

Handa, Ichitarō, ed. 1968. *Hachirōgata—Kantaku to Shakai Hendō.* Tokyo: Sōbunsha.

Hane, Mikiso. 1982. *Peasants, Rebels, and Outcasts: The Underside of Modern Japan.* New York: Pantheon.

Hanson, Victor Davis. 2007. "Please—Not Another Farm Bill." *Victor Davis Hanson.com* (5 November) (http://victorhanson.com/articles/hanson110507C1PF.html, retrieved Feb. 20, 2008).

Hayami, Yujiro. 1988. *Japanese Agriculture under Siege.* New York: St. Martin's Press.

———. 1991. "Institutional Aspects of Agricultural Development." In *The Agricultural Development of Japan: A Century's Perspective*, ed. Yujiro Hayami and Saburo Yamada. Tokyo: University of Tokyo Press, pp. 61–108.

Hoagland, Alison K., and Margaret M. Mulrooney. 1991. *Norvelt and Penn-Craft, Pennsylvania: Subsistence Homesteads of the 1930s.* Historical American Buildings Survey/Historical American Engineering Record. Washington, DC: National Park Service.

Hōjō, Hisashi. 1969. "Hachirōgata Chūōkantakuchi (Ōgata-mura) ni Okeru Einō to sono Mondaiten." *Chirigakkairon* 42(11): 713–718.

———. 1976. "Hachirōgata Chūōkantakuchi (Ōgata-mura) no Suii to Shūhen no Henyō." *Nōgyōdobokugakkaishi* 44(5): 321–326.

Horiguchi, Kenji. 1990. "Kome no Kokusai Shijō to Gatto." In *Jiyūka ni Yuragu: Kome to Shoku Kanseidō*, ed. Nōsanbutsu Shijō Kenkyūkai. Tokyo: Tsukuba Shobō, 25–55.

Ichinoseki, Kinjūrō. 2007. "Fukōki Saibai to Naebako Sehi ni Torikumi Hajimete 15 Nen." In *Atarashii Suiden Nōhō e no Charenji: Ogata-mura ni Okeru Sangaku Kyōdō no Seika*, ed. Atarashii Suiden Nōhō Henshūiinkai. Tokyo: Atarashii Suiden Nōhō Henshūiinkai. pp. 31–33.

Idei, Nobuo. 2005. *Shitei Kanrisha Seido.* Tokyo: Gakuyō shobō.

Ikebata, Tetsuo. 2007. "Yūkimai no Seisan to Hanbai: Ikebataryū Aigamo Nōhō." In *Atarashii Suiden Nōhō e no Charenji: Ogata-mura ni Okeru Sangaku Kyōdō no Seika*, ed. Atarashii Suiden Nōhō Henshūiinkai. Tokyo: Atarashii Suiden Nōhō Henshūiinkai. pp. 52–59.

Ikuma, Hitoshi. 2002. *Dai-san Sekutā o Risutora Seyo*. Tokyo: Nikkan Kōgyō.

Ishida, Takeshi. 1984. "Conflict and Its Accommodation: Omote-Ura and Uchi-Soto Relations." In *Conflict in Japan*, ed. Ellis S. Krauss, Thomas P. Rohlen, and Patricia G. Steinhoff. Honolulu: University of Hawaii Press, pp. 16–38.

Itō, Abito. 2007. *Bunkajinruigaku de Yomu Nihon no Minzoku Shakai (Anthropological Introduction to Japanese Folk Society)*. Tokyo: Yūhikaku.

Ivy, Marilyn. 1995. *Discourses of the Vanishing: Modernity, Phantasm, Japan*. Chicago: University of Chicago Press.

Japan Statistical Association. 1988. *Historical Statistics of Japan, Vol. 4*. Tokyo: Japan Statistical Association.

JSIDRE. 1976. "Hachirōgata Kantaku no Seika." *Nōgyō Doboku Gakkaishi* 44(5): 283–351.

Jussaume Jr., Raymond A. 1991. *Japanese Part-Time Farming: Evolution and Impacts*. Ames: University of Iowa Press.

Kaneda, Yoshihiro. 2007. "Shinka Suru Fukōki Saibai." In *Atarashii Suiden Nōhō e no Charenji: Ogata-mura ni Okeru Sangaku Kyōdō no Seika*, ed. Atarashii Suiden Nōhō Henshūiinkai. Tokyo: Atarashii Suiden Nōhō Henshūiinkai. pp. 227–230.

Kelly, William W. 1986. "Rationalization and Nostalgia: Cultural Dynamics of New Middle Class Japan." *American Ethnologist* 13(4): 603–618.

———. 2006. "Rice Revolutions and Farm Families in Tōhoku: Why Is Farming Culturally Central and Economically Marginal?" In *Wearing Cultural Styles in Japan: Concepts of Tradition and Modernity in Practice*, ed. Christopher S. Thompson and John W. Traphagan. New York: SUNY Press, pp. 47–71.

Kirby, Peter Wynn. 2011. *Troubled Natures: Waste, Environment, Japan*. Honolulu: University of Hawaii Press.

Kishi, Hiroaki. 1988. "'Ogata-mura' Kurose-shi yo Ogoru Nakare." *Chūō Kōron* 103(6): 178–183.

Knight, John. 1994a. "The Spirit of the Village and the Taste of the Country." *Asian Survey* 34(7): 634–646.

———. 1994b. "Town-Making in Rural Japan: An Example from Wakayama." *Journal of Rural Studies* 10(3): 249–261.

———. 2003. "Repopulating the Village?" In *Demographic Change and the Family in Japan's Aging Society*, ed. John W. Traphagan and John Knight. New York: SUNY Press, pp. 107–124.

Kome Mondai Kenkyūkai. 1990. *Kome no Jiyūka Mondai o Kangaeru*. Tokyo: Daiichi Planning Center.

Kudō, Kichijirō. 1969. "Hachirōgata Kantakuchi ni Okeru Shin-sonraku." *Shūdai Chiri* 16: 1–6.

Kurose, Tadashi. 1988a. "Ware Nōsuishō to Kaku Tatakaeri." *Chūō Kōron* 103(4): 186–193.

———. 1988b. "Nōsuishō no Mōron o Futatabi Warau." *Chūō Kōron* 103(4): 224–230.

Kushner, Barak. 2010. "Imperial Cuisines in Taishō Foodways." In *Japanese Foodways, Past and Present*, ed. Eric C. Rath and Stephanie Assmann. Urbana: University of Illinois Press, pp. 145–165.

Kusumoto, Masahiro. 2007. *Shūraku Einō*. Tokyo: Nōbunkyō.

Kuwayama, Takami. 2004. *Native Anthropology: The Japanese Challenge to Western Academic Hegemony*. Melbourne: Trans Pacific Press.

Kyodo News. 2011a. "Rice Futures' Revival OK'd after 72 years." *Daily Yomiuri* (2 July): 6.

———. 2011b. "Firms Angling for Slice of Green Energy Pie." *Japan Times* (19 April): 3.

Latour, Bruno. 1993. *We Have Never Been Modern*. Trans. Catherine Porter. Cambridge, MA: Harvard University Press.

MAFF (Norin-shō Kōzōkaizen-kyoku). 1977. *Hachirōgata Shinnōson Kensetsu Jigyōshi*. Tokyo: Nihon Doboku Gakkai.

——. 2005. Nōgyō Keiei Kaizen Keikaku no Einō Ruikeibetsu Nintei Jōkyō (Heisei 17 Nen). (http://www.maff.go.jp/j/ninaite/n_nintei/zyokyo/index.html, retrieved Mar. 30, 2012).

——. (Statistics Division). 2006. (http://www.maff.go.jp/toukei/sokuhou/data/sakutsuke-suitou200610/sakutsuke-suitou200610.pdf, retrieved Feb. 29, 2008.)

——. 2007. *Akita Prefecture Municipal Merger Information*. (http://www.akita.info.maff.go.jp/nousei/genntijouhou/syuraku/misato_yajinaka.htm, retrieved Nov. 24, 2007.)

——. 2010. Nōgyō Keiei Kaizen Keikaku no Einō Ruikeibetsu Nintei Jōkyō (Heisei 22 Nen). (http://www.maff.go.jp/j/ninaite/n_nintei/zyokyo/index.html, retrieved Mar. 30, 2012).

Matanle, Peter, Anthony S. Rausch, and the Shrinking Regions Research Group. 2011. *Japan's Shrinking Regions in the 21st Century: Contemporary Responses to Depopulation and Socioeconomic Decline*. Amherst, NY: Cambria Press.

McConnell, David L. 1996. "Education for Global Integration in Japan: A Case Study of the JET Program." *Human Organization* 55(4): 446–457.

——. 2000. *Importing Diversity: Inside Japan's JET Program*. Berkeley: University of California Press.

McMillan, John. 2002. *Reinventing the Bazaar: A Natural History of Markets*. New York: W.W. Norton & Company.

Media Productions Group. 1991. *As Iwate Goes, Is Culture Local?* (video) Center for Educational Media Institute for Education on Japan. Earlham College, Richmond, IN 47374.

Mishima, Tokuzoh. 2004. "Revision of Japan's Basic Law on Agriculture and its Features— Improvement of Food Self-sufficiency Ratio and Agricultural Price Policy." *Review of Agricultural Economics* 60: 259–271.

Miyamoto, Tsuneichi. 2008. *Wasurerareta Nihonjin*. Tokyo: Iwanami Shoten.

——. 2010. *The Forgotten Japanese: Encounters with Rural Life and Folklore*. Trans. Jeffrey S. Irish. Berkeley, CA: Stone Bridge Press.

Miyara, Takahiro. 1984. *Hokkaidō o Saguru: Nishioka Tokushū—Sapporo-shi Toyohira-ku Nishioka no Shakai to Minzoku*. Sapporo: Hokkaidō Minzoku Bunka Kenkyūkai.

Miyazaki, Makoto, and Koichi Uetake. 2010. "Govt Pushing on with Agricultural Reform." *Daily Yomiuri* (1 December): 3.

Mizuki, Yoh. 2002. *"Nihon no Saisei" no Genba o Iku*. Tokyo: Shinchōsha.

Mock, John. 1999. *Culture, Community and Change in a Sapporo Neighborhood, 1925–1988: Hanayama*. Lewiston, NY: Edwin Mellen.

——. 2006. "The Social Impact of Rural–Urban Shift: Some Akita Examples." In *Wearing Cultural Styles in Japan: Concepts of Tradition and Modernity in Practice*, ed. Christopher S. Thompson and John W. Traphagan. New York: SUNY Press, pp. 25–46.

Moon, Okpyo. 1989. *From Paddy Field to Ski Slope*. Manchester: Manchester University Press.

Moore, Richard H. 1990. *Japanese Agriculture: Patterns of Rural Development*. Boulder: Westview Press.

——. 1991. "Strategies for Manipulating Japanese Rice Policy: Resistance and Compliance in Three Tohoku Villages." *Research in Economic Anthropology* 13: 19–65.

——. 1993. "Resistance to Japanese Rice Policy: A Case Study of the Hachirōgata Model Farm Project." *Political Geography* 12: 278–296.

Morimoto, Takahito. 2012. "Ogata-mura no Dantai ni Daijin-shō: Kankyō Hairyo-shita Yūkisaibai Hyōka." *Akita Sakigake Shimbun* (28 Mar.): 26.

Mulgan, Aurelia George. 2000. *The Politics of Agriculture in Japan*. London: Routledge.

———. 2005a. "Where Tradition Meets Change: Japan's Agricultural Politics in Transition." *Journal of Japanese Studies* 31(2): 261–298.

———. 2005b. *Japan's Interventionist State: The Role of the MAFF*. London: Routledge Curzon.

Mutō, Tetsujō, ed. 1940. *Akita-gun Yūgyotan*. Tokyo: Attic Museum.

Nagahama, Ken'ichirō. 2011. "Akita-ken Ogata-mura ni Okeru Kobetsu Shotokuhoshō Seido Dōnyū no Imi to Kadai." *Government of Japan, National Diet Library*. (http://www.ndl.go.jp/jp/data/publication/refer/pdf/072906.pdf, retrieved Mar. 30, 2012).

Nara, Hiroshi. 2006. *Akita no Chiiki-zukuri*. Akita: Kappanpuran.

Near, Henry. 2008. *The Kibbutz Movement: A History, Volume 1*. Oxford: Littman Library of Jewish Civilization.

NHK. 2007. *Rice Shock: Who Will Produce Your Staple Food?* (14, 15 October).

Nishida, Yoshiaki, and Kazutoshi Kase, eds. 2000. *Kōdo Keizai Seichō-ki no Nōgyō Mondai: Sengo Jisakunō Taisei e no Chōsen to Kiketsu*. Tokyo: Hyōronsha.

Nonaka, Takeshi. 2011. *TPP Bōkokuron*. Tokyo: Shūeisha.

Norbeck, Edward. 1978. *Country to City: The Urbanization of a Japanese Hamlet*. Salt Lake City: University of Utah Press.

Nozoe, Kenji. 1994. *Dokyumento Dekasegi*. Tokyo: Shakai Shisōsha.

———. 2006a. *Dekasegi: Shōnen Bassaifu no Kiroku*. Tokyo: Shakai Hyōronsha.

———. 2006b. *Akita Sugi o Hakonda Hitotachi*. Tokyo: Shakai Hyōronsha.

Occhi, Deborah J. 2006. "Heartbreak's Destination: Tōhoku in the Poetic Discourse of Enka." In *Wearing Cultural Styles in Japan: Concepts of Tradition and Modernity in Practice*, ed. Christopher S. Thompson and John W. Traphagan. New York: SUNY Press, pp. 151–170.

Ogata-mura. 1994. *Ogata-mura Sonseiyōran Shiryōhen*.

———. 1998. *Ogata-mura Guidebook*.

———. 2001. *Ogata-mura Nōgyō Kankyō Dētabukku*. Ogata-mura Kankyō Sōzō 21.

———. 2007. *Ogata-mura Nōgyō no Shōkai*, ed. Ogata-mura Nōgyō Kyōdōkumiai Einōshien Sentā.

———. 2010. *Kōhō Ogata* (April).

———. 2011a. *Hachirōgata Chūō Kantakuchi "Ogata-mura" ni Okeru Nōson Shūraku no Kensetsu to Murazukuri no Hensen*.

———. 2011b. *Kōhō Ogata* (December).

Ohnuki-Tierney, Emiko. 1993. *Rice as Self: Japanese Identities through Time*. Princeton, NJ: Princeton University Press.

Onoda, Tetsushi. 2007. "Local Tax Grants Set to Be Shaken up." *Daily Yomiuri* (21 March): 3.

Partner, Simon. 2009. *The Mayor of Aihara: A Japanese Villager and His Community, 1865–1925*. Berkeley: University of California Press.

Pomfret, Richard. 1996. *Asian Economies in Transition: Reforming Centrally Planned Economies*. Cheltenham: Edward Elgar.

———. 2002. *Constructing a Market Economy: Diverse Paths from Central Planning in Asia and Europe*. Cheltenham: Edward Elgar.

Pryor, Frederic L. 1992. *The Red and the Green: The Rise and Fall of Collectivized Agriculture in Marxist Regimes*. Princeton, NJ: Princeton University Press.

Rausch, Anthony. 2001. *A Year with the Local Newspaper: Understanding the Times in Aomori, Japan, 1999*. Lanham: University Press of America.

——. 2005. "Municipal Mergers in Rural Japan: Easy on the Powerful, Severe on the Weak." *Electronic Journal of Contemporary Japanese Studies* (http://www.japanese studies.org.uk/discussionpapers/2005/Rausch.html, retrieved Nov. 11, 2009).

Robertson, Jennifer. 1991. *Native and Newcomer: Making and Remaking a Japanese City*. Berkeley: University of California Press.

Rucker, Philip. 2011. "An Anti-Subsidy Call from the Heartland: Kansas Congressman Tells Farmers to 'Expect Less,' and Finds Bipartisan Agreement." *Washington Post* (21 June): 10.

Rutherford, John. 1984. *Rice Dominant Land Settlement in Japan: A Study of Systems within Systems*. Sydney: University of Sydney Department of Geography.

Ryang, Sonia. 2004. *Japan and National Anthropology: A Critique*. New York: Routledge Curzon.

Sachs, Jeffrey. 1994. *Poland's Jump to the Market Economy*. Cambridge, MA: MIT Press.

Saitō, Kōkichi. 1969. *Koshō no Kantaku*. Tokyo: Kokonshoin.

Saitō, Tadahiro. 2001. *Kokoro o Komete: Ogata-mura, Saitō Nōjō, Sanchoku Jūnenki*. Akita: Mumyōsha.

Sakamoto, Shinichirō. 1990. *Kome-tori Monogatari*. Tokyo: Kage Shobō.

——. 1991. *Kome Jiyūka Yurusazu*. Tokyo: Ochanomizu Shobō.

——. 1998. *Nihon Nōson Dai Risutora*. Tokyo: Ochanomizu Shobō.

——. 2006. *WTO wa mō Iranai*. *Akita Sakigake Shimbun* (20 January): 7.

Samuels, Richard J. 1983. *The Politics of Regional Policy in Japan: Localities Incorporated?* Princeton, NJ: Princeton University Press.

Sanger, David. E. 1991. "Japan's Unlikely Rebels: The Fabled Rice Farmers." *New York Times* (http://www.nytimes.com/1991/11/04/world/ogata-journal-japan-s-unlikely-rebels-the-fabled-rice-farmers.html, retrieved Jul. 22, 2011).

Satō, Haruo. 1966. "Akita-ken ni Okeru Dekasegi no Chigakuteki Kenkyū." *Shūdai Chiri* 13: 28–32.

Satō, Kōnosuke. 1997. *Akita: Kieta Mura no Kiroku*. Akita: Mumyōsha.

——. 2001. *Akita: Kieta Bunkō no Kiroku*. Akita: Mumyōsha.

——. 2005. *Akita: Kieta Kaitakuson no Kiroku*. Akita: Mumyōsha.

Schnell, Scott. 1999. *The Rousing Drum: Ritual Practice in a Japanese Community*. Honolulu: University of Hawaii Press.

——. 2005. "The Rural Imaginary: Landscape, Village, Tradition." In *A Companion to the Anthropology of Japan*, ed. Jennifer Robertson. Malden, MA: Blackwell, pp. 201–217.

Scott, James C. 1985. *Weapons of the Weak: Everyday Forms of Peasant Resistance*. New Haven, CT: Yale University Press.

——. 1989. "Everyday Forms of Resistance." In *Everyday Forms of Peasant Resistance*, ed. Forrest D. Colburn. New York: M.E. Sharpe, pp. 3–33.

——. 1990. *Domination and the Arts of Resistance: Hidden Transcripts*. New Haven, CT: Yale University Press.

——. 1998. *Seeing Like a State: How Certain Schemes to Improve the Human Condition Have Failed*. New Haven, CT: Yale University Press.

Shichōson Jiji Kenkyūkai. 2002. *Zenkoku no Shichōson Yōran*. Tokyo: Daiichi Hōki.

Shimizu, Tei. 1978. *Ogata-mura: Janarisuto no Mita Moderu Nōson*. Akita: Mumyōsha.

Shimomura, Naoya. 1996. "Sōrāmanshippu o Taisetsu ni." *Akita Sakigake Shimbun* (29 August): 14.

Shimpo, Mitsuru. 1976. *Three Decades in Shiwa: Economic Development and Change in a Japanese Farming Community*. Vancouver: University of British Columbia Press.

Shioya, Junji, Yasutoki Togashi, and Tatsuo Furuuchi. 2001. *Akita-ken no Rekishi*. Tokyo: Yamakawa.

Shirai, Yoshihiko. 1976. "Nōson Keikaku no Tenkai Katei." *Nihon Doboku Gakkaishi* 44(3): 170–174.

Smith, Patrick. 1997. *Japan: A Reinterpretation*. New York: Vintage.

Smith, Robert J. 1978. *Kurusu: The Price of Progress in a Japanese Village, 1951–1975*. Stanford, CA: Stanford University Press.

Smith, Robert J., and Ella Lury Wiswell. 1982. *The Women of Suye-Mura*. Chicago: Chicago University Press.

Smith, Thomas C. 1959. *The Agrarian Origins of Modern Japan*. Stanford, CA: Stanford University Press.

Solt, George. 2010. "Rāmen and U.S. Occupation Policy." In *Japanese Foodways, Past and Present*, ed. Eric C. Rath and Stephanie Assmann. Urbana: University of Illinois Press, pp. 186–200.

Stanbury, Pamela. 1987. "Agricultural Land Settlement along the Indira Ganghi (Rajasthan) Canal." *Research in Economic Anthropology* 9: 281–304.

Suzuki, Hikaru. 2000. *The Price of Death: The Funeral Industry in Contemporary Japan*. Stanford, CA: Stanford University Press.

Suzuki, Nobuhiro, and Junko Kinoshita. 2011. *Yoku Wakaru TPP 48 no Machigai*. Tokyo: Nōsangyosonbunkakyōkai.

Tabuchi, Hiroko. 2010. "Japan's Farmers Oppose Pacific Free-Trade Talks." New York Times (http://www.nytimes.com/2010/11/12/business/global/12yen.html?_r=1&pagewanted=print, retrieved Apr. 17, 2012).

Takata, Wakizō. 2000. *Konsen Kaitaku to Ijū Kenkyū*. Kushiro, Hokkaido: Kushiro City.

———. 2001. "Formation and Change of the Tondenhei Village in Eastern Hokkaido: A Case Study of Ota Village in Akkeshi Town." *Kushiro Public University Research Papers* 10: 97–113.

Takarajimasha. 2012. Hogo Seisaku wa Tadashii! TPP wa Amerika no Sakuryaku da! Tokyo: Takarajimasha.

Takenaka, Akira. 2004. "Land Transaction under the Expansion of Farm Size in Tokachi, Hokkaido: A Case Study of N Block at Otofuke Town." *The Review of Agricultural Economics* 60: 225–237 (in Japanese).

Takeuchi, Toshimi. 1948. *Koshō Gyogyōshi Kenkyū—Hyōjō Gyogyō ni Tsuite*. Tokyo: Suisan Jijō Chōsajo Kan.

Talmon, Yonina. 1972. *Family and Community in the Kibbutz*. Cambridge, MA: Harvard University Press.

Tanaka, Daisuke. 2007. "Conceptualizations of Death in a Commercial Context: The Funeral Business in Present-Day Japan." *Research in Economic Anthropology* 25: 173–197.

Tamanoi, Mariko. 1998. *Under the Shadow of Nationalism: Politics and Poetics of Rural Japanese Women*. Honolulu: University of Hawaii Press.

TDK Corporation. 2011. "Joining Forces with the Community towards a Low-Carbon Society." *TDK Home Page* (http://www.global.tdk.com/csr/csr_report/pdf/rep10007.pdf, retrieved Apr. 27, 2011).

Thompson, Christopher S. 2003. "Depopulation in Rural Japan: 'Population Politics' in Tōwa-chō." In *Demographic Change and the Family in Japan's Aging Society*, ed. John W. Traphagan and John Knight. New York: SUNY Press, pp. 89–106.

Thompson, Christopher S., and John W. Traphagan, eds. 2006. *Wearing Cultural Styles in Japan: Concepts of Tradition and Modernity in Practice*. New York: SUNY Press.

Torsello, Davide. 2002. "The Paths to Difference: Social and Economic Choices in Three Post-war Agrarian Settlements of North-eastern Japan." *Social Science Japan Journal* 5(1): 37–53.

Tozawa, Tetsutarō. 1993. *Mō Hitotsu no Ogata-mura.* Akita: Akita Bunka Shuppan.

Traphagan, John W. 2000. *Taming Oblivion: Aging Bodies and the Fear of Senility in Japan.* New York: SUNY Press.

Traphagan, John W., and John Knight, eds. 2003. *Demographic Change and the Family in Japan's Aging Society.* New York: SUNY Press.

Traphagan, John W., and Christopher Thompson. 2006. "The Practice of Tradition and Modernity in Contemporary Japan." In *Wearing Cultural Styles in Japan: Concepts of Tradition and Modernity in Practice,* ed. Christopher S. Thompson and John W. Traphagan. New York: SUNY Press, pp. 2–24.

Traphagan, Tomoko W. 2006. "Negotiating Internationalization in Kitasawa." In *Wearing Cultural Styles in Japan: Concepts of Tradition and Modernity in Practice,* ed. Christopher S. Thompson and John W. Traphagan. New York: SUNY Press, pp. 96–123.

Tsuchiya, Keizō. 1976. *Productivity and Technological Progress in Japanese Agriculture.* Tokyo: University of Tokyo Press.

Ueba, Hiroyuki. 2007. "Farmers Hope Luxury Food Exports Will Save Industry . . . Japan Needs Large-Scale Farms to Compete." *Daily Yomiuri* (8 December): 1,20.

Ueda, Kazumi. 2003. "Impoldering Works (*Kantaku*) in Japan." *Workshop on Hydroenvironmental Impacts of Large Coastal Developments* (http://wave.skku.ac.kr/ACECC_TC1/PDF/20_ueda.pdf, retrieved Feb. 29, 2008).

Vogel, Steven K. 2005. "Routine Adjustment and Bounded Innovation: The Changing Political Economy of Japan." In *Beyond Continuity: Institutional Change in Advanced Political Economies,* ed. Wolfgang Streeck and Kathleen Thelen. Oxford: Oxford University Press, pp. 145–168.

Wakui, Tōru. 2007. *Nōgyō wa Yūbō Bijinesu Dearu!* Tokyo: Tōyō Keizai Shinpōsha.

Williams, Brian. 2010. "Satoyama: The Ideal and the Real." *Kyoto Journal* 75: 24–29.

Wood, Donald C. 1999a. *Ancestral Land, Inheritance, and the Revitalization of Rural Japan: The Case of Ogata Village.* Unpublished M.A. thesis, Department of Anthropology, Texas A&M University.

———. 1999b. "The Rural Revival Movement in Japan: A Comparison of Two Communities." *Bulletin of the National Association of Student Anthropologists* 11(1–2): 8–16.

———. 2003. "Fragmented Solidarity: Commercial Farming and Rice Marketing in an Experimental Japanese Village." *Research in Economic Anthropology* 22: 145–167.

———. 2004. *From Paper to Practice: Social Solidarity, Political Economy, and Change in a Planned Japanese Farming Village.* Unpublished Ph.D. dissertation, Department of Cultural Anthropology, University of Tokyo.

———. 2005. "The Polder Museum of Ogata-mura: Community, Authenticity, and Sincerity in a Japanese Village." *Asian Anthropology* 4: 29–58.

———. 2007. "Introduction." *Research in Economic Anthropology* 25: 1–23.

———. 2009. "Children as a Common-Pool Resource: Change and the Shrinking Kindergarten Market in a Japanese City." *Research in Economic Anthropology* 29: 341–379.

Yamamoto, Shōzō, Akira Tabayashi, and Yoshihiro Kitabayashi. 1987. *Nihon no Nōson Kūkan: Henbōsuru Nihon Nōson no Chiiki Kōzō.* Tokyo: Kokonshoin.

Yamano, Akio. 2003. "The Development Process of Agriculture on Reclaimed Land in Hachirogata, Akita Prefecture." *Chigaku Zasshi* 112(1): 114–130 (in Japanese).

———. 2006. *Nihon no Kantakuchi.* Tokyo: Nōrin Tōkei Kyōkai.

Yamashita, Kazuhito. 2004. "Chokusetsu Shiharai de Nōgyō Kaikaku." *Nihon Keizai Shimbun* (26 August) (http://www.rieti.go.jp/jp/papers/contribution/yamashita/05.html, retrieved Jun. 27, 2006).

Yamashita, Kiyomi. 1987. "Hachirōgata Chūōkantakuchi—Ogata-mura ni Okeru Nōgyō Keikan to Tochi Riyō." *Shūdai Chiri* 34: 19–26.

Yano, Christine R. 2002. *Tears of Longing: Nostalgia and the Nation in Japanese Popular Song*. Cambridge, MA: Harvard University Press.

Yomiuri Shimbun. 2007a. "Akita Village Hopes to Be Radioactive Waste Site." *Daily Yomiuri* (25 July): 2.

——. 2007b. "Regions to Get 500 Bil. of City Tax Revenues." *Daily Yomiuri* (31 October): 3.

——. 2007c. "Ishihara OK's Redistribution of Tokyo Tax Revenues." *Daily Yomiuri* (12 December): 2.

——. 2007d. "Govt to Urge Farmers to Be More Competitive." *Daily Yomiuri* (7 November): 3.

——. 2009. "'Shibuya-gyaru' Help Make Rice Cool." *Daily Yomiuri* (12 July): 10.

Yoshitake, Yasumi, and Ryōichi Ura, eds. 1976. *Kenchiku Keikakugaku 7: Nōka Jūtaku*. Tokyo: Maruzen.

INDEX

M

Machida, Hiroaki (son of Nobuhiro Machida),
196, 197, 198
Machida, Nobuhiro (fifth-wave settler from
Toyama)
and adjustment to Ogata-mura, 193, 196,
198
background and settlement of, 56–57, 201
business attitude of, 125, 141, 144, 201, 204,
209, 210, 211
business practices of, 141, 144–145, 212
family of, 196–198
farming practices of, 129, 218
household of, 196–198
and Nōyū, 135, 201
political beliefs of, 125, 144, 145, 165,
195–196, 198, 204, 209, 210
prosecution of, 96
and the SKK, 95, 135, 197
Machida, Takako (wife of Nobuhiro Machida),
56, 145, 165, 195–196, 197, 198
MAFF (Ministry of Agriculture, Forestry and
Fisheries), 2, 21, 33–36, 40–41, 42n12, 45,
96, 124n5, 202–203, 208, 217
Manchuria, 1, 147, 169
Meiji (era) (1868–1912), 9, 22, 24, 26, 27, 45,
213
Mie Prefecture, 72, 74, 77, 80, 148
Minshutō. *See* Democratic Party of Japan
Miyagi Prefecture, 6, 32, 72, 74, 77, 79, 80, 218,
220n5
Miyata, Seiki (Ogata-mura mayor,
1978–2000)
administration of, 91, 92, 95, 101, 123, 142,
168, 193
background of, 94–95, 99, 192
campaigns of, 134
cooperative farming group of, 152
election of, 94–95, 163, 164, 166, 184
leadership of, 99, 103, 107–108, 111, 119,
123, 143, 163–166, 169, 171, 183
political legacy of, 173–175, 177, 185, 186,
187, 188n2, 226
political philosophy of, 100, 191
political retirement of, 167, 188n2
post-retirement positions of, 173, 186, 227
projects of, 101–123, 133, 164, 166, 167,
173–175, 192, 195–196, 199
Miyazaki, Sadayoshi (head, Ogata-mura JA),
162, 172, 188n7
background of, 140
and connections with Tōru Wakui, 166–167,
180, 183, 185, 205, 209
and the convenience store plan, 181–184
and the election of Yukiko Kusakabe, 169
as political opponent of Kita Kurose,
183–184, 185, 187, 193
as political supporter of Kita Kurose,
167–168, 177, 180, 183–184

Mizuho (rice marketing corporation), 135, 148,
185, 211
modernization, 9–10, 14, 24n2, 40
modernity, 10, 14, 15, 24n2, 91
See also Hachirōgata reclaimed land area and
modernity
Moore, Richard, 6, 16, 17, 23, 24n4, 30, 42n2,
93, 124n3, 124n6, 161n15
municipal amalgamation (*gappei*), 30, 36–37,
38, 41, 42n9, 175–176, 177, 178, 185, 186,
196
mura-okoshi (village revitalization), 133
mura-zukuri (village-building), 31
musenmai (rice that needs no washing), 132,
133, 135, 145, 218
museum (see Polder Museum of Ogata-mura)

N

Naka-umi (Shimane Prefecture), 44
naming of Ogata-mura, 48
Nanohana Festival, 121–123, 164, 165, 173,
174–175, 178
nanohana flowers, 121, 122, 124n12, 175
National Comprehensive Development Plans,
43
National Land Development Act (1950), 43
natural soap, 107, 167, 169, 172, 214
nature (*shizen*), 10–11, 17, 103, 123, 214
Netherlands, The
Dronten, 119, 124n10
Dutch engineers, 1, 46, 88
Dutch land reclamation technology, 1, 46
New Food Control Act (Shin Shokuryō Kanri
Hō–1995), 32, 33, 130, 135, 143
new communities, 18 –19, 190
NHK (Nippon Hōsōkyoku), 201–206, 207, 214
Niigata Prefecture
and Koshi-hikari rice, 202
Ogata-mura settlers from, 17, 53–55, 62, 69,
72, 74, 77, 78, 79, 80, 151, 168, 171, 193,
195
Niigata Prefecture group (association), 67, 169,
170
ninaite. See designated producer
nintei nōgyōhōjin. See accredited farming
corporation
nintei nōgyōsha. See accredited farmer
nishi nichōme, 50, 53, 72, 77, 82, 88, 138,
145–158
Nitahara, Yutaka, 169–170, 171, 187
Nōgyō Kobetsu Shotoku Hoshō Seido, 209
Nōkyō (JA). *See* Agricultural Cooperative
Association
noncompliant faction ("party"), 94, 133, 136,
140, 191, 193, 210
divisions within, 179–184, 187
election strategies of, 167–168, 170, 177,
185
and house type, 142, 146, 154–157, 161n14